THE GOA INQUISITION

THE GOA INQUISITION

BEING
A QUATERCENTENARY COMMEMORATION STUDY
OF THE INQUISITION IN INDIA

BY
ANANT KAKBA PRIOLKAR

WITH
ACCOUNTS GIVEN BY
DR. DELLON AND DR. BUCHANAN

VOICE OF INDIA
NEW DELHI

First Published: 1961
First Reprint by Voice of India: 1991
Second Reprint: 1998
Fourth Reprint: 2019
Fifth Reprint: 2020
Sixth Reprint 2021

ISBN 978-81-85990-56-9

www.voiceofin.com

Published by Voice of India, 2/18, Ansari Road, New Delhi – 110 002
and printed at Replika Press Pvt. Ltd.

CONTENTS

ILLUSTRATIONS

Illustrations Nos. 1, 2, 5, 6, 7 are taken from Picard's *Exact description of outward Rites, Ceremonies and Customs of the Peoples of the World* (Amsterdam 1727-38); Nos. 3, 4 from Féréal's *Mystéres of L'Inquisition* (Paris 1845), and Nos. 8, 9, 10 from *Voyages de Dellon avec la Relation de L'Inquisition de Goa*, (A Cologne 1709).

DEDICATED TO THE MEMORY OF

Dr. J. H. Cunha Rivara

(*The Late Chief Secretary to the Government of Goa*, 1855-1870)

Liberal Portuguese savant whose example served as inspiration to many contemporary Indians to undertake research into the activities of the Portuguese in Asia and who facilitated the work of succeeding generations of research-workers by publishing documents available in the official archives of Goa.

INTRODUCTION

THE Inquisition was established in Goa in 1560. Although known as the Goa Inquisition, its jurisdiction extended to all the Portuguese colonial possessions to the East of the Cape of Good Hope. Four hundred years have now elapsed since its establishment and the present volume, therefore, has been described as a Quater-Centenary Commemoration Study.

It is more than two decades since I first thought of writing an account of the Goa Inquisition. A volume on the early history of the Printing Press in India, intended to commemorate the quater-centenary of the establishment of the first printing press in Goa by the Portuguese in 1556, which was planned much later, was published three years ago. It is true that the establishment of the printing press in India took place earlier than that of the Inquisition. But the book on the Inquisition was not deliberately delayed to make its publication coincide with the quater-centenary of its establishment. The delay in its publication is in a large measure due to the fact that the task of writing a history of the Inquisition was more difficult and much less pleasant and it was undertaken after considerable hesitation. The history of the printing press in India is a record of achievement and progress and an Indian writer who traces it is called upon to discharge the pleasant duty of acknowledging with gratitude the debt which India owes to the pioneering work of the Portuguese and other Europeans. On the other hand, the story of the Inquisition is a dismal record of callousness and cruelty, tyranny and injustice, espionage and blackmail, avarice and corruption, repression of thought and culture and promotion of obscurantism and an Indian writer who undertakes to tell it can easily be accused of being inspired by ulterior motives. From this point of view, it would have been appropriate if the task had been undertaken by a Portuguese historian of the stature of Oliveira Martins, Pinheiro Chagas, Alexandre Herculano or Cunha Rivara. Such a writer would also have done fuller justice to the subject. But in the present circumstances there is little chance that a popular work of this nature from the pen of a Portuguese writer would be forthcoming in the near future. Works of historical research like those by Antonio Baião, which have been drawn upon in the preparation of the present volume, are likely to interest the student of history rather than the general reader. In the present volume scrupulous care has been taken to eschew bias and present a dispassionate and objective account of the working of the Goa Inquisition. Inspite of this, the picture which emerges is undoubtedly grim. But this could not be helped as truth had to be told. In situations of this nature the historian should be guided by the following memorable words of Pope Leo XIII :

> " Endeavour most earnestly to refute all forgeries and false statements, after investigating the sources of the subject-matter. The historians should keep foremost in their minds the fact that the first law of history is that no one should dare to utter falsehood and hesitate to state the truth." (" *Enitendum magnopere, ut omnia ementita et falsa, adeundis rerum fontibus, refutentur ; et illud imprimis scribentium observetur animo, primam esse historiae legem, ne quid falsi dicere audeat, deinde ne quid veri non audeat.*" —Letter of Leo XIII of 18th August 1883 to the Cardinals : De Luca, Pitra Hergeuraether).

The records of the Inquisition should have formed the most important source of information for writing an account of its working. Unfortunately, they are not available either in Goa or in Portugal and there is reason to believe that they were destroyed. In the absence of these, it became necessary to draw mainly upon the documents in the official archives in Goa, and published contemporary correspondence of Inquisitors and Jesuit missionaries. Some information relating to the Goa Inquisition which is available in the records of the Inquisition of Portugal has also been published. Occasional references to it are also found in the accounts of contemporary European travellers to India. Another major source of information is the *Relation de l' Inquisition de Goa* by Dr. C. Dellon (Paris, 1688) in which the writer gives an account of his own sufferings as a prisoner of the Inquisition of Goa. An English translation of this work is reprinted in the second part of this volume.

It will be seen that the account given in this volume is to a large extent presented in the words of the original documents on which it is based. In my view this procedure not only adds to the accuracy and authenticity of the narrative but also helps to recapture the contemporary atmosphere.

An extract from the *Christian Researches in Asia* by Dr. Buchanan, who visited the Inquisition of Goa in 1808, is also printed in Part II. Dr. Buchanan's writings contributed to bring about the abolition of the Inquisition of Goa.

Some particulars about Dr. Dellon and his account of the Inquisition of Goa are given in Chapter IV of Part I of this volume. I have also shown in the same chapter that doubts about the authenticity of Dr. Dellon's account raised by some scholars in India are baseless. The English translation of Dr. Dellon's account which is reprinted in Part II was published in 1812.

The immediate cause of the establishment of the Inquisitional tribunals in Spain and Portugal was the tendency to apostasy noticed among the enforced converts to Christianity from Judaism. These were known as New Christians and the slightest suspicion of adherence to any of the ancestral customs of Judaism on their part, whether of religious significance or not, sufficed to justify arrest and trial. The story of the Inquisition, which forms an integral part of the age-long heroic struggle of Judaism for survival in the face of pitiless persecution and countless miseries, will, therefore, always prove of special interest to the Jews. In the sixteenth century the New Christians of Portugal largely availed themselves of the opportunities provided by the colonial trade in the East and established themselves in Goa and its dependencies. The atmosphere of comparative freedom there encouraged them to observe less caution in their day to day life than at home. Scandalised at this laxity, the Portuguese missionaries demanded the establishment of a Holy Tribunal in the East and it was, therefore, natural that the New Christians should have been the objects of the solicitude of the Goa Inquisition also. In the East there were also the native converts, a large majority of whom had been brought within the Christian fold by threat of force or lure of material rewards. It was inevitable that many of these should also continue to adhere in secret to their ancestral beliefs and practices and the energies of the Inquisition of Goa were also directed towards the prevention, detection and punishment of these heretical tendencies. As a consequence, the life of these new converts was rendered so insecure that many of them left the land of their birth and settled down in the adjoining territories outside the jurisdiction of the Inquisition. The Hindus living within the Portuguese dominion, were forbidden to observe their ancestral rites and customs, even behind closed doors, and subjected to many other discriminatory laws. The Inquisition took a prominent part in enforcing these measures and the resulting harassment was so great that many of the Hindus also emigrated to neighbouring territories. Thousands of Konkani-speaking families, both Hindu and Christian, who are found scattered in various centres in Mysore, Kerala and Madras today are the descendants of these emigrants. The present volume should be of special interest to them as it would help them to trace the history of their ancestors and explain the circumstances in which their families were forced to leave their original homes.

I wish to thank the Board of Trustees of charitable institutions and funds of the Goud Saraswat Brahman Community of Bombay for the grant given for the publication of this volume. I also acknowledge my indebtedness to the Poona University for the grant-in-aid towards the cost of publication of this work.

I am indebted to many friends for their valuable assistance in bringing out this volume. I wish, however, to refrain from mentioning them by name, as I am afraid this would cause embarrassment to many of them and might even place some of them in difficulties. It must be remembered that the Inquisition has been abolished but the spirit which guided its activities is not entirely extinct.

I wish to thank the authorities of various institutions who allowed me to make use of books in their libraries in the preparation of this volume. I am grateful to the authors of standard works on the subject which, as the footnotes to the text would indicate, I have freely drawn upon. In particular, I have taken the liberty to include in the volume pictures appearing in some of the old standard works. I must also place on record my appreciation of the excellent work done by the Bombay University Press.

BOMBAY, 1ST JULY, 1961. A. K. PRIOLKAR

Part I

THE GOA INQUISITION

CHAPTER I

THE SPANISH INQUISITION

THE Inquisition was established in India in 1560, four centuries ago. Its activities ceased for a while in 1774, due to the efforts of Marquez de Pombal, the liberal minister of Portugal, but it was revived five years later in 1778 during the reign of D. Maria, queen of Portugal. It was only in 1812 that it was finally abolished.

The Inquisition may be described as an ecclesiastical tribunal for the suppression of heresy and punishment of heretics. It is officially styled " the Holy Office." Writers differ as to the date on which the institution first came into existence. Some would trace it back to the days of Adam and Eve, assigning to God the role of the First Inquisitor. For instance, the Sicilian writer Paramo in his book *De Origine et Progressu Inquisitionis* states : " God was the first Inquisitor and his condemnation of Adam and Eve furnished the model of the judicial forms observed in the trials of the Holy office. The sentence of Adam was the type of the Inquisitorial reconciliations ; his subsequent raiment of the skins of animals was the model of the san-benito, and his expulsion from Paradise the precedent for the confiscation of the goods of the heretics."[1] A less fanciful view is to trace it to the beginning of the thirteenth century of the Christian era and to regard it as the aftermath of the Crusades. William Prescott writes : " Acts of intolerance are to be discerned from the earliest period in which Christianity became the established religion of the Roman empire ; but they do not seem to have flowed from any systematized plan of persecution, until the papal authority had swollen to a considerable height. The popes, who claimed the spiritual allegiance of all Christendom, regarded heresy as treason against themselves and as such deserving all the penalties which sovereigns have uniformly visited on this, in their eyes, unpardonable offence. The crusades, which in the early part of the thirteenth century, swept so fiercely over the southern provinces of France, exterminating their inhabitants and blasting

[1] William H. Prescott, *History of the reign of Ferdinand and Isabella the Catholic of Spain*, vol. I, London 1838, p. 345.

the fair buds of civilization, which had put forth after the long feudal winter, opened the way to the inquisition; and it was on the ruins of this once happy land that were first erected the bloody altars of that tribunal. After various modifications, the province of detecting and punishing heresy was exclusively committed to the hands of the Dominican friars, and in 1233, in the reign of St. Louis, and under the pontificate of Gregory IX, a code for the regulation of their proceedings was finally digested. The tribunal, after having been successively adopted in Italy and Germany, was introduced into Aragon, where in 1242, additional provisions were framed by the Council of Tarragona, on the basis of those of 1233, which may properly be considered as the primitive instructions of the holy office in Spain."[2]

A. Herculano, a writer on Portuguese Inquisition, observes: "The year 1229 was the correct date of the establishment of the Inquisition. ...Romano de S. Angelo, the legate of Pope Gregory IX, convened in this year a *Concilio Provincial*—an assembly of bishops and divines to determine matters of religion—at Tolosa. Forty-five resolutions were passed at this assembly, eighteen of which related to heretics and persons suspected of heresy. It was determined that Bishops and Archbishops should appoint in each parish a clergyman with two, three or more secular assessors all sworn to investigate into the existence of heresiarchs or any persons who followed or protected them and denounce them to the respective bishops or secular magistrates, taking necessary precautions to ensure that they did not run away. These commissions were to be permanent. Besides, barons and owners of land and prelates of monastic orders were enjoined to look for such persons in their dependent districts and territories, in inhabited areas as well as in woods, in human habitations as well as in secret hide-outs and caverns. One who permitted one of these wretches in his lands would be condemned and would lose the lands and receive corporal punishment. A house in which a heretic was found was to be demolished. Further provisions analogous to these, completed a system of persecution which was worthy of the heathens when they sought to strangle nascent Christianity in its cradle. At the same time, Louis IX promulgated a decree, which not only harmonised with the substance

[2] *Ibid.*, pp. 344-6.

of the provisions of the Council of Tolosa, but in which he also ordered immediate punishment of the condemned heretics and held out threats of confiscation and dishonour against their abettors and protectors. In this manner the spirit of the legislation of Frederick II, which already prevailed in Germany and a part of Italy, spread itself to France and enhanced the dreadfulness of the measures taken at the Assembly of Tolosa."[3]

It will be seen that, as a result of the active cooperation of Church and state, a ruthless machinery of systematic persecution of persons considered as heretics had been evolved in the thirteenth century. This formed the background for the establishment in Spain of what is known as the Spanish or the Modern Inquisition during the reign of Ferdinand and Isabella.

At this time in Spain the Jewish community occupied the foremost positions in many fields—trade, scholarship and politics. This provoked the envy of their Christian brethren and interested parties succeeded, by spreading all manner of malicious rumours and calumnies against this unfortunate race, in inciting the crowds to indiscriminate massacres and pillage. Prescott writes:

" Stories were circulated of their contempt for the Catholic worship, their desecration of its most holy symbols, and of their crucifixion or other sacrifice of Christian children, at the celebration of their own passover. With these foolish calumnies, the more probable charge of usury and extortion was industriously preferred against them, till at length, towards the close of the fourteenth century, the fanatical populace, stimulated in many instances by the no less fanatical clergy, and perhaps encouraged by the numerous class of debtors to the Jews, who found this a convenient mode of settling their accounts, made a fierce assault on this unfortunate people in Castile and Aragon, breaking into their houses, violating their most private sanctuaries, scattering their costly collections and furniture, and consigning the wretched proprietors to indiscriminate massacre without regard to sex or age.

" In this crisis, the only remedy left to the Jews was a real or feigned conversion to Christianity. St. Vincent Ferrier,

[3] A. Herculano, *Historia da Origem e Estabelecimento da Inquisição em Portugal*, Tomo I, Lisboa (Edited by David Lopes), pp. 38-40.

a Dominican of Valencia, performed such a quantity of miracles, in furtherance of this purpose, as might have excited the envy of any saint in the calendar, and which, aided by his eloquence, are said to have changed the hearts of no less than 35,000 of the race of Israel, which doubtless must be reckoned the greatest miracle of all."[4]

The marriage of Ferdinand, king of Aragon, to Isabella, queen of Castile, had resulted in the union of these two kingdoms. Torquemada (1420-1498), a Dominican monk, who was the confessor to Isabella since her childhood, played a prominent part in bringing this about. He also played a central role in the early history of Spanish Inquisition. A Portuguese writer traces the psychological origin of his fanatical zeal to an incident in his early youth :

" In the course of his travels, while he was very young, he fell in love with a woman of Cordova. Either through lack of knowledge or means he failed to win her and a Moor, whom she preferred, took her to Granada. Thus germinated and took root in the heart of Torquemada his life-long hatred for the Moors. Thence he went to Saragoça, where he studied Theology and with the assistance of a priest who admired him, he entered the convent of the Dominicans. There, while looking into the archives, he acquainted himself with the authority which the Inquisitors enjoyed. The hatred, ambition and desire for revenge which he harboured, thereupon raised before him an idea, well defined and grandiose, which required to be translated into reality, viz., the establishment of the Inquisition. "[5]

Prescott describes the character of Torquemada and the part he played in bringing the Spanish Inquisition into existence, in the following words :

" This man, who concealed more pride under his monastic weeds than might have furnished forth a convent of his order, was one of that class with whom zeal passes for religion and who testify their zeal by a fiery persecution of those whose creed differs from their own ; who compensate for their abstinence

[4] Prescott, *op. cit.*, pp. 358-4.

[5] *A Inquisição* (Enciclopédia pela Imagem), Porto, (Date of publication not given).

from sensual indulgence, by giving scope to those deadlier vices of the heart, pride, bigotry, and intolerance, which are no less opposed to virtue, and are far more extensively mischievous to society. This personage had earnestly laboured to infuse into Isabella's young mind, to which his situation as her confessor gave him such ready access, the same spirit of fanaticism which glowed in his own. Fortunately this was greatly counteracted by her sound understanding and natural kindness of heart. Torquemada urged her, or indeed, as is stated by some extorted a promise, that 'should she ever come to the throne, she would devote herself to the extirpation of heresy, for the glory of God, and the exaltation of the Catholic faith.' (Zurita, *Anales de Aragon*, tom. IV, fol. 323). The time was now arrived when this fatal promise was to be discharged."[6]

As stated earlier, many Jews at this time were forced to embrace Christianity, as this was the only way to save their life and property As would be expected, though Christians in outward appearance, they remained loyal to their old faith at heart and practised in secret the rites and usages associated with that faith. The position was described by the Curate of los Palacios at Andalusia as follows :

"This accursed race were either unwilling to bring their children to be baptized, or if they did, they washed away the stain on returning home. They dressed their stewes and other dishes with oil instead of lard ; abstained from pork ; kept the passover ; eat meat in Lent ; and sent oil to replenish the lamps of their synagogues, with many other abominable ceremonies of their religion."[7]

There were loud and persistent demands for the establishment of the Inquisition for remedying this state of things. Foremost in pressing these demands were Alphonso de Ojedo, a Dominican, who was the prior of the Monastery of St.Paul in Seville and Diego de Merlo, Assistant of that city. The reactions of the Royal couple to these repeated importunities varied. Prescott writes :

"These persons, after urging on the sovereigns the alarming

[6] Prescott, *op. cit.*, pp. 361-362.
[7] *Ibid.*, p. 357.

extent to which the Jewish leprosy prevailed in Andalusia, loudly called for the introduction of the holy office as the only effectual means of healing it. In this they were vigorously supported by Nicolas Franco, the papal nuncio then residing at the Court of Castile. Ferdinand listened with complacency to a scheme which promised an ample source of revenue in the confiscations it involved; but it was not so easy to vanquish Isabella's aversion to measures repugnant to the natural benevolence and magnanimity of her character.

"It was not until the queen had endured the repeated importunities of the clergy, particularly of those reverend persons in whom she most confided seconded by the arguments of Ferdinand, that she consented to solicit from the pope a bull for introduction of the holy office into Castile. Sixtus IV who at that time filled the pontifical chair, easily discerning the sources of wealth and influence which this measure opened to the Court of Rome, readily complied with the petition of the Sovereigns, and expedited a bull bearing date November 1st, 1478, authorising them to appoint two or three ecclesiastics, inquisitors for the detection and suppression of heresy throughout their dominions."[8]

Owing to her natural aversion for the abuses to which the Inquisition would lead, the queen postponed action on the authority given to her for some time, and as an alternative, asked the Archbishop Cardinal Mendoza to prepare a Catechism with the object of educating the new converts into the tenets of the Christian faith. However, ultimately, the Royal couple had to give their consent to the establishment of the Inquisition and that Tribunal started operations on January 2, 1481. Within four days of its establishment took place the first *Auto da Fé* in which four persons were burnt to death. During 1481, about 300 persons were condemned to be burnt at the stake in Seville and 80 to imprisonment for life. In the rest of the province and the bishopric of Cadiz, 2000 persons were condemned to be burnt to death, and 17000 others were given diverse penalties.[9]

In 1483, Pope Sixtus IV appointed Thomas de Torquemada as the Inquisitor General of Castile and Aragon and assigned to

[8] *Ibid.*, pp. 362-3.
[9] Herculano, *op. cit.*, Tomo I, p. 84.

him the task of preparing a new constitution of the Inquisition. This code came into effect in October 1484. Considerable literature on the working of this dread Tribunal is available. For instance, *A History of the Inquistion of Spain* by H. C. Lea would be accessible to most of the readers.[10]

Many Jews and new converts escaped to neighbouring territories like France, Italy and Africa in order to escape the terror of the Spanish Inquisition. Strong attachment to their land of birth, their people or their property, however, prevented many others from doing so and they preferred to remain in Spain even at the risk of attracting the attentions of that dread Tribunal. The Jews offered to pay 30,000 ducats to Ferdinand for the privilege of being allowed to remain in the country on any terms. Ferdinand, out of avarice and Isabella out of magnanimity were inclined to accept this offer. Torquemada entered the palace at this stage, and throwing a Crucifix on the table, exclaimed : " Judas Iscariot sold his master for thirty pieces of silver. You wish to sell him for 30,000 ducats. Here he is, take him and sell him ". This dramatic gesture had the desired effect and the Royal couple changed their minds. On March 31, 1492 it was decreed that Jews should be banished from the Kingdom. The decree allowed them four months within which to wind up their affairs and leave the country, failing which they would be liable to capital punishment and their property confiscated. Even conversion to Christianity did not mean security gainst the unkind attentions of the Inquisition. The plight of these unfortunate people when faced with the decree of banishment and their fate in the countries where they sought refuge are described in the following passage :

" All such as remained after that date incurred the penalty of death, and of confiscation of their entire property to the royal treasury.... They were to be allowed to export their wealth and substance either by sea or land, with the exception of gold, silver, or other articles prohibited by law....

" In proportion as the day of their departure drew near, and the means of realisation became more difficult, their anxiety to dispose of their worldly goods grew greater ; valuable plots

[10] Henry Charles Lea, *A History of the Inquisition of Spain*, 4 vols. The Macmillan Company, New York 1906-7.

of land were sold for a few pieces of cloth, fine houses were exchanged for a couple of mules, and in many cases the riches of the Israelites melted away with those few articles, which they could carry with them, and the beasts, which were to transport them. Moreover convents and public institutions, the nobles and persons of every class, were largely indebted to the Jews, and as no provision was made for the collection of the debts becoming due to them after the date of their enforced departure, their losses from this source were almost incalculable, and the gain to the debtors was of course proportionately enormous. Some of them amid tears and lamentations removed many of the tomb-stones of their fathers, and carried them with them in their long wanderings. The fate of the exiles was varied in the different lands where they sought refuge. Those who escaped to Morocco and Algiers found an inhospitable reception; many were sold into slavery; some starved to death, whilst others were ripped open in the hopes of finding gold pieces in their bodies and a few prefered to return to Spain and receive baptism. In Turkey they were well received. The major part emigrated to Portugal, the noble Rabbi Isaac Aboab having obtained permission of king John II to their entering the country, though only in consideration of each immigrant paying a capitation tax and the understanding that within eight months they should leave the country."[11]

During the regime of Torquemada 8,800 New Christian converts were condemned to be burnt at the stake and 96,504 others to various other penalties by the Spanish Inquisition.[12] These figures are given by Don Juan Antonio Llorente, who was the Secretary of the Inquisition at Madrid during the period 1790 to 1792 and by virtue of this position had access to all departments of the Inquisition. After the Inquisition had been abolished in 1808, he examined the records of its working in the city and in other provinces. The activities of the Inquisition were a dread mystery carefully hidden under a veil of secrecy and Llorente is said to be the only contemporary writer who dared to lift the veil.

[11] F. D. Mocatta, *The Jews of Spain and Portugal and the Inquisition*, London 1877, pp. 49-54.

[12] Prescott, *op. cit.*, pp. 380-4.

CHAPTER II

The Portuguese Inquisition

IT was but natural that the Jewish community in Spain, when faced with the order to leave Spain within four months, should turn to Portugal for help in their difficulties, not only on account of the geographical contiguity of these two countries but also because of their intimate ties with the Jewish community in Portugal, who till that time continued to enjoy the protection of law. They approached the King or Portugal with a request for temporary asylum in that country until they could finalise arrangements for ultimate migration to other suitable territories and offered to pay large sums as consideration for this favour. When this request was discussed at the council of the royal advisers at Cintra, King D. João II expressed himself in favour of its acceptance and use of the moneys received for defraying the expenses of wars in Africa. Many of the members of the council were also inclined to accept the proposal, either out of deference for royal wishes, or humane considerations or in view of the financial aspect of the transaction. There were however, some fanatics who opposed it vigorously as they felt that it would be shame for Portugal to show itself more lukewarm in matters of faith than Castile. They pleaded that the request should either be refused outright, or granted only on condition that the emigrants should agree to their children being baptised. However, the views of D. João II ultimately prevailed and the Jews were allowed to enter Portugal on condition that they leave the country within 8 months and pay a certain sum per head as capitation tax. It was also agreed that ships for further journeys should be made available to them when they left the country. There are different views among historians as to the precise amount of the capitation tax. For instance, according to Marina it was 8 gold *escudos*, while according to Goes it was 8 *cruzados*. It has been recorded that about 1,50,000 persons took advantage of this offer. Of these, 600 rich families secured the privilege of permanent domicile in Portugal on payment of 600,000 *cruzados*. This privilege was also granted to certain artisans. Unfortunately, at this time an epidemic of plague appeared in Spain and the immigrants carried the contagion to Portugal. As the pestilence spread among the local residents, the ill-will which the common people already harboured towards these unfortunate visitors, increased considerably. D. João II thereupon compelled them to leave Portugal even before the expiry of the stipulated period and, as agreed, provided ships for their further journeys. But the captains and crew of the ships, taking advantage of the helpless conditions of these travellers, robbed them and abandoned them at various places on the African coast. Here some perished of hunger and others became slaves of the Moors. There was an absurd story current in Spain that the Jews in order to salvage their gold, reduced it to powder and swallowed it. This had spread to Africa and the Moors are said to have killed many a traveller with the hope of finding gold in his entrails.[1] Some of the Jews who could not afford to pay the capitation tax or wished to evade it had entered the country surreptitiously. When caught they were reduced to slavery and distributed among those who asked for them. Under an order of D. João II children between the ages of 3 and 10 of these unfortunate Jews were snatched away from their parents, and sent to the island of St. Thome which was then being colonised.

These actions of the Portuguese king caused great concern among the local Jewish community. • There had been a long tradition of tolerance of Jews in Portugal and the Jewish community, as a result of their superior intelligence, habits of hard work and thrift had carved out for themselves a position of considerable influence and power in that country. From very early times, they functioned as the farmers of public revenues. However, the distinction between the followers of the dominant religion and those of a religion which was merely tolerated was made clear beyond doubt in certain humiliating disabilities from which the latter suffered and great care was taken to see that they did not abuse their vast resources and influence to pervert the religion of the former. Their synagogues could not hold real estate as the Christian Churches did. In addition to the general imposts, all Jews had to pay a special poll tax. (This formed the precedent for a similar tax imposed on Hindus in Goa during the early Portuguese regime). If the son of a Jew embraced Christianity, not only was the father not permitted to disinherit him, but, on

[1] A. Herculano, *Historia da Origem e Estabelecimento da Inquisição em Portugal* (Edited by David Lopes), Tomo I, Lisboa (?), p. 135.

the other hand, the son was entitled to receive immediately a share in the paternal and maternal estates it being presumed for this purpose that both the parents were dead ; as a consequence, if the son was the only child, he immediately received two-thirds of the family property.[2] This measure proved very effective as an incentive to conversion. The Jews were forced to live in segregation in separate parts of towns which were known as *Judarias* and were administered by committees of their representatives known as Communes. They were not allowed to employ Christians as servants. They could not wear silk garments or jewels and could not ride horses. However, they had the freedom to follow their religion and to use its practices in their synagogues and were governed in relations of personal law by their own customs.

D. João II, inspite of the harsh treatment which the Spanish Jews met at his hands, was firmly opposed to the establishment of the Inquisition in Portugal. He was fully alive to the varied benefits accruing to the country from the intelligence and wealth of the Jewish community, and would not countenance any move to banish them. The lower strata of the Christian citizens, however entertained a deep-rooted feeling of ill-will towards the Jewish community. This had its origin in envy for the superior wealth and influence of the Jews, resentment against the extortions which members of that comunity practised as creditors, farmers of taxes, etc., as well as in religious prejudice. The common people were also profoundly influenced by the systematic persecution of Jews in Spain as well as the cruel treatment meted out to the Jewish immigrants in Portugal. At this juncture, D. João II died in 1495. His only son D. Affonso had died four years earlier as a result of a fall from the back of a horse. He was, therefore, succeeded by a nephew, D. Manoel. The latter was of a tolerant disposition and for some time the Jews received protection and fair-play at his hands. However, he soon developed a passionate attachment for D. Isabella, the widow of his cousin D. Affonso, and wished to marry her. D. Isabella, who was the eldest daughter of Ferdinand and Isabella of Spain, entertained a fanatical hatred for the Jews and ardently desired that in its policy towards that race Portugal should follow in

[2] *Ibid.*, p. 116.

the footsteps of her royal parents. One of the conditons on which the Spanish Court agreed to offer the hand of Isabella to D. Manoel was that the Jewish fugitives from the attentions of the Spanish Inquisition, who had sought refuge in Portugal, should be expelled. It was stipulated in the marriage contract, which was signed in 1497, that their expulsion should be completed within one month, and it was only after verifying this fact that D. Isabella agreed to the union.

The Spanish monarchs would not, however, be satisfied with the banishment of the Jews of Spanish origin from Portugal. They desired that the Jews who belonged to Portugal should also be expelled. To meet their wishes, D. Manoel, while he was on a hunting party at Muge in December 1446, issued an order that all the Jews who were not converted to Christianity should leave the country within ten months. Failure to comply would entail death penalty and loss of all property, which would pass to the informer. Those who left the country were, however, to be allowed to carry with them all their possessions and were assured that they would be provided with the necessary means of transport. The order was originally intended to apply to the Muslims also; but they were later excluded from its scope for fear of provoking reprisals from neighbouring Muslim countries. It was found that a large majority of the Jews preferred exile to conversion to Christianity. Another order was, therefore, issued to the effect that children below 14 years of age should be forcibly taken away from all the Jews who left the country and handed over to persons who would bring them up in the Christian faith. While this tyrannical order was being executed, other more direct impediments were also being placed in the way of the escape of the the victims. It was originally provided that the Jews would be allowed to leave the country from one of three ports, viz., Oporto, Lisbon and Algarve. This was altered and Lisbon was fixed as the only port of embarcation. Further, matters were so arranged that at this port there would be a scarcity not only of ships but also of clothes and provisions for the journey. A. Herculano describes this breach of royal promise as "the height of villainy."[3] Refering to the order to take away the children of the Jews who left the country, he writes: "When the extent of

[3] *Ibid.*, p. 150.

the popular malevolence against that unhappy race is borne in mind, it is easy to imagine how this cruel order would be executed. The shrieks of mothers from whose arms children were snatched away, the laments and fury of fathers and mothers, the resistance put up by bolder members of the community and the supplications and tears of the more timid, turned the country into a kind of a theatre, where an incredible, fantastic and diabolical drama was being enacted. Those members of the community whose hearts were more hardened or spirits more ardent carried the resistance to the point of delirium and preferred to tear their children to pieces, strangle them or drown them in wells, to handing them over to the officers of the king. "[4] (It is recorded that similar scenes were enacted in Goa when a similar order directed against the Hindus was promulgated there during the early Portuguese regime).[5] The scope of the inhuman order, which as stated above originally applied only to children upto age 14, was subsequently enlarged so as to bring within it children of ages upto 20.

As the period allowed for the departure of the Jews was nearing its end, heads of principal Jewish families who had not succeeded in secretly leaving the country pressed the king to provide them with ships or at least to permit them to hire ships at their own cost. They were asked to gather in Lisbon where the royal promises would be fulfilled. Accordingly, it is said that more than 20,000 of them assembled at Estaos, a palace in Lisbon. Here, a cruel fate awaited them. Children who had not already been taken away by the king's officers, were snatched away from their parents without regard to age or sex, and, thereafter, even older men of all ages were baptised by force. A. Herculano writes :

" In a kind of delirium, after having forcibly baptised the Jewish youth, they passed on to full-grown men and old men. Those who offered resistance, were dragged by the hair to the baptismal font. A majority of these unfortunate individuals, placed between the threat of death to which the law condemned them if they did not leave the country and the obstacles raised

[4] *Ibid.*, p. 151.

[5] J. H. Cunha Rivara, *Archivo Portuguez Oriental*, Fasciculo IV, Nova Goa 1862, p. 92.

by the law-maker himself so as to render compliance with the law impossible, bowed down their heads and allowed themselves to be engulfed. Out of more than twenty thousand persons, hardly seven or eight, whose names time has hidden, resisted fearlessly till the end. Tyranny recoiled in the face of such constancy worthy of a better cause, and government ordered that these seven or eight individuals should be provided with a ship to carry them to Africa."[6]

This inhuman episode was not only an affront to Christian religion but also a reversal of the policy of tolerance which had prevailed in Portugal for over four centuries. It produced a reaction of remorse in the heart of the king. On May 30, 1497, he ordered that the new converts should be allowed a period of twenty years for familiarising themselves with the new faith and forgetting their old beliefs and that during this period no proceedings should be taken against them on account of their religious behaviour. Even after the expiry of this period, if a new convert was accused of following Jewish practices he was to be tried in accordance with due processes of law and if he was condemned to the loss of his property, it would pass to his Christian heirs and not to the public exchequer. The king promised that never again he would enact laws in regard to Jews as a distinct race.[7]

Despite these evidences of royal indulgence, the situation of the new converts continued to be far from happy: " Followers of the Mosaic law, were compelled to keep up in their outward behaviour the pretence of conforming to the duties of good Catholics, and it was only in solitude, in the privacy of their homes or under the darkenss of night, that they could invoke in a submissive voice the name of the God of Israel. The very letter of the law which was intended to protect them, proved that the law-maker himself did not believe that their conversion was real, and, like him, no one else did. "[8] Pretence of conforming to the Christian practices on the part of persons who remained Jews at heart, meant sacrilege and blasphemy in the eyes of the Christians and this intensified considerably the popular malevolence towards the Jewish community which had its origin mainly in material

[6] Herculano, *op. cit.*, Tomo I, p. 155.
[7] *Ibid.*, p. 157.
[8] *Ibid.*, p. 158-9.

considerations. There were many in Portugal who looked with favour upon the working of the Inquisition in the neighbouring country and conditions in Portugal were now such that they felt keenly the need for similar institutions in Portugal. The more far-seeing among the new converts were well aware of this impending danger and as the only escape lay in migration to countries like Italy, Flanders or the Orient where they could hope for greater tolerance and security, by way of preparations for the exile, they started converting their immovable property into cash and other movable assets. Perturbed at these effects of past violence, Government decided to put a stop to them by resorting to more violence. On April 21 and 22, 1499 were published two edicts by which local residents as well as foreigners in the country were forbidden to have exchange dealings over cash or merchandise with the New Christians and required to report those already effected within eight days. It was laid down that no one should buy real estate from the New Christians without a special royal licence and that New Christians should not leave the country with wife, sons or household without express permission of the king. Failure to comply with these provisions entailed the penalty of confiscation.[9]

In 1506, while the country was in the grip of a famine, an epidemic of plague broke out. People gathered in Churches to invoke divine mercy against these terrible scourges. On the altar in the Church of Bom Jesus in Lisbon, there was a crucifix and by its side a small receptacle covering the consecrated host. A member of the congregation saw a strange light playing on this receptacle and in his religious fervour took it to be a miracle. The news of the miracle spread far and wide during the next few days and on the following Sunday there was a large concourse to watch the supposed miracle. There were many among those present in whose minds doubts about its authenticity arose. Among these there was a New Christian who was so indiscreet as to let some words slip his lips which gave expression to his doubts. This blasphemy roused the mob to frenzy and its author was assassinated and his body consigned to flames. Two friars emerged from the Church, one carrying a cross and the other

[9] *Ibid.*, p. 161.

a Crucifix, inciting the mob with shouts of "Heresy! Heresy!"[10] Guided by these the mob massacred Christians, wounded others and threw their bodies into pyres lighted in different parts of the city. More than 300 persons were burnt on that day. The scenes were repeated with increased violence on the next day when the number of victims exceeded a thousand. Some Old Christians were also mistaken for New Christians and killed. The houses of the New Christians were forcibly entered and men, women and children killed indiscriminately. Children were snatched away from the breasts of their mothers and holding them by their feet, their skulls were dashed against walls. Plunder and pillage followed. Temples and altars did not serve as sanctuary to those who had sought refuge there. Virgins and married women who were expelled from such sanctuary were raped and then thrown into the flames.[11] The carnage continued for three days and more than 2000 persons perished therein. At this stage the government succeeded in establishing order. The two dominican friars who had incited the mob were hanged and their bodies burnt. Dominican friars were expelled from the convent in Lisbon and it was handed over to secular clergy. Stern punitive measures were taken against the rioters and their abettors. Lisbon was deprived of its ancient privileges on account of the cowardice and indifference shown by its inhabitants.

The atrocities described above filled D. Manuel with remorse. He extended further the period allowed to the new converts to familiarise themselves with the new faith till 1526. The orders which prohibited the New Christians from leaving the country without royal permission, from selling real estate, and converting capital into letters of exchange were revoked. The remainder of the reign of D. Manuel, which ended with his death in 1521, was a period of comparative peace for the New Christians.

On the death of D. Manuel, his eldest son D. João III succeeded to the throne. He was of a fanatical disposition and entertained a profound hatred for the Jewish race. According to A. Herculano, the intolerance by which his reign was marked had its origin principally in the character and inclinations of the king himself. During the early years of his reign he actually confirmed

[10] *Ibid.*, p. 174.
[11] *Ibid.*, p. 177.

the privileges and immunities which his father had conferred on the New Christians. However, he was planning all the time to break his word and actively searching for excuses to justify a policy of persecution. In 1524, he assigned to George Themudo the task of investigating secretly into the religious habits of the New Christians in Lisbon, which was considered to be the principal focus of Judaism. The latter's adverse report was based on information provided by the curates of various parishes. Later a similar assignment was given to Henrique Nunes, who was a New Christian himself and had for some time worked in Spain as a servant of the notorious Inquisitor Lucero. Nunes insinuated himself into the hearts of the families of New Christians and under the guise of friendship wormed out information about their true religious beliefs and secret practices and conveyed it to the king. The king expressed appreciation of his services by giving him the nick-name "Firm of Faith." His betrayed victims soon discovered that he was a spy and he was murdered. This added to the popular anger against the New Christians. During this period accusations against the New Christians of committing sacrilege and insulting the Christian religion continued to multiply and there were frequent violent manifestations of popular ill-will against them. The anti-Jewish faction received powerful support from the queen D. Catherine. She was the sister of Charles V, King of Spain, and was brought up from her infancy to view the Inquisition as an essential institution for the maintenance of the true faith. Through her, the influence of dominican friars in the Portuguese Court also grew. These factors encouraged the enemies of the Jews to redouble their efforts to introduce the Inquisition in Portugal. Ultimately, early in 1531, the king issued instructions to his ambassador at the Papal Court in Rome to move secretly to secure a Papal bull which would serve as the basis for the establishment of the Inquisition in Portugal. The bull was issued on December 17, 1531. The awful prospect created terror in the hearts of the New Christians in Portugal and by straining all their resources to the utmost they succeeded in postponing the evil day for a decade. Duarte de Paz, himself a New Christian, who was sent to Rome as their representative to safeguard their interests at the Papal Court, betrayed his employers to the king. However, he incurred the displeasure of the Pope and was imprisoned. After his release, he migrated to Turkey, where he died as a Muslim. As stated above, the efforts of the New Christians did not succeed in averting the calamity. The Portuguese Inquisition started functioning in 1541 and in October of that year took place the first *Auto da Fé* in Portugal.

In the following passage, the Portuguese historian Oliveira Martins gives a vivid account of the working of that dread Tribunal:

" Its processes infringed all the elementary rules of justice and good sense. The accusers made use of sons as witnesses to give evidence against their parents, and parents against their children; the accused could not communicate with his advocates, nor did he know who his accusers were. The charge was always applauded and spying considered to be a virtue. The *familiars* ingratiated themselves with families, as medical men, confessors, intimate friends and advisers to worm out secrets and report them. There was neither appeal against the sentence nor revision.

" In prisons there was no period of limitation, and the prisoner remained for months, for years, often for the rest of life, without knowing what crime he was accused of. Traps were set for him; and he was waylaid with treachery. Prison guards were bribed to worm out secrets and pretended to be sympathetic, to favour him and to pity him in his distress. They did thus win his confidence, and he was inclined to be confidential. The Inquisiton was a horror, a plague! To extort confession of faults, often times imaginary, the inquisitors pretended to soften and tone down, promised pardons and help, and cajoled until the poor wretch confessed all that he did, or did not do.

" Everytime the prison-gate was opened, the prisoners quailed with fear, or with a faded hope. They were taken tied with ropes to the house of torture; and while they went down the tortuous steps, their cries were smothered. Their judgment clouded and their ideas mixed up, they could not distinguish the real from the unreal. They looked upon themselves as monsters, and persuaded themselves that they were guilty of all they were accused of: they had seen the devil in prison,they had sold their souls to him, they had smashed a crucifix with a hammer, etc. The inquisitor, cold and funereal, sitting at the back of a vaulted building, dimly lit by lights fixed to the walls by iron rings, would he believe in the devil and his appearances ? Why not ? It was a mad man who tortured an idiot ; and in the dark background of a crypt, the lunacy of men had its terrible repercussions.

" In these dark tragedies the wretch often died, while under torture or in prison ; he was then buried in the palace graves, the corpse being first unfleshed, religiously, in order that the bones might figure in the next *auto-da-fé*, and burnt in the fire."[12]

The famous liberal minister of Portugal Marquez de Pombal, as a result of a measure of reform passed in September, 1774, rendered the Inquisition practically defunct and it was finally abolished in 1820. Until 1732 it condemned 23000 persons to various forms of punishment and burnt at he stake 1454 persons. There is no record of the number of persons who lost their lives as a result of tortures to which they were subjected during the trials.

[12] J. P. Oliveira Martins, *Historia de Portugal*, Tomo II, Lisboa 1886, pp. 33-4.

CHAPTER III

Advent of the Inquisition in India

AFTER the Portuguese had established colonies in India many Jews from Portugal settled down therein with the object of taking advantage of the new opportunities for trade and commerce. Later on, when the Portuguese Jews were forcibly converted to Christianity and the life of the new converts in Portugal became increasingly precarious as a result of the growing ferocity of the popular odium against them and threats of organised persecution at the hands of the Church and the State, others sought refuge in the Indian colonies in quest of greater security and tolerance. There were also Jewish communities who had made their home in India from ancient times. Many Jews were employed in the army of the King of Cochin, who, according to Padre Lucena, was, as a consequence, known as the King of the Jews. However, even in India, they were persistently pursued by the hatred and intolerance of their Christian brethren. The Inquisition, as stated earlier, started functioning in Portugal in 1541 and it was established in India in 1560. However, Gaspar Correia, records in his *Lendas de India*, that an *Auto de Fé* took place in India as early as in 1543. The circumstances in which this occurred are described by him as follows :

" In this very year (1543) it came to pass that a bachelor of medicine residing in Goa, named Jeronimo Dias, of the caste of New Christians, in the course of familiar discourses with his friends, spoke of certain things which were against our holy faith. The bishop, on being informed of this, ordered that he should be arrested and tried and that witnesses should be examined. When arrested, together with certain other persons who had discoursed with him, he continued to uphold certain things of the old law against our holy faith, all of which showed clearly that he was a Jew, and the proceedings were concluded. The bishop thereupon went to the residence of the Governor where a council was held, at which were also present the teacher Diogo (Borba), friar Antonio, commissary of St. Francis and preacher, another dominican preacher and the Vicar General (Minguel Vaz). Having seen the papers of the case, they pronounced sentence, which was signed by the bishop and ran as follows : 'Having seen the sentence of the Holy Church, in which bachelor Jeronimo Dias, stands condemned in a case of heresy, the justice of our sire the King, pronounces sentence to the effect that in respect of the said case, by public proclamation your body be burnt alive and reduced to ashes, for heresy against our holy Catholic faith. In case you seek pardon and repent and confess your error and desire to die as a Christian, you shall be first strangled to death so that you may not feel the torments of fire.' While the case was thus being dealt with by the Governor's council, teacher Diogo spoke to the Bachelor and sternly rebuked him. As a result, the latter was made to repent and realise his error, so that when the secular sentence was pronounced as stated above, he heard it patiently, thus accusing himself of his sin in public. Soon he was sent to the prison, where he asked for confession and was confessed by teacher Diogo. He was taken to the pillory, accompanied as an act of mercy by teacher Diogo who accompanied him until he was strangled, and was burnt and reduced to ashes.

" Soon thereafter, on the following Sunday, the bishop preached at the Cathedral church. From the pulpit he read the bull of the Holy Inquisition, and gave information only of the penalty of excommunication in order that all those who learnt of the errors of Christian men and women who in their lives or usages practise heresies against our Holy faith should disclose the same ; the other provisions of the Holy Inquisition would not be used for the present until express orders of our sire the king were received."[1]

The first demand for the establishment of the Inquisition in Goa was made by St. Francis Xavier. In a letter addressed from Amboina (Moluccas) to D. João III, king of Portugal, on May, 16, 1545, he wrote :

" The second necessity for the Christians is that your majesty establish the Holy Inquisition, because there are many who live according to the Jewish law, and according to the Mahomedan sect, without any fear of God or shame of the world. And since there are many who are spread all over the fortresses, there is

[1] Gaspar Correa, *Lendas da India*, Livro quatro, Tomo IV, Lisboa 1864, pp. 292-4.

the need of the Holy Inquisition and of many preachers. Your majesty should provide such necessary things for your loyal and faithful subjects in India."[2]

D. João III did not pay heed to the request of St. Xavier and the Inquisition was not introduced in Goa during his reign. However, similar demands continued to be addressed to the authorities in Portugal and Rome from different quarters. For instance, P. M. Nunes Barreto, a Jesuit priest, in a letter addressed on January 15, 1551 to the Father General in Rome writes as follows :

" This is to inform Your Paternity that the Inquisition is more necessary in these parts than anywhere else, since all the Christians here live together with the Muslims, the Jews and the Hindus and, also the largeness of the country itself causes laxness of conscience in persons residing therein. With the curb of the Inquisition they will live a good life. And since the people of this country set store by their honour, if they do not mend their ways from consideration of what they owe to God, they may do so at least out of fear of the disgrace and shame of prison and other penalties. "[3]

The Inquisition was not introduced in Goa during the reign of D. João III, but soon after his death in 1557, conditions in Portugal became propitious for the establishment of the Inquisition in Goa and in 1560, Aleixo Dias Falcão was sent to Goa as Inquisitor. H. C. Lea describes in the following passage the circumstances which led to the introduction of the Inquisition in India and the historical consequences of the " sinister renown as the most pitiless in Christendom " which this tribunal soon earned :

" João died June 11, 1557, leaving the crown to his grandson Don Sebastian a child in his third year, under the regency of the dowager Queen Cataliana, who resigned it, in 1562, in favour of Cardinal Henrique. The Regency was more mindful of the spiritual needs of the Indies than the late King and, in March, 1560, Henrique sent to Goa as inquisitor Aleixo Diaz

[2] Silva Rego, *Documentação para a Historia das Missões do Padroado Portugues do Oriente*, Vol. III, Lisboa 1950, p. 351.

[3] Joseph Wicki, *Documenta Indica*, vol. IV, Rome 1956, pp. 229-30.

Falcão who, by the end of the year, founded a tribunal which in time earned a sinister renown as the most pitiless in Christendom. When Lourenço Pirez, the ambassador at Rome, learned through Egypt of this establishment, he expressed to the Regency his apprehension that this zeal for religion would prove a disservice to God and to the kingdom, for it would drive to Bassorah and Cairo many who would aid the enemy in both finance and war. His prevision was justified more fully than he anticipated for, to the activity of the tribunal was largely attributable the decay of the once flourishing Indian possessions of Portugal. After exhausting the New Christians it turned its attention to the native Christians, who rewarded so abundantly the missionary labors of the Jesuits, for Portugal did not follow the wise example of Spain in exempting native converts from the Inquisition. It was impossible for these poor folk to abandon completely the supersticious practices of their ancestors, and any relapse into these however trifling was visited with rigour with which were treated similar lapses by the Conversos of the Peninsula."[4]

The eminent Jesuit historian, Fr. Francisco de Souza, describes in the following passage an incident which served as the immediate cause for the introduction of the Inquisition in Goa :

" Whilst in the island of Goa, heated efforts were made to destroy Hinduism, father Provincial Gonsalvo da Silveira and bishop Belchior Carneiro were moving about in Cochin persecuting the insidious Judaism. These priests came to know how in that city were living some descendants of the Israelite people, rich and possessing much, but infected with Judaism, as a consequence of their proximity to and communications with the Jews of Cochin, who had been converted to Judaism from Hinduism many centuries ago. Since the tribunal of Inquisition had not been introduced in these parts and since the bishop D. João de Albuquerque was already dead, there was no one who would inquire into their lives, and they lived in freedom of conscience, secretly observing the Law of Moses. Fr. Silveira commenced to preach against these rebellious and obstinate people. As he was well versed in the holy scriptures and knew the Greek and the Hebrew languages, with great erudition and copious variety of passages taken from the oldest authors he proved how the Messiah

[4] H. C. Lea, *op. cit.*, vol. III, New York, 1907, pp. 260-61.

had already come and he could not be anyone else but Jesus Christ. Also from clear texts taken from the Old Testament he showed to them that the Messiah was God and that there was Trinity of persons with the Unity of Essence. With this preaching the Jews felt very badly cornered and they came out and started speaking against the priests. When one of them renounced Judaism the others told him publicly that it was great imprudence that a man should abandon the Law he had professed. This bold act led others to indulge in the rashness of placing in the boxes, kept in the churches, writings full of blasphemy against the Divinity of Christ, the Catholic Church, and the Society of Jesus. The priests could not tolerate such outrages in a city of Catholics, and they applied to the Vicar Pero Gonsalves, a great friend of St. Francis Xavier, on the grounds that there was no bishop in India nor the tribunal of the Holy Office, who might proceed against these atrocious blasphemies, and if necessary arrest the delinquents. The Vicar agreed to these just requests and helped by the priests, started taking necessary action. One day, whilst in the Cathedral church witnesses were making depositions, the Captain of the City, induced by the New Christians entered and told the Vicar that it was not expedient to make inquiries about these cases and therefore he should at once dissolve the tribunal. The Bishop appointed for this purpose replied with great firmness, 'You go back to the fortress and do not interfere in matters of Faith.' The Captain at once obeyed and the result was that at the end of rainy weather, twenty or more New Christians from among the rich of the City, were arrested and taken to Goa. Fr. Silveira accompanied them to support the case. It was good that he acted so, because the Goan authorities wanted to release the prisoners on bail. This priest opposed this proposal with such strength, that many other New Christians were arrested in Goa, and were sent to Portugal where they were judged and punished as Jews. The result of these actions and the letters that priests wrote, was to send immediately to India in the year 1660 the tribunal of the Holy Inquisition, the first Inquisitors being Alex Dias Falcão and Francisco Marquis, both well-versed in Canon Law."[5]

[5] Francisco de Souza, *Oriente Conquistado a Jesus Christo*, Part I (Second Edition), Bombay 1881, p. 82, (Conq. 1, Div. 2, § 29).

It would appear that Fr. Souza has based his account of the incident described in the passage quoted above on the information contained in a book on the history of the Society of Jesus written in the sixteenth century by Alessandro Valignano (1539-1606). A printed edition of this book, which was in manuscript form, has recently been brought out by Fr. J. Wicki of Rome. Referring to the incident of the New Christians who were sent from Cochin to Goa, Fr. Valignano, after stating the facts narrated by Fr. Souza, adds :

" They were sent to the Holy Inquisition in Portugal where some were burnt and others awarded punishments according to their offences.

" And with this, His Highness, having understood what was happening in India, took the opportunity to send here the Holy Office, which with the passage of time found so many guilty and burnt and awarded other punishments to so many of these New Christians,...,thereby cleansing India of so much corruption and wickedness.

" And thus he sent two apostolic Inquisitors who were ordered to go to India, as from the letters which he had received from these parts he was informed that there were many New Christians who practised Judaism and had separate synagogues. Some prominent persons from among these were sent to him during the preceding year with documents setting forth their guilt, as there was none there who could pronounce sentence on them. And along with this there existed many other things against the glory of God, and good Christian customs, to which it was necessary to attend diligently, in order that they might not go further. Hence soon a reference was made to the Pope to send to these parts the Holy Inquisition."[6]

François Pyrard, a French traveller, was in Goa during the period July 1608 to January 1610. In his account of his travels he gives the following information of the Inquisition of Goa :

" The Inquisition consists of two fathers, who are held in great dignity and respect ; but the one is much greater man than

[6] Alessandro Valignano, *Historia del Principio y Progresso de la Compañia de Jesus en las Indias Orientales* (Edited by Fr. J. Wicki), Rome 1944, pp. 343-4.

the other, and is called Inquisitor Major. Their procedure is much more severe than in Portugal ; they often burn Jews, whom the Portuguese call Christianos noeuous, that is to say, 'New Christians.' The first time they are taken before the holy Inquisition, all their goods are seized at the same time ; they are seldom arrested unless they are rich. The king supplies the cost of this process to everyone who has not wherewithal. But ordinarily they attack them not except they learn that they have massed much property. Nothing in the world is more cruel and pitiless than this process. For the least suspicion, the slightest word, whether of a child or of a slave who wishes to do his master a bad turn, is enough to hang a man ; and they give credence to a child, however young, so only he can speak. Sometimes they are accused of putting their crucifixes in the cushions whereon they sit and kneel ; sometimes of striking the images, or of refraining from eating bacon ; in short that they are still secretly observing their ancient law, though they conduct themselves in public as good Christians. I verily believe that whatever is desired is assumed of them. Only the rich are put to death, while the poor get off with some penance. And, what is most cruel and wicked, a man who would do evil to another will, in revenge, go and accuse him of his crime. When the other is arrested, there is no friend will dare say a word for him, or will visit him, or lift a hand in his behalf, no more than for a person charged with high treason. The people durst not speak in public of this Inquisition but with very great honour and respect ; and if a chance word should escape a man, having but the smallest reference to it, he must forthwith go, accuse and denounce himself, if he suspect that anyone has heard him. Otherwise, if another denounce you, you will be at once arrested. It is a terrible and fearful thing to be there even once for you have no proctor or advocate to speak for you, while they are judges and parties at once. The form of the procedure is all the same as in Spain, Italy and Portugal. Sometimes men are kept prisoners two or three years without knowing the cause, visited by none but officers of the Inquisition, and in a place where they never see a fellow-creature. If they have no means of livelihood, the king gives it them. The Indian Gentiles and Moors, of whatsoever religion, are not subject to this Inquisition unless they have become Christians, and even then are not so rigorously dealt with as the

Portuguese or New Christians from Portugal, or other Christians from Europe. But if peradventure an Indian, Moor, or Gentile inhabitant of Goa, had dissuaded or hindered another that was minded to become Christian, and that was proved against him, he would be punished by the Inquisition, as would be he who has caused another to quit Christianity; such cases often happen. The reason why they treat these Indian thus rigorously is that they suppose that they cannot be so steadfast in the faith as the old Christians; also that it will prevent the rest from being led astray. For the same reason, too, they permit them to retain some of their petty Gentile and Mahomedan superstitions, such as not eating pork or beef, not drinking wine, and keeping to their former dress and ornaments, that is among men as well as women that are become Christians.

"It would be impossible to calculate the number of all those put to death by this Inquisition in ordinary course at Goa. I shall content myself with the single example of a Hollander jeweller or lapidary, that had resided there five-and-twenty years and more, and was married to a Portuguese Metice, by whom he had an exceeding pretty daughter of marriageable age, and had amassed goods to the amount of about thirty or forty thousand crusadoes. Being at that time on bad terms with his wife, he was accused of having the books of the pretended religion, whereupon he was arrested and his goods seized. One half was left to his wife, the other to the Inquisition. I know not what befell him, but I am inclined to believe that he was put to death, or at the least lost all his property; he was a Hollander. They did not treat in like sort a Portuguese soldier, who had married both in Portugal and in the Indies; but he was poor. They sent him in our carrack to Portugal as a prisoner to Lisbon; had he been rich, they had never taken the pains to send him. For the rest, all the other Inquisitions of the Indies depend upon that of Goa. It is upon all the great feast-days that they carry out their judgments. Then they cause all these poor culprits to march together in shirts steeped in sulphur and painted with flames of fire; the difference between those that have to die and the rest being that their flames are turned upwards and the others downwards. They are led straight to the great church or *A Sce* which is hard by the prison, and are there during the mass and the sermon, wherein they receive the most strenuous remonstrances. Thereafter they are conducted to the *Campo Sancto Lazaro*, where the condemned are burned in the presence of the rest, who look on."[7]

The Portuguese jurist, Coelho de Rocha, in his *Ensaio sobre a historia de Governo e legislatura de Portugal* (Essay on the history of the government and the legislature of Portugal) observes :

" There is however nothing which can equal the impropriety of establishing the Holy Office in Goa, where all considerations demanded avoidance of religions severity in the treatment of ignorant persons who had been converted very recently and were living in a mercantile centre where nations as varied in creeds as in orgin and colour carried on trade."[8]

J. C. Barreto Miranda, a Goan historian, speaks of the cruelties of the Inquisition of Goa in the following words :

" The cruelties which in the name of the religion of peace and love this tribunal practised in Europe, were carried to even greater excesses in India, where the Inquisitors, surrounded by luxuries which could stand comparison with the regal magnificence of the great potentates of Asia, saw with pride the Archbishop as well as the viceroy submitted to their power. Every word of theirs was a sentence of death and at their slightest nod were moved to terror the vast populations spread over the Asiatic regions, whose lives fluctuated in their hands, and who, on the most frivolous pretext, could be clapped for all time in the deepest dungeons or strangled or offered as food for the flames of the pyre."[9]

There are many well-known books dealing with the working of the Inquisition in countries like Spain and Portugal, but there exists no comprehensive account of the Inquisition in Goa, which is known to have surpassed all its counterparts in severity. Minguel Vicente de Abreo records that the eminent Goan historian, Felipe Nery Xavier, had announced in the *Boletim do Governo* (No. 78) in 1864, his intention to bring out a book under the title

[7] *The Voyage of François Pyrard to the East Indies, the Maldives, the Molucas and Brazil* (Trans. by Albert Gray) vol. II, pt. i, London 1888, pp. 92-95.

[8] *Narração de Inquisição de Goa* (Translated by Minguel Vicente D'Abreu), Nova Goa 1866, p. 8.

[9] C. B. Barreto Miranda, *Quadros Historicos de Goa*, Cadernete I, Margão 1863, p. 145.

"*Memoria Historica de Tribunal da Inquisição de Goa*" (Historical Record of the Tribunal of the Inquisition of Goa) which would "deal at length with the origin, progress, decadence and extinction of that colossal monument, which lived in these latitudes a long life of two and a half centuries." This work, however, did not see the light of the day.

One can visualise two main difficulties in the way of a historian of the Holy Office in Goa. First, the Inquisition continued to inspire terror in the hearts of contemporaries for a long time even after its power was on the wane and they would naturally prefer not to speak of it or to disclose what they knew of its dark deeds to the curious historian. Second, records of the Inquisition and other authentic documentary material were not available. It may be expected also that the authorities of the Church and the State in Portugal would prefer to hush up the excesses committed by this tribunal and they would frown at any attempt to bring to the light of the day this dark chapter in the history of that country. I hence believe that in the present conditions few Goan savants would dare to undertake the task and it would be only a historian of Portuguese birth, like A. Herculano, Oliveira Martins or Cunha Rivara, who may some day do full justice to it.

A vivid idea of the feelings of deep-rooted terror with which the Holy Office in Goa was viewed by the common people is provided by the following story recounted by F. Nery Xavier:

"The terrible acts of the Inquisition during the early period of its existence had caused terror to be so deeply rooted in the memories of the people that none dared to name the place where it was housed as the house of the Inquisition, but gave it the mysterious appellation "*Orlem gor*" (the Big House). While we were once passing by the riverside, not having understood the aforesaid mystery, we were desirous of knowing the situation of the mysterious house which was not in sight, but they did not consent to our pointing our fingers in that direction—and this at a time when the tribunal retained hardly its name!"[10]

I have always felt it a pity that there should be no authentic account of the Inquisition in India and have given some thought

[10] *Instrucçãs do Marquez de Alorná as seu successor* (Edited by F. Nery Xavier), 3rd ed., Goa 1903, p. 38.

to the problem of filling up this lacuna in our history. A quarter of a century ago, during a visit to Goa, I made some enquiries about the basic material for the purpose. I examined all printed material available in Goa and proceeded to look for any manuscript documents. The main source for an authentic account would obviously be the records of the proceedings of the Inquisition. In response to my enquiries, Shri P. Pissurlencar, Director of the Historical Archives of the Goa government, informed me that these records were not available in Goa. I must admit that at the time a passing suspicion as to whether this official denial might have been made in pursuance of the policy of the government or motivated by a desire on the part of the officer not to embarrass the Portuguese government by giving away inconvenient secrets, arose in my mind. The ground for this suspicion was provided by an assertion of Mr. Braz Fernandes, former Secretary to the Bombay Historical Society. In support of his contention that Dr. Dellon's account of his incarceration at the hands of the Inquisition of Goa was a fabrication, Mr. Fernandes, had stated that he had personally examined the records of the Inquisition which were housed in a Church in Goa and verified that the papers relating to the case of Dr. Dellon did not exist in the records of the year 1674. I also contacted the persons in charge of the various churches in Goa and was informed that the records of the Inquisition were not housed in any of these Churches. I next met Dr. A. B. Bragança Pereira, President of the Archaeological Commission of the Goa government, but he too confirmed that these records were not available in Goa. From information which became available later, there is reason to believe that these records were deliberately burnt.

The first occasion when plans to destroy these records were made arose in 1739, when Goa was attacked by the Marathas. Details of this incident are available in a note made by Salvador Ribeiro, Adjutant to the Inquisition, under the orders of the Inquisitor Antonio de Amaral Coutinho. On January 23, 1738, as a result of an attack by the Marathas, the Portuguese had to leave Margão and other villages of Salsete with the exception of the fort of Rachol. It was feared that during the following week the Marathas would attack Goa also. The Inquisitor thereupon ordered that all the contents of the archives of the

Inquisition—codes, indexes, ornaments and a mass of processes as recent as possible, should be placed in boxes and sent to the fort of Mormugão. Later on, the Marathas conquered Bardez, and as Goa was considered to be in imminent danger, the viceroy issued orders that women and children from Goa should proceed to Mormugão. In the resulting commotion, transport could not be spared for carrying the remainder of the papers of the Inquisition to Mormugão and these papers were, therefore, deposited in the corridors of the prison-house with dry leaves spread underneath, the intention being to set fire to the records if necessary. The luck of the Portuguese rulers, however, held on this occasion and the need to destroy the records as planned did not arise.[11]

In 1774, when the Inquisition was suspended, the more important of its records were carried to Portugal. In a letter dated March 9, 1782, addressed from Portugal to Goa, it is stated that ten boxes containing these records were returned to Goa in 1779, when the Inquisition was revived.[12] When in 1812, it was finally decided to abolish the Inquisition the authorities were faced with the problem of the disposal of these records. The viceroy, Conde de Sarzedas in a letter dated December 20, 1812, addressed to the King expressed his views on the subject as follows :

" The papers which comprised the archive of that tribunal were found to be a vast mass, and there was no room in the office of the Secretary of State to permit of their being received, as I had decided. I, therefore ordered, that they be kept in the building of the Royal arsenal, being deposited in large sacks which would be sealed with the royal arms by the Inquisitor, and that the building be closed with three keys, one of which would remain with me, another at the secretariat, and the third in the hands of the intendant of the navy. I considered it was proper to take all these precautionary measures in respect of these records as I am informed that in them exist papers relating to all the suits tried by the Holy Office since its inception, and if they are not guarded with all care, therein would be found motives to defame, even falsely, all the families in the state and these would provide

[11] Panduranga S. Pissurlencar, *Roteiro dos Archivos da India Portugueza*, Bastorà 1955, (Introduction, pp. vii-xviii).

[12] Antonio Baião, *A Inquisição de Goa*, Vol. I, Lisboa 1945, p. 14.

occasions to feed the enmities and intrigues which so much abound in this country. It is meet that your Royal Highness should determine what should be done with this mass of papers and processes. As I am persuaded that it is not expedient that they should be seen by any person, it appears to me that it would be appropriate to burn them."

In reply to this communication dated September 27, 1813, contained the following directions on this point :

" As regards the huge mass of papers existing in the archive of the Inquisition, as it does not appear wise to burn them without some kind of review, nor to commit them to the care of a person who is not in the secret of the said papers, His Royal Highness decided for this purpose to order that the Promoter, in whom are found the talent and probity necessary for this task, should be placed in charge of such examination and as soon as he has finished and has made the necessary separation of those papers which are worthy of being preserved, you will arrange to burn the rest, and remit those which are retained under proper security to this office of the Secretary of the State. "[13]

The task of selecting the important papers from this archive was assigned to Fr. Tomas de Noronha. There is however no way to find out how he carried it out. Antonio de Baião, author of *A Inquisição de Goa* writes that no indication can be found that these selected papers were ever sent to Portugal. Nor can any trace of these papers be found in Goa.

[13] *Ibid.*, p. 16.

CHAPTER IV

Dellon's Account of the Inquisition of Goa: A Fabrication?

THE circumstances in which the records of the Inquisition of Goa were destroyed have been described in the previous chapter. The working of the Inquisition was always shrouded in secrecy and in the absence of these records, whic should have provided the main material for a history of that institution, it has become almost impossible to write a comprehensive account of its working. Fortunately, a glimpse into its organisation and procedures can be obtained from the recorded experiences of a contemporary French traveller, Dr. Dellon, who was its prisoner for a period of nearly three years. Some research-workers in India have, however, questioned the authenticity of Dr. Dellon's account, and it is proposed at this stage to examine briefly the grounds advanced by them in support of this view as well as other evidence bearing on the question.

Dr. Charles Dellon was born in 1649. He took up employment with the French East India Company and started for India on March 20, 1668. On arrival in India, he served for some time on the ships and in the factories of the Company. In 1673 he resigned from the service of the Company, as a result of differences with M. Flacourt, the head of the French factory at Tellicherry, and started medical practice at Damaun, which was under Portuguese rule. After a stay of five or six months in that city, he was arrested under the orders of the Inquisition and taken to Goa in the beginning of the year 1674. He remained in the prison of the Inquisition of Goa for two years and was then condemned to serve on the Galleys in Portugal for five years. He left for Lisbon on January 27, 1676 and was set at liberty by the Inquisitor General in Lisbon in June 1677, on condition that he leave for France immediately.

He wrote two books about his experiences in India; or, in the words of Dr. Gerson da Cunha, two books "are said to have been written by him." The first of these, which is an account of his travels in India was published in Paris in 1785 under the title *Relation d'un Voyage fait aux Indes Orientales.* This went into many editions and an English translation bearing the title

Voyage to the East Indies published in London is also extant. The second book bears the title *Relation de l'Inquisition de Goa* and was published in 1687. This book also went into many editions. Two English translations of this book, both published in London, the first in 1688 and the second in 1812, are extant and the later translation is reprinted in the second part of the present volume.

Dellon visited Goa twice in the course of his stay in India, first when he was travelling northwards from Mangalore and later when he was taken there from Damaun as prisoner of the Inquisition. In his first book he devotes four chapters to describe his first visit to Goa. The serial numbers and the titles of these chapters are as follows :—

Serial No.	*Title*
IX	Our Arrival at Goa
X	Of the City of Goa
XI	Of the Inhabitants of Goa
XII	Concerning our Stay at Goa.

In chapter X, he refers to the Inquisition in the following worlds:

"Just opposite to the Cathedral in a great square stands that Famous House, whose very Name makes many thousands Tremble in those parts ; this is the Court of Inquisition called by the Portuguese *Santa Casa* or *Casa do Santo Oficio.*"[1]

In the same book, he describes his second visit to Goa in the following words :—

"We staid in Bassaim about five or six days and then set sail for Goa, where we arrived on the fourteenth day of January towards Night. I went on shoar the next day, and by the advantageous offers made by Friends, was prevailed upon to stay near three whole years in this great City, of which I have given a description before."[2]

It will be seen that although particulars of this second visit, such as the period of stay at Bassaim and date of arrival in Goa, agree with those mentioned in the second book, in the account

[1] Dellon, *Voyage to the East Indies,* Part II, London 1698, p. 161.
[2] *Ibid.*, Chap. XXII, p. 193.

given in the first book Dellon not only omits to state that his visit was involuntary and made as a prisoner of the Inquisition, but also adds that he was prevailed upon to stay in the city of Goa " by the advantageous offers made by friends. " This departure from truth need not cause any surprise to those conversant with the methods of the Inquisition and the terror which remained permanently implanted in the hearts of its victims. In the opening chapter of the second book Dellon refers explicitly to the " dread of the horrid tortures inflicted on those convicted of breaking the oath of secrecy imposed before their liberty is restored. " He also describes in the same chapter the prolonged hesitation which preceded his decision to risk the displeasure of the Holy Office by breaking the oath of secrecy :

" I have long hesitated as to the publication of this account, for eight years have elapsed since my return to France, and upwards of four since the account was written. I was afraid to offend the Holy Office and to break my oath,..."[3]

It also appears that in the first edition of this book the name of the author was not disclosed in full but mentioned in the form "D+ + +." In the editions of the book which appeared after the death of the author, the publishers probably replaced this arrangement by his full name. The first English translation of this book, to which we have already referred, was carried out in 1688 by Daniel Horthemels in Paris. In this translation the name of the author appears in the form " D+ + + " in the author's " Dedication." It also appears in the same form in " An Extract of the Priviledge of the King, " which runs as follows :

" By the Grant and Priviledge of the King, given at *Versailles* the 21st day of *August* 1687. Signed, *by the King in his Council, Poullain*, it is permitted to the Sieur D+ + + to cause a Book to be imprinted, Intituled, *A Relation of the Inquisition of Goa,...*"[4]

No scholar in Portugal or any other European country appears to have questioned the authenticity of Dellon's account of the Inquisition. To my knowledge the first attempt to do so was made by Dr. Gerson da Cunha, a well-known research-worker and author of *The Origin of Bombay* and other books.

[3] *Vide* Part II, p. 6.

[4] *The History of the Inquisition as it is exercised at Goa*, London 1688, (Preface).

In a paper read under the auspices of the Bombay Branch of the Royal Asiatic Society on December 18, 1888, Dr. Cunha observed :

" For all these reasons I think the narrative which goes by the name of M. Dellon is a fabrication, a forgery, a fraud, although based on his genuine travels. If I were to recapitulate all the arguments to doubt its fidelity or to repudiate its authenticity, it would take much time, which, unfortunately, I cannot spare. I shall be glad, however, if this humble contribution as a protest against the truthfulness of a work that has deceived several generations of scholars will invite the attention of other students of Indian history to the true character of the work."[5]

A similar view is also expressed by Fr. Heras, S.J., in a footnote appearing in a paper read on March 27, 1927, which runs as follows :

" There are founded suspicions that the whole work of Dellon is a tremendous forgery. It seems that he was actualy in Europe when supposed to be in the dungeons of the Inquisition at Goa."[6]

A more elaborate attempt in the same direction was made by Braz H. Fernandes, a former secretary to the Bombay Historical Society in a series of articles published under the title *Dellon and the Inquisition of Goa* in *The Anglo Lusitano*, a Bombay weekly. This was subsequently published in book form in 1936. In the concluding paragraph of this book the author wrote :

" We have briefly examined and exposed the forgery known as Dellon's *History of the Inquisition in Goa*, which has deceived several generations of scholars, and which will most likely, go on deceiving."[7]

After a careful study of these attempts to establish that Dellon's account of the Inquisition was a fabrication, I felt they were based on arguments which were far from convincing as the

[5] J. Gerson da Cunha, " M. Dellon and the Inquisition of Goa ", *J. B. Br. of the Royal Asiatic Society*, Vol. XVIII, Part II (1887-1889) Bombay 1889, p. 52.

[6] H. Heras, " The Decay of the Portuguese Power in India, " *Journal of the Bombay Historical Society*, Vol. I, Bombay 1928, p. 35.

[7] Braz A. Fernandes, *Dellon and the Inquisition of Goa*, Bombay 1936, p. 63.

approach adopted was that of an advocate arguing in favour of a preconceived case rather than that of an impartial and disinterested historian in search of truth. The controversy would be resolved if independent contemporary documentary evidence could be produced to show that Dellon was actually a prisoner of the Inquisition. An obvious source of such evidence should have been the records of the Inquisition of Goa relating to the period 1674-76 but as stated earlier, these have been destroyed. Another possible source was indicated by a reference in Chapter XII of Dellon's account to a visit paid to him at Damaun by the famous French traveller Abbé Carré. Dellon writes :

"M. l'Abbé Carré passing through Damaun, on his return from St. Thomas's, with much difficulty obtained permission to see me ; and had the goodness to come to me on Christmas eve, and also the next day, when he departed for Surat."[8]

I had read that Abbé Carré was an admirer of Shivaji and had left an account of the latter in a book describing his travels. It occured to me that if Abbé Carré mentioned in the book that he visited Dellon while the latter was a prisoner of the Inquisition, this would provide conclusive evidence of the authenticity of Dellon's own story. My search for a copy of Abbé Carré's book proved fruitless for a long time, and it was only during the period of the last world war that I could obtain definite information about it. Late Sir Sitaram Patkar, a judge of the High Court of Bombay, sent for me at this time and informed me that a former colleague of his, Sir Charles Fawcett, had written to him in connection with an annotated English translation of the French account of Abbé Carré's travels, which Sir Charles and his wife proposed to bring out. They had come across certain obscure passages in this work and Sir Sitaram handed over the letter to me and asked me to try my hand at elucidating their difficulties. I spent about a week on the work and handed over to Sir Sitaram written answers to all the queries raised in the letter. I resisted the temptation to use this opportunity to enquire whether Abbé Carré in his book had referred to his visit to Dellon, lest this appear as asking for a favour in return for the small service I had rendered. I knew that the translation would soon be published

[8] *Vide* Part II, p. 18.

and I could satisfy my curiosity then. The book has been published in three volumes by the Hakluyt Society in London during 1947-48 and in the first volume the help given by Sir Sitaram has been acknowledged. On reference to these volumes I found that my previous impression that Abbé Carré's book had been published in French in the seventeenth century was wrong. The English translation has been based on the French manuscript of the book available at the India Office, which was purchased by the Court of Directors on November 3, 1820 for £ 40 from one John Walker.

I was very happy to note that Abbé Carré has given a detailed account of the background of the misfortunes of Dellon and their meetings at Damaun. It is interesting to note in this connection that Braz Fernandes, in his book referred to earlier, has tried to establish that Dellon's story of his having been visited by Abbé Carré was fictitious. In the foot-note No. 31 on p. 36, Braz Fernandes writes as follows :

" It is extremely doubtful that Abbé Carré was in Damaun on Christmas day 1673. He arrived at Surat in 1668, and went home via the Persian Gulf in 1671. He returned to India again in 1672 and went straight from Surat to Madras—H. R. (G) Rawlinson. *Source Book of Maratha History* (Bombay, 1929), 205."[9]

On reference to the *Source Book* by Rawlinson, from which the information about the movements of Abbé Carré given in the above foot-note would appear to have been drawn, I could trace no mention therein of Abbé Carré having proceeded to Madras from Surat.

Abbé Carré's account of his stay in Damaun and his visits to Dellon is reproduced hereunder in full.

JOURNEY TO DAMAN AND SURAT

FRIDAY, 22 *December*, (1673) I left Tarapur two hours before dawn, and by making my people march rapidly, we got to Dahanu at daybreak. This is a large Portuguese aldea, to which Donna Petronella and her daughter, the wife of the

[9] Braz A. Fernandes, *op. cit.*, p. 36.

unfortunate Dom João, had lately come and were living in a house of their own. Without stopping, I then passed by several other pleasant aldeas and rivers ; and in the evening I met three or four Portuguese fidalgos, who joined me. We all slept at Nargol, a large aldea belonging to the Paulist Fathers of Daman and yielding them a large revenue. It is inhabited by Hindus and some Christians, subjects and slaves of these Fathers.

The next day, 23rd, we left before daybreak and, after crossing three rivers, followed the seashore, arriving at Daman about ten o'clock in the morning. At first I went to stop with M. Nicholas Vidal of Provence, as I usually did when passing through this place, but I soon saw that there was trouble and unpleasantness in his family on account of his wife. I drank a glass of wine with him and, though he pressed me to stop there, I withdrew to the house of Senhor Antonio Guiard, the father-in-law of M. Mariage, a French merchant of our Company, who had had the fantastic idea of marrying a young Portuguese lady, the cause of his ruin and the loss of all his wealth in India. I shall recount this story later when I have finished that of M. Vidal.

The latter had been married in Daman for fifteen years and had amassed great riches and honour by the annual voyages which he made to Eastern kingdoms as commander of both Moor and Portuguese ships. Nevertheless, he was not better off on this account, as his wealth, wife, and family were at Daman, and he could never remove any of them from Portuguese territory. By this wife he had only a small son, now eight years old and his chief consolation next to his wife, who was very handsome. Until now he had always thought her virtuous, because she had so well hidden her love affairs, of which he had only slight suspicions. But this year, on his return from a ten months' voyage to Mozambique, as captain of a vessel belonging to the Governor of Daman with whom he had an interest in the venture, he was much astonished to find his wife seven months gone with child, and he learnt with extreme displeasure that she had led an immoral and disgraceful life, both in her own house and also in that of the Governor, where she went every night. The Governor, who was a near relation of the Viceroy, thus set a fine example. Not only had he a wife and a twenty-years-old son with him, but also a troop of concubines ; and besides he now debauched married women, without even excepting the wife of an honourable man, who had exposed his life at sea to peril in voyages to gather riches and goods for his employer. The worst of the affair was that M. Vidal, seeing no other remedy for this miserable business, resolved not to go to sea again. He contemplated living quietly at home with his wife, hoping by his presence to overcome her bad habits and immoral inclinations. The poor man did not know that it is impossible to cure a woman who has once got into the habit of illicit pleasures : you might as well try to make a nigger's head white by washing it. The Governor, well knowing that this woman could not live without her love affairs, resolved on his side to make use of all his power and credit. To succeed in this he at first cajoled M. Vidal with hopes of great gains, so as to make him do another voyage in his ship ; but, failing in that because of the latter's resolve never to go to sea again, he tyrannically threatened to confiscate all his goods and to ruin him entirely. if he did not undertake the trip. The poor man was in a terrible consternation, not knowing what to decide. Sometimes in his despair he thought of stabbing his wife, who was thus disgracing his honour ; sometimes he contemplated making the voyage and losing the Governor's ship and goods in Moor territory, as a punishment for the wrong and insult done to him by the robbery of his honour and the possession he held the dearest in the world. He restrained himself, however, as he was an upright and God-fearing man. He also still had a great tenderness for his wife, whom he had always loved from the first day he lived with her. But what touched him most deeply was his little boy, beautiful as a cherub, whom he could not take away from Portuguese. So by the advice of his friends and particularly of an influential Portuguese companion of his at Daman, who promised to look after his wife in his absence, he decided to make this voyage. It was, however, the same as if a wolf were left in charge of a lamb, for all the Portuguese at Daman were so devoted to the Governor that they would not oppose any of his desires, no matter what they were.

About this time there was a young Parisian Frenchman, a M. Deslong (Dellon), who in 1668 had left France for India in the ship *La Force* as surgeon's mate. Ater serving several years in the factories and ships of the French Company, he left its service six months ago, as he could not get on with M. Flacourt, the head of the Tellicherry factory. He then retired to the town of Daman, where he was considered to be the cleverest doctor in India, though all his science consisted in knowing how to bleed ; but on the other hand he had other qualities to recommend him, which soon gave him an *entrée* in Portuguese society. He was young, good-looking, and intelligent. His knowledge and use of a few Latin words gave him great prestige in this town, where several families treated him like a relation, so much was he liked and appreciated. They gave him lodgings, food and his expenses ; and, being French, he freely visited the family of M. Vidal, where he became like a son of the house. The Portuguese Governor, madly jealous of him, resolved to do something unexpected to prevent his visits to this house, where the Governor's own affections were deeply involved, especially when he saw that M. Vidal on his return treated the young man with all the courtesy and esteem due to a compatriot. Besides this jealousy, the Governor feared that he might give M. Vidal some drug to do away with his wife secretly. So, knowing the habit of this young surgeon to argue about our religion with the Portuguese, he asked him civilly to bleed his son, and laid a trap for our young doctor by attaching an ivory figure of St. Antony to the boy's arm. This Portuguese plot succeeded as they had hoped for before the doctor began to put a ligature on the arm of the Governor's son, he asked the boy to take off his St. Antony, as it hindered the operation. Thereupon the boy replied that he would not do so, as St. Antony would prevent any mistakes or accidents that might happen during bleeding. The young doctor did not fail to say that it was an absurd superstition to imagine that St. Antony had any effect on the operation. So from these and other words there arose a sharp quarrel on the merits of St. Antony, and M. Dellon spoke a little carelessly, though without malice.

The witnesses, who had been placed there for this purpose, went at once, on behalf of the Governor, to the Father Rector of the Paulists, who was also the local Commissary of the Inquisition at Goa. They accused the French doctor of heresy and uttering words against the Holy Faith. The Father had formerly been very friendly with the doctor on account of some services he had rendered, and did not wish him to know that he was to be arrested by the Rector's order, so he went off to Goa, where he had some business, and left instructions that, as soon as he was out of the town, the Frenchman was to be secured. This was promptly done, and he was thrown into the town prison with the common criminals. He was there for a long time and was not allowed to see or speak to any one. After this *coup* the Governor still feared that M. Vidal would get poison elsewhere or would try in some other way to rid himself of the wife who had disgraced him. He therefore issued orders to all persons living in the same street to spy on M. Vidal's actions and on everything that happened in his house, and that he was to be arrested at the least sound of lamentations or cries raised by his wife.

This was the state in which I found these two poor Frenchmen of Daman on my arrival. M. Vidal poured out his sorrows to me in a most heartbreaking way, and also asked my advice. I replied that, in similar cases, even the most discreet people were at their wits' end over it, and that he could never hope to make his wife virtuous by force, if she did not wish this herself; so that I considered the most expedient thing was for him, first of all, to escape, if possible, with his goods and son, from Portuguese territory, as they would never cease to disturb and vex at him in every way they could, in the hope of causing his death and seizing all his wealth.

Being in the town of Daman, where I was obliged to stay for two days so as not to lose the opportunity of making my devotions on Christmas Day. I should have been very glad to avoid paying a visit to this Governor. This was not only on account of his conduct towards M.Vidal and the French surgeon, but also because of his having refused my request to him in the preceding year to release some Frenchmen of our Company, whom he had taken into his service. Neverthless, as I wished to speak to M. Dellon, whom he had kept in prison for five months and the Governor's permission was required for this, I decided to force myself to pay him the civility of a visit.

Sunday, 24 December. In the morning I went to visit the Governor of Daman, whom I found surrounded by the principal men of the town. From the latter I received many courtesies, but I found the Governor very frigid and a litle anxious, as he imagined I might be visiting him with the same object as in the previous year, or else to speak about his bad treatment of our Frenchmen. However, he became more cordial, when I had spent half an hour in talking of other things and giving him news of what had occurred in the countries I had just visited. I left till the last the real object which had obliged me to come and see him. On his rising to conduct me to the door, being thus a little withdrawn from the rest of the company, I said to him casually, " They tell me sir, that there is a young French surgeon in prison here. Will you be gracious enough to tell me something about it, and whether you would permit me to speak to him, so as to see if there is any chance of rescuing him from this misery. It is indeed a disgrace to our nation that any Frenchman should be detained in a Portuguese prison, they being our allies and friends." " Truly ", replied the Governor, " I should much like to be of use to you in every way, but this business is risky for both of us, since if we show any desire to help this young Frenchman, we run great danger of being ourselves arrested, as he had been. It is a matter of the Holy Inquisition, and relations and friends are not allowed in any way to solicit the deliverance of those who have been apprehended by its orders. Neverteless, I will make a suggestion, which may help you in what you wish. Go and see the Father Rector of St. Paul, who has just returned from Goa and is at the head of the Inquisition here." Therefore, having taken leave of the Governor I went at once to the Paulist Fathers, though with some reluctance, fearing that they might try to find a pretext for putting me also under the Inquisition, from which it is not easy to escape once you are in their clutches, no matter who or what you are. Also it would be foolish to mention the subject which had brought me there.

Having arrived, I was led into a high room, very well built like a cloister in the European style. Here I spent half an hour alone, walking up and down, while awaiting the Father Rector, who was engaged with some farmers of their aldeas. Finally I saw him approach with a severe and grave aspect, which did not however, prevent me saluting him very politely. I told him that I was very much obliged to the priests of his Order for the good education, in learning and manners, that I had received from them in my youth, and that I never failed to pay my respects, in recognition of those benefits, to the Houses they had in whatever country I found myself. I had, therefore, in passing through Daman taken the liberty of coming to offer my humble services and regards to him, as one of my benefactors. The Father replied very politely to this discourse, and we spent a long hour in conversation on affairs in Europe, as to which I was enchanted to be able to give him some details of what was going on there. Finally he demanded news of the St. Thomé affairs, and how it was possible for the French to hold out so long against all the power of the Golconda kingdom and the Dutch forces, whom they had been unable to resist in former wars. On that I let him know that our French were at present stronger than ever in the place and were quite able to resist all the powers in the East, notwithstanding that many flighty and dishonourable Frenchmen had left the service of their king for that of foreign nations, where by Heaven's just punishment they found themselves reduced to utter want. "It is quite true," said the Father, "that we have a great many of them in our Portuguese towns, but they are not so unhappy as you imagine. Our Viceroy at Goa makes much of them, but what is really sad is that most of them are heretics and unbelievers. They discuss and argue on our holy religion, and this we cannot allow here any more than in our own country. There is one here in our holy prison whose case much pains me, because he is so intelligent and very skilful in the art of medicine, which is his profession. This is not rare, because nearly all these doctors are inclined to be heretics and atheists." I then appeared astonished, as if I had never heard of the matter. "What!" I said "my Reverend Father, you have a French doctor here! You do surprise me, for I do not know of any other in India but the one at Bassein (Dr. Seguineau), who had married a mistress (MS. *creade*) of the Governor there." "It is true, nevertheless," replied the Father; "he is a fine young man and says he has been five years in the service of your Company, which he left only six months ago. He then came to this town, where he acquired great credit and esteem among our Christians, and says he is the son of one of the cleverest doctors in France." "Perhaps", I replied to the Father, "you can give me his name, and I may be able to enlighten you about him. I know all the officers who have served our Company in India ever since it was established." Thereupon the Father, who desired to know all about the genealogy of everyone (this is a principal feature of the Holy Inquisition), went to his room, and having opened his register, wrote on a small piece of paper his name, age, height, visage, hair, parents, and all that is elicited by the interrogation of any person arrested by the Holy Chamber.

He had no sooner shown me this note than I assured him that I knew all about the young man; that he was of an honourable and god-fearing family, good Roman Catholics ; and that I had never heard of any of them doing anything against our holy faith, also that only last year, before I left France for the East, his father had given me some letters for his son, urging him to serve God in everything and to do his duty as a true Christian ; but that, as I now heard he was in prison for offences against the service of God and our holy faith, I should not trouble myself about him, nor would I bother myself to send this news to his parents. Consequently, while I showed the Father Commissary of the Holy Inquisition the indifference I felt towards this man's affairs, he came himself to the goal I desired, and said to me very obligingly that he would be glad if I would go and see the young man before I left, and give him a reprimand and some good advice to be more restrained in the future in talking of our holy faith. He also said that they intended sending him soon to Goa, to recieve the punishment due for his offence, which would be to make a humble apology, torch in hand, in the church of the Holy Inquisition there, and afterwards to be flogged through the streets of Goa, this being the mildest treatment he could expect for his indiscretion respecting our religion and St. Antony. These last statements almost put me off from visiting the surgeon, knowing how dangerous the Inquisition was ; but in view of the goodwill of the Father, who had himself invited me to go there I pretended I had great repugnance to visiting this young Frenchman, and that I was doing so only out of consideration for his parents, to see if he wished to reply to their letters which I had brought him from France the preceding year.

I took leave of the Father much pleased at my success, and went to find M. Vidal to whom I gave an account of the visits I had just paid and their object. He showed great pleasure at my having managed the affair so well. I then went to the prison, accompanied only by my little boy. Orders had been sent to let me see and speak freely to M. Dellon, and I had a long hour's conversation with him through a double grille, in which he told me of his bad luck and the reason for his detention that I have already described. As there was nobody there who understood French, he opened his heart freely and told me a pleasing story of his happiness among the Portuguese before his imprisonment. I found it an amazing thing that all the other prisoners came in a body to the grille, to beg me not to try to rescue or deliver M. Dellon, because during the five months he had been with them they had lacked for nothing, calling him their father-provider. This was due to three or four families at Daman, who being fond of this young Frenchman and much grieved at his misfortune, but not daring in any way to procure his liberty, had the satisfaction and consolation of sending him food and clothes, (MS, *victum et vestitum*), so that every day he received enough to support those who were incarcerated with him. He told me he had been warned that he would shortly be sent to Goa to appear before the tribunal of the Inquisition, but he did not expect to receive the severe penance predicted for him. I did not wish to speak of it either, as I had not visited him in order to increase the chagrin and sorrow he was in; so he was quite consoled by my visit, and was moreover given liberty to write a letter in reply to his parents, which he sent that evening to my rooms.[10]

The foregoing passage from Abbé Carré's book should set at rest all honest doubts regarding the authenticity of Dellon's story. It will be seen that the accounts of Dellon's misfortunes given by Abbé Carré agrees in essentials with that given by Dellon himself. In fact Abbé Carré provides many more details of the episode which led to Dellon's incurring the "jealousy and malice" of the Governor of Damaun. There are, however, some minor discrepancies in the two accounts, which can easily be explained as having arisen as a result of lapse of memory on the part of Abbé Carré or his having misunderstood some details of what Dellon related to him. Abbé Carré writes that the Governor

[10] *The Travels of the Abbé Carré in India and the Near East* (1672 *to* 1674), vol. III, Translated by Lady Fawcett and Edited by Sir Charles Fawcett, the Hakluyt Society, London, 1947, pp. 748-759.

asked Dellon to bleed the Governor's own son and attached an ivory figure of St. Anthony to the son's arm. Dellon, on the other hand, states that the incident occurred " at the house of a Portuguese gentleman, whose son was to be bled for some indisposition " and that he " observed that the youth had an ivory image of the Holy Virgin in his bed, which he reverenced much, and often kissed and addressed himself to it."[11]

Further evidence showing that Dellon was tried and sentenced by the Inquisition in Goa, drawn from the records of the Inquisition itself, has also been published by Antonio Baião, an eminent Portuguese research-worker and member of the Academy of Sciences of Lisbon. A volume giving the correspondence of the Inquisitors of India (1569-1630) edited by Baião was published by the Academy in 1930. In another volume intended as an introduction to this correspondence which was published in 1949, Baião mentions that among 16,172 cases tried by the Inquisition of Goa during 1561 to 1774 was the case of Dellon. Baião writes :

" Item No. 15·028 of the Inquisition of Lisbon is a list of the *Auto da Fé* of January 12, 1676 and in it is found : under No. 70, age stated being 23 years, Charles Dellon, French surgeon, a Native of d'Aguede in the kingdom of France, living in this state, bachelor, son of Luiz Dellon, for heresy, 5 years to the Galleys of Portugal and (banishment) for all time from the State of India."[12]

Baião also gives a reproduction of the name of Dellon, as it is found written in the records of the Inquisition of Portugal.[13]

It will be seen that the contentions of Dr. Gerson da Cunha and Braz Fernandes that the story of Dellon's imprisonment by the Inquisition of Goa is a fiction cannot stand in the face of incontrovertible contemporary evidence. It is indeed an irony of history that some of the descendants of the " New Christians " in Goa, who suffered cruelly at the hands of the Inquisition, should be so anxious to prevent the truth about the working of the institution from coming to light.

[11] *Vide* Part II, p. 9.
[12] Baião, *op. cit.*, vol. I, pp. 434-5.
[13] *Ibid.*, p. 293.

CHAPTER V

Conversions—From Conviction, for Convenience or by Force?

WE have seen how the Inquisition had to be introduced in Portugal mainly for the purpose of dealing with the tendency on the part of the New Christians, who had been forcibly converted from Judaism, to revert to the practices of their old faith. The Inquisition in India had to play a similar role not only in relation to the new converts drawn from Judaism but also those drawn from Hindu and Muslim religions. It has been the generally accepted view that the main instruments which were responsible for the conversion of the latter were the lure of material rewards and threat of violence and force and that religious conviction played a comparatively minor role in effecting such conversions. This explains why these converts continued to adhere in secret to their old faiths and tended to indulge in beliefs and practices which were heretical from the Christian point of view. However, some attempts have been made from time to time to demonstrate that the conversions to Christianity during the early Portuguese regime were primarily motivated by religious conviction. It is, therefore, proposed to examine in this chapter the nature of the policies of proselytism followed during this period, as these provided the background against which the Inquisition in Goa functioned.

Penrose describes in the following passage how "bribery, threat and torture" were used freely as instruments of proselytism:

"Religious bigotry and proselytism, fostered by the Inquisition, sapped the vitals of the empire while mere cruel terrorism took the place of the strength—albeit cruel strength—on which the early giants had relied. In so far as any one date can be taken as of prime importance in the ruin of the Portuguese empire, it is 6 May 1542, when Francis Xavier set foot ashore at Goa. From then on the Jesuits did their worst, using every form of bribery, threat, and torture to effect a conversion. Burton, writing 80 years ago, refers to "fire and steel, the dungeon and the rack, the rice pot and the rupee," which played "the persuasive part in the good work...assigned to them." Facetious as this quotation may seem it sums up in nutshell the methods used, and the satisfaction at the result, for the Jesuits were fanatics, and like all fanatics they did irreparable harm."[1]

Recently, Fr. H. Heras, S. J., made a gallant effort to refute the statements of Penrose and other historians holding similar views, in two essays dealing with *Decay of Portuguese Power in India* and *The Conversion Policy of the Jesuits in India* which were published in book form. He was kind enough to present me copies of these essays and later enquired whether I agreed with his conclusions. On hearing that I remained unconvinced by his arguments, he accused me of being prejudiced against the Catholics under the influence of the writings of Protestant historians. I smilingly replied that, although I did plead guilty to having read the works of Protestant writers, the main basis of my own convictions in the matter was my study of material available in Portuguese archives in Goa. It may be mentioned that in the essay on the Conversion Policy of the Jesuits, Fr. Heras, after quoting passages from Jesuit historians like Fr. Francisco Souza and such extracts from the writings of contemporary travellers as support his case, arrives at the following conclusion :

" After reading these extracts one remains with the impression that at least in most cases, if not in all, the work of the Jesuits was only *a posteriori*, viz. work of instruction and of baptism, after the Hindus themselves had decided to join the Church. The *a priori* work—say the work of invitation, of persuasion, of moral compulsion—seems to be left almost entirely to God's grace and call."[2]

To illustrate the religious freedom enjoyed by the Hindus at the time, Fr. Heras points out that the practice of *Sati* was permitted to the Hindus during the Portuguese regime.[3] In support of this contention he mentions an actual instance where a widow was burnt alive on the funeral pyre of her deceased husband. It is found, however, that this incident took place in Vengurla, which was never under the Portuguese rule.[4] Although

[1] Boies Penrose, *Sea Fights in the East Indies in the years* 1602-1639, Cambridge, Massachusetts 1931, p. 14.

[2]. H. Heras, *The Conversion Policy of the Jesuits in India*, Bombay 1933, p. 55.

[3] *Ibid.*, p. 26.

[4] *Tavernier's Travels in India*, vol. I., (Tr. by V. Ball), London 1925, pp. 175-6.

not directly relevant to my present purpose, I am tempted to mention here a few historical facts relating to the attitude of the Portuguese to the practice of *Sati*.

Tomé Pires, writing about the custom of *Sati* in Goa, states sometime during 1512 to 1515:

"It is mostly the custom in this kingdom of Goa for every heathen wife to burn herself alive on the death of her husband. Among themselves they all rate this highly, and if they do not want to burn themselves to death their relatives are dishonoured and they rebuke those who are ill disposed towards the sacrifice and force them to burn themselves. And those who will not burn themselves on any consideration become public prostitutes and earn money for the upkeep and construction of temples in their district, and they die in this way."[5]

Even before the Portuguese had embarked on a policy of systematic religious persecution in India, Affonso de Albuquerque had himself forbidden the practice of *Sati* on humanitarian grounds.[6] Later when Bardez and Salsete came under the Portuguese rule, the viceroy promulgated an order forbidding the practice in those territories also:

"No Hindu woman, living in the territories of Salsete or Bardez, or in this island of Goa or any other island annexed thereto, shall burn herself alive on account of the death of her husband. Any person who causes such a woman to be burnt alive, or for that purpose render an advice or help, be he a relation of the woman who has burnt herself or not, shall be liable to the penalty of loss of his entire estate, one half to the person who denounces him and the other for the works of the home of Apostle St. Thomas, and imprisonment for life."[7]

In statement made on May 28, 1766, by José Antonio Ribeiro, Promotor to the Inquisition, it is recorded that, as a result of pressure from influential Hindus and new converts, the governor

[5] *The Suma Oriental of Tomé Pires and the Book of Francisco Rodrigues*, vol. I, (Translated from the Portuguese by Armando Cortesão), The Hakluyt Society, London, 1944, p. 59.

[6] *The Commentaries of Afonso Dalboquerque* (Translated and Edited by W. De G. Birch) Vol. 11, London 1877, p. 94.

[7] Silva Rego, *op. cit.*, vol. VIII, Lisboa 1952, p. 40, (Doc. 14).

Francisco Barreto had permitted the practice of *Sati* round about 1551.[8]

The king of Portugai enjoined from time to time that proselytisation should be based on free consent and persuasion and should not be effected by compulsion and force. As we shall see later, the laws actually enacted from time to time were inconsistent with these liberal sentiments. The *Concilio Provincial*, an assembly of bishops and divines which laid down the lines on which the missionary work should be carried on also in theory expressed itself in favour of conversions by free consent. But, in their case also, there was a wide divergence between precept and practice. For instance the first resolution passed by the *Concilio Provincial* at its session of 1567 contained the following passage :

" In the first place it is hereby laid down that it is not lawful to bring to our faith and baptism any person by force with threats and terror, because no one comes to Christ by faith unless brought by the Celestial father with voluntary love and prevenient grace. Just as a person if by his free will he succumbs to the temptations of the Devil, perishes, so also if he responds to the call and grace of God he saves himself. The unbelievers should be brought to the true faith by the example of our lives, preaching of the truth of our law and the confutation of their errors so that by recognition of these things, they will give up their lies, and be received in Christ, who is the way, the truth and the life. Those who wish to bring the unbelievers to the true faith must also seek to cultivate gentleness and goodness in order that they may win persons to Christ, not merely by their preachings but also by kindness, courtesy and service."[9]

The following account given by the contemporary traveller François Pyrard also indicates how care was taken to give an impression that the conversions were free and voluntary :

" There is another house of these same Fathers adjoining this second Church ; it is called *Cathecumenos* and is for catechising and teaching the new Christians; they are fed and supplied with

[8] Cunha Rivara, *Archivo Portuguez Oriental*, Fasc. VI, suppl. 2, p. 501, (Doc. 185).

[9] Cunha Rivara, *op. cit.*, Fasc. IV, pp. 7-8.

clothing there, until such time as they are instructed and baptised : over these the Father of the Christians has charge, as over the whole house.

" From this place, one day of the Feast of the Conversion of St. Paul, I saw come forth about 1,500 Indian persons, men. women and children, habited in Christian fashion, to make their procession through the streets of the town, marching two and two, each having a bough or branch of palm in his hand, to distinguish them from the others, as being still unbaptised. Thence they went to the first Church and college of St. Paul of the Jesuits, where they were all baptised.

"Before they were baptised one of the Jesuit Fathers, as I saw, gave them an appropriate sermon upon the excellence of the Christian religion, that none should come there by constraint, that if any one of them had any regrets he was free to withdraw and go forth of the church. Then all answered with one voice that they were well satisfied and that they were willing to die in the Christian faith. Being baptised everyone retired to his own house : if any of these were poor, to him the Jesuit Father gave some money by way of alms. This is repeated every year with the like pomp and solemnity as above, besides that many are baptised every day in private. I have also seen many a time great numbers baptised in the church of the Franciscans, on the morrow of Christmas, even as many as eight hundred."[10]

It is easy to see how the brave words in the sermon to the effect that if any one of the neophytes had any regrets he was free to withdraw, in the circumstances of the case, could be only an empty gesture. Those who had proceeded so far on their way to conversion stood not the least chance of being accepted back into Hindu society and it was hardly likely that they would at this stage dare to incur the displeasure of the authorities by refusing to take the last leap !

Dr. Antonio Noronha, a former Judge of the High Court of Goa, in his essay " The Hindus and the Portuguese Republic," which is based on a careful study of contemporary official record referring to the foregoing account given by Pyrard, comments as follows :

[10] *The Voyage of François Pyrard*, vol. II, pt. i, London 1888, pp. 60-1.

"None should come there by constraint " what pious comedy! As though they had not been snatched violently from their families and interned in the house of Cathecumens for being indoctrinated with whip and ferule " ![11]

Dr. Noronha sums up in the following words the manner in which conversions actually took place :

" Until 1560 in Salsete there existed but one church and mission house in the fort of Rachol. In the course of less than 30 years a major part of the inhabitants of that province had embraced Christianity and 28 parishes had been established. It is known how such rapid and extensive conversions took place : some by fear of physical force ; others from moral cowardice ; many because they could not overcome the love for the country of their birth from which they would otherwise be expelled ; not a few to avoid the loss of their properties and interests ; some with their eyes on lucrative jobs—and almost none from conviction. The conviction, the faith, these would come later...."[12]

The following letter written in Spanish on October 10, 1547 from Goa by a Jesuit priest Fr. Nicolau Lancilotto to Fr. Ignatio Loyola should also prove of interest as contemporary evidence that conversions were mainly motivated by reasons other than religious conviction and hence there was a tendency for the converts to revert to their old faiths.

" The people of this country who become Christians do so purely for temporal advantage, as is inevitable in a land where slavery reigns. Slaves of the Moors or Hindus seek baptism in order to secure their manumission at the hands of the Portuguese. Others do so to get protection from tyrants, or for the sake of a turban, a shirt, or some other trifle they covet, or to escape being hanged, or to be able to associate with Christian women. The man who embraces the faith from honest conviction is regarded as a fool. They are baptized whenever or wherever they express a wish for the Sacrament, without any instruction, and many revert to their former paganism...."[13]

[11] *A India Portuguesa*, Vo. II, Nova Goa 1923, p. 227.
[12] *Ibid.*, p. 261.
[13] J. Wicki, *Documenta Indica*, Vol. I, Rome 1948, pp. 183-4. (Vincent Cronin, *A Peart to India*, London 1959, p. 29)

There were cases where Brahmins embraced Christianity so that they could marry women of lower castes. An instance of this type is mentioned by Irmão Gomes Vaz in the "*Carta Geral do Collegio de Goa*", dated December 12, 1567 :

"A Hindu who lived in the lands of the Muslims came here for being converted to Christianity and brought with him and took for his wife a dedicated servant of a temple, notwithstanding that she belonged to a low caste, which he could do only because she like him became a Christian, he being a much-honoured Brahman."[14]

Fr. James Brodrick, well-known biographer of St. Xavier and himself a Jesuit, while writing about Minguel Vaz, a co-worker of St. Xavier, states how the policy followed by Vaz in effecting conversions involved "a great deal of pressure, social and financial" and resulted in breeding a hatred of Christianity :

"Minguel Vaz Coutinho. Strange to say, this dignitary, who in effect ruled the Church in Portuguese India, was a layman. St. Francis held in him the highest regard and so did the King of Portugal. A zealous and honest man, the 'true father of the Indian Christians', as the Saint described him, he was yet narrow-minded and very oppressively hostile to the native religion. It was not as he imagined, by destroying Hindu Sanctuaries in Portuguese territory and applying their revenues to the building of churches that the Indians would be won to Christianity. No Hindu in Goa, Cochin, Malacca and other centres was ever forced by that policy to accept the faith, but a great deal of pressure, social and financial, was exercised to 'persuade' them to do so. Of course, it had exactly the opposite effect and bred a hatred of Christianity. All said, however, it was but the application in India of the accepted motto of European politics, *Cajos regio, illius religio*."[15]

It is interesting to contrast the foregoing views of Fr. Brodrick with the conclusions drawn by Fr. Heras from his researches.

The candour of Fr. Brodrick's critical views as set forth in his biography of St. Xavier, is indeed reassuring in that it illustrates

[14] Silva Rego, *Documentação, op. cit.*, Vol. X, 1953, p. 308.
[15] James Brodrick, *Saint Francis Xavier*, London 1952, p. 201 (Foot Note).

how even a Jesuit historian, who has to secure the permission of his religious superiors before bringing out any publication, is not always prevented from presenting facts, the disclosure of which might be expected to be inexpedient or embarrassing from the point of view of his order. The following passages in which Fr. Brodrick describes the limitations of the understanding and outlook of St. Xavier himself are significant in this connection :

" St. Francis Xavier's knowledge of Hinduism was, if possible, even less adequate than his few biased notions of Mohammedanism. Though the Portuguese had been in India for over forty years, none of them appears to have made the slightest attempt to understand the venerable civilization, so much more ancient than their own, on which they had violently intruded.

" Francis did admit to his Roman friends that Goa, reckoned by the widely travelled Tavernier the finest port in the world after Constantinople and Toulon, was a *cosa para ver*, but he had his special non-aesthetic reasons for the judgement. Goa was a sight to be seen because it was a city wholly Christian, with a populous Franciscan friary, a Cathedral of much distinction and many canons, as well as numerous other churches. That was as far as he was prepared to move in the realms of Baedeker, and a quarter of the information is incorrect. Goa at that date was by no means entirely a city and island of the baptized. Like Sheppey and Thanet, it is an island only by courtesy of the two rivers which encircled it, Mandovi and Juari, and in those days their blue waters still served the ancient Gods. The Moslems were back also for trade, undeterred any longer by the menacing ghost of Albuquerque. Francis neither knew nor probably cared to know that for more than a millennium Goa had been a centre of Hindu learning, wealth and splendour, and then, falling to the Moslems, had become one of the leading markets of the East from whose quays thousands of devout souls departed annually on the pilgrimage to Mecca. Such a place was not to be easily christianized, as Francis himself discovered."[16]

As further evidence of the important role which considerations other than religious played in the conversion of the Hindus, the following passage from the pen of Fr. Alexandre Valignano, who

[16] *Ibid.*, pp. 114-5.

occupied the position of the *Visitador de Provincia da India*, in which he explains what practical measures a Father of Novices (*Pae dos Christãos*) should adopt for discharging his duties, viz., the conversion and salvation of souls of the unbelievers and education and support of the newly converted, is revealing :

"As regards the first duty, viz., conversion of unbelievers, in these parts of India this does not commonly occur as a result of sermons and doctrine, but is effected by other just means, such as, obstructing the idolatrous practices of the unbelievers and meting out just punishment therefor, refusing them favours which can justly be refused, and offering them to those who are newly converted, and honouring, assisting and protecting the latter in order that others might thereby get converted. The Father of Novices should try his best to see that none of these means is left unavailed of and thus help the conversion of unbelievers. Since almost all of these means have already been approved by the sessions of *Concilio Provincial* in Goa and in the measures promulgated by the king of Portugal and his viceroys of India in favour of Christianity, the Father of Novices should strive to be thoroughly versed in all these things and try hard to see that all comply therewith and implement them, inasmuch as experience has shown that many are thus converted."[17]

I am sure that the evidence set forth in the foregoing paragraphs should suffice to convince any unprejudiced reader that religious persuasion played but a very insignificant role in the conversions of the Indians to Christianity effected during this period. It was only to be expected that persons so dragged into the new religion would have little understanding thereof or love therefor. This provided a fertile breeding ground for 'heresy' and there was thus vast scope for the activities of the Inquisition. As the records of the Inquisition have been destroyed, it is not possible to obtain an idea of the numbers of the new Christians who were burnt at the stake or subjected to other penalties. Filipe Nery Xavier, in his periodical *Gabinete Literatorio* mentions an instance in which under the orders of the Inquisition an entire family of Bassein were burnt at stake and their home razed to the ground He writes :

[17] Cunha Rivara, *Archivo Portuguez Oriental*, Fasc. V, pt. III, Nova Goa 1866, pp. 1436-7. (Doc. 1022),

" In this same district (Bassein) we discovered in 1840, a part of a flat stone raised in 1780 on the site of a house which the Inquisition had ordered to be razed to the ground. This carried an inscription which read as follows :

" They, being dogmatists of the said sect, practised rites and ceremonies with the participation of many other persons, and for this were condemned by the Holy Office and being delivered to secular justice burnt in the *Auto de Fé* celebrated on December 30, 1747. It was ordered that their houses should be demolished and ploughed with salt and this stone erected in detestation of the said crimes."

This action was according to the rule laid down in the code of the Inquisition.[18] F. Nery Xavier states that in 1865 this stone was lying on the road broken in two parts.

[18] *Regimento de Santo Officio, da Inquisiçam dos Reynos de Portugal,* Liv. III, Tit. 2, § 4, Lisboa 1640, f. 156.

CHAPTER VI

Evolution of the Policy of Religious Persecution in India

We have seen how the fact that conversions to Christianity in Goa were generally motivated by reasons other than religious conviction, was responsible for the widespread tendency on the part of new converts to revert to the practices of their old religion. The Inquisition came into existence for the purpose of checking this tendency. A history of the Inquisition in India must, therefore, include a review of the policy of systematic religious persecution adopted by the Portuguese in India, the object of which was to convert the native population to Christianity. During recent years considerable contemporary material has come to light which enables the development of this policy to be traced clearly. It is proposed to present in this and the next two chapters a review of the evolution of the policy of religious persecution adopted by the Portuguese. Strictly speaking, a review as full as is herein given would not be relevant in its entirety for the purpose of delineating the background against which the Inquisition functioned. However, the subject is obviously intimately related to the theme of this book and a large majority of the readers would be interested in the additional information for its own sake. Also, a succinct account of this aspect of the history is not easily available elsewhere. It is hence felt that it will not be inappropriate to include such a detailed review in the present book.

Before Affonso de Albuquerque conquered Goa, it was under the rule of Yusuf Adilshah of Bijapur and the local Hindu community suffered from the tyrannies of his Turkish and Rumes officers. The Hindus therefore appealed to Timoja, who was the commander of the navy of the Hindu King of Onor (Honawar), to attack Goa. Timoja, however, did not dare to enter on this enterprise single-handed. He called on Albuquerque, while the armada of the latter was lying at anchor in front of the castle of Cintacora on its way to Ormuz, and advised him to attack Goa. Braz de Albuquerque, son of Affonso de Albuquerque, in his book *Commentaries of Afonso Dalboquerque* describes the meeting between his illustrious father and Timoja in the following words :

" Afonso Dalboquerque enquired of him the reason that had moved him to come and advise him to take Goa. Timoja answered, that the principal head-men of the natives that were established in the land had written to tell him that the death of the Çabaio was certain and that all were very well pleased at hearing of it on account of the numerous robberies and tyrannies which he had practised upon them, and that during the year last passed he had murdered and robbed more than two hundred merchants, and that on this account the whole land had risen up in mutiny and in quarrels one against another. " And," he continued, " if I wanted to possess myself of Goa, I have only to go there with my men and they would yield themselves up to me of their own accord."[1]

Gaspar Correa, one of the secretaries of Affonso de Albuquerque, states that Timoja addressed Albuquerque in the following words :

" The merchants have been robbed and are not allowed to leave the city as though they were slaves. They are in such a mood that if you enter the river with this armada and take a position in front of the city, they will soon surrender it to you in order to see themselves free from the wrongs which the *Rumes* do. I know all this from many letters which the numerous friends and relatives which I there have write to me."[2]

Albuquerque decided to take Timoja's advice and changed the course of his armada. According to Gaspar Correa he replied to Timoja as follows :

" Timoja, only on your word and as I have confidence that you are good and true in the service of our master the king, I take your counsel and give up another which had brought me on this voyage. I promise you that if you guide me well into Goa, my master the king will repay your good services by giving you the principal office, the most honoured in the land which can be given, and other major rewards."[3]

Things turned out as anticipated by Timoja and in the words of Pissurlencar " the city of Goa surrendered peacefully to the

[1] *The Commentaries of the Great Afonso Dalboquerque*, vol. II, p. 85.

[2] Gaspar Correa, *Lendas da India*, Livro segundo, Tomo II, Lisboa, 1860, p. 51.

[3] *Ibid.*, p. 52.

Portuguese."[4] Damião de Goes in his "*Cronica de D. Manuel*" (Pt. II, Chapter XI, 1926) writes that on the very next day Krishna, the leader of the citizens of Goa, called on Albuquerque and prayed for an assurance of security to Brahmins and other residents of the city and this was readily granted. Castanheda also confirms that such an assurance of security was given by Albuquerque "only to merchants and natives of the land, muslims, brahmans and canarins" and this was received with great satisfaction by both the Hindus and the Muslims.[5]

There is evidence to show that Timoja's intention was not to replace the rule of the Muslims in Goa with that of the Portuguese. He had fondly hoped that the Portuguese would agree to hand over Goa to him and leave the country, if he agreed to pay tribute. Albuquerque, however, had other plans and he proceeded to build the walls of the fort and make other arrangements which clearly indicated that he had come to stay. After these measures had sufficiently advanced, he asked Timoja to advise the inhabitants of Goa to pay taxes to the Portuguese king as they had previously done to their old rulers. Braz de Albuquerque describes Timoja's reactions to this move in the following passage :

"Timoja replied that he would call them together and acquaint them of this matter. But nevertheless he was not pleased to find that Afonso de Dalboquerque had resolved to retain Goa, for he had, some days before this, privately requested him to hand over the place to him, with all its lands, and he would pay a certain sum every year by way of revenue for it, sustaining the place at his own risk. And Afonso Dalboquerque always made a point of deferring to give any reply to this request of his, without giving any account of it to the Captains, by reason of the necessity he had of using Timoja's men for the work of the building."[6]

Having realised that Albuquerque was unlikely to change his mind Timoja tried to obtain the support of Albuquerque's captains to his demands. They tried unsuccessfully to persuade Albu-

[4] P. S. S. Pissurlencar, *Colaboradores Hindus de Afonso de Albuquerque*, Bastorá 1941, p. 9.

[5] Fernão Lopes de Castanheda, *Historia dos Descobrimentos e Conquista da India pelos Portugueses*, Livro III (Editor-Pedro de Azevedo), Coimbra 1928, p. 25.

[6] *The Commentaries of the Great Afonso Dalboquerque*, vol. II, p. 102.

querque to hand over Goa to Timoja on condition that the latter should pay an annual tribute of 20,000 *pardaos*. Albuquerque offered to Timoja a high position under the king of Portugal. His son writes that he told Timoja that " in return for the numerous services that he had rendered on these parts, he would, in the king's name make him a present of the whole of the revenues of the lands of Mergeu paid in the factory of Goa, and would appoint him to be Chief *Aguazil*, and captain of all the people of the land." Timoja, however, remained disgruntled and left the city. Braz de Albuquerque writes that even thereafter his friends tried to bring pressure on Albuquerque by threatening to follow him out of Goa, and further states: " Three days after that Timoja had gone away, some Hindoos came to tell Afonso Dalboquerque that he was in the land of Salsete, and that as soon as he had got there every Hindoo had gone over to him and had come to a determination of going withersoever he went and deserting the land. Afonso Dalboquerque knew that this was a piece of spite brought about by Timoja, but concealed his thoughts from the Hindoo messengers, and made as though he did not understand the drift of what they said." Albuquerque however remained firm in his resolve.

Later, Adilshah attacked Goa and Albuquerque had to withdraw from the city. He recaptured Goa on 25th November, 1510, and ordered an indiscriminate massacre of its Muslim population by way of punishment for their treachery. His son writes :

" ...Afonso Dalboquerque told the captains to reconnoitre the whole of the island and to put to the sword all the Moors, men, women and children, that should be found, and to give no quarter to any one of them; for his determination was to leave no seed of this race throughout the whole of the island. And he did this, not only because it was necessary for the security of the land that there should be none but Hindoos within it, but also as a punishment for the treachery of which the Moors had been guilty when he took the city for the first time. And for four days continuously they poured out the blood of the Moors who were found therein; and it was ascertained that of men, women, and children, the number exceeded six thousand."[7]

[7] *Ibid.*, vol. III, 1880, p. 16.

João Barros writes that some of the Muslims, in order to escape from the terror jumped into the river with a view to crossing it by swimming, as no boats were available, and a good many were drowned. He adds : " In this massacre, the principal officer was Medeo Rao, the Hindu captain of Timoja's company, who had come to Affonso d'Albuquerque. Timoja himself arrived later with three thousand persons, apologising for not having been able to come before the incident."[8] It appears from this that Medeo Rao was not a native of Goa but one of Timoja's officers. During this period of insecurity in Goa the Hindus had taken refuge in adjoining territories. Albuquerque invited them by public crier to return, " notifying to them that they could till their hereditary lands and occupy houses, after paying taxes in accordance with the usage of the land, inasmuch as he was not at war with native people other than the Muslims." Timoja was appointed as the captain of the Hindu inhabitants, but it appears that he was not popular among them. João de Barros writes : " But Timoja continued in this position only for a little while as the Hindus felt very bad that they were governed through him, as he was a man of lowly origin but on the contrary hed raised himself to the status of a Captain." Albuquerque probably appreciated the risk involved in retaining such an unpopular person in that responsible position and replaced him with Melrao, a nephew of the King of Onor, who, " the people of the land wished to have as their governor, as he was an individual of royal blood." According to the custom of Onor, a king was succeeded to the throne by his sister's son and Melrao later became the king of Onor.[9] It is believed that Timoja went to Vijayanagar and died there at the hands of a poisoner. Padre Leonardo Paes in his book *Promptuario das Diffinições Indicas* states that the wife and children of Timoja came to Goa from Onor and were later converted to Christianity.[10]

It will be seen from the above that the relations between Albuquerque and the Hindu population of Goa were friendly and cordial. Until recently it was the general belief among students of history that Albuquerque remained true to his promise to the

[8] João de Barros, *Da Asia*, Decada II, Livro V, Lisboa 1777, p. 543.
[9] *Ibid.*, pp. 546-7.
[10] Pissurlencar, *Colaboradores Hindus*, *op. cit.*, p. 15.

Hindus and until his death the Hindus continued to receive a fair deal. However, late Dr. Bragança Pereira, President of the Department of Archaelogy of Goa, recently published a document which indicates the possibility that this belief might be erroneous. This is a letter written to Duque Giuliano de Medicis on January 6, 1515 from Cochin by André Corsali in which he refers to the destruction of a temple by the Portuguese during the lifetime of Albuquerque in the following words :

"In this land of Goa and of the whole of India there are innumerable ancient edifices of the gentiles and in a little neighbouring island that is called Divari, the Portuguese in order to build the land (town) of Goa, have destroyed an ancient temple called a pagoda which was built with wonderful skill, with ancient figures of a certain black stone worked with very great perfection, of which some are standing, ruined and spoilt, but which these Portuguese hold in no esteem. Should I have in hand any (figure) thus ruined, I shall send it to Your Highness that Your Highness may see how in ancient times sculpture was appreciated everywhere ."[11]

It is true that the incident mentioned by André Corsali occurred before the death of Albuquerque on December 5, 1515. However, from the published correspondence of Albuquerque it is seen that during the period between November 15, 1514 to January 12, 1515 he was absent from Goa visiting areas around Cananor, Cochin and Calicut and there is a possibility that the act of vandalism referred to by Corsali might have been perpetrated during his absence.[12] There is, however, no doubt that Albuquerque was a firm believer in the need to convert Indians to Christianity. In a letter addressed to the King of Portugal on December 20, 1514, he has not only expressed his keen interest in the matter but gives an account of his own efforts to convert the king of Cochin.[13]

According to Lucena, the persecution of the Hindus and the movement to destroy Hindu temples and other vestiges of

[11] A. B. Bragança Pereira, *Historia Religiosa de Goa*, vol. I, Bastorá (n.d.), p. 44.

[12] *Cartas de Affonso de Albuquerque*, Tomo VI (Academia das Sciencias de Lisboa), Lisboa 1915.

[13] Silva Rego, *op. cit.*, vol. I, p. 228.

Hindu religion was initiated by Minguel Vaz and Diogo Borba, after 1540. There is, however, evidence to show that even before this date pressure was being exerted on the Hindus to ensure their conversion and that the Franciscans were already planning to rid Goa of all vestiges of Hinduism. In a letter addressed to the king of Portugal on November 4, 1518, Friar Antonio writes :

"You will be rendering great service to God if from this island you send to Portugal a Hindu individual Krishna by name, a great servant of yours, who is here sunk in heathenism but has come very near to Christ as I have spoken many times to him, and gives no excuse other than that in Portugal after seeing Your Majesty he will convert himself to Christianity.

"Your Majesty should order that the poor mendicants who are known as *Joguis* should not enter this island from the mainland, because they bring flowers used in worship and other relics of their temples and devils with which they restore the heathenism of local people.

"In this island of Goa a friar has placed some crosses in the Hindu temples and the Hindus say that others come and tell them that they are already Christians and the latter would not speak with them any longer.

"Sir, there is a great temple in this island of Divar which has much freestone and a large part of it is already destroyed. We pray Your Majesty to make a gift of it to this monastery."[14]

The temple of Divar which is mentioned here is probably the same as the one referred to by André Corsali.

In a report submitted to the king from Cochin on January 12, 1522, Bispo de Dumense wrote as follows:

"Around the territories of the neighbours of Goa, there exist in that island temples in which statues of the enemy of the Cross are worshipped and every year their festivals are celebrated. These are attended by many Christians, both Europeans and natives, which is very wrong in that it promotes idolatry.

"It will be service to God if these temples in the island of Goa are destroyed and in their stead churches with saints are

[14] *Ibid.*, p. 354.

erected, and it is ordered that whosoever desires to live in this island and have house and lands there should become a Christian, and if he does not wish to be one should go out of the island. I assure Your Majesty that there would then be no individual who did not turn to the faith of Our Lord Christ, because if exiled from this island he will have no means of livelihood."[15]

In a letter dated November 13, 1521, in which Diogo Mariz, Escrivão da Camara de Goa, reports to the king of Portugal about the Churches in Goa, he writes that "many natives of the lands have been and are being converted to Christian faith."[16] It is unlikely that all these would be Muslims. It appears probable that many Hindus too, especially those belonging to the lower castes, had already been converted at this time by the use of temptations and pressures in various forms. The deplorable condition of these New Christians as well as of their religious instructors is described by Friar Vincente de Laguna in a letter addressed to the king of Portugal on November 29, 1532 :

"Senhor, many Christians from these parts are badly instructed in things pertaining to faith, which is in charge of the vicars of the Church who do not wish to teach and the people have started again to adore in their temples. Your Majesty should remedy this state of affairs.

"Now arrives the new vicar General sent by Your Majesty. I have advised him of this, and your Majesty should order that he should work to praise the name of God.

"Over this part of India, many priests lead a dissolute life, causing damage to themselves as well as to the whole world by their bad example. Your Majesty may make a general enquiry and send such of the priests as cause scandal here to Portugal."[17]

The new vicar general mentioned in the foregoing passage, was Minguel Vaz. His predecessor in that office was Sebastião Pires whose tenure was marked by laxity and mismanagement into which an inquiry was subsequently ordered.[18] Minguel Vaz may be said to have laid the foundation of the policy of systematic religious persecution in Goa.

[15] Silva Rego, *op. cit.*, Vol. I, pp. 452-3.
[16] Silva Rego, *op. cit.*, vol. II, Lisboa 1949, p. 188.
[17] *Ibid.*, p. 230.
[18] *Ibid.*, p. 304.

In 1534 Goa was raised to the status of a Bishopric but the number of Christians living therein was not large as the policy of proselytism had not yet made sufficient headway. It was therefore decided in 1541 that the policy of " Rigour of Mercy " (*Rigor de Misericordia*) should be followed in Goa. In this year Hindu temples were destroyed and various leaders of the Hindu Community were made to agree of " their free volition " that the income of the lands belonging to the temples which had been destroyed might be applied to the upkeep of Christian churches and Christian missionaries. A resolution adopted by the leaders of the Hindu community in 1541 runs as follows :

" On the 28th of June of 1541 in his own dwelling at Goa, Fernão Rodrigues de Castello Branco, Veedor da Fazenda (Controller of Finances) and in the absence of the Governor D. Estevão de Gama himself governing the land, at the time being present Chrisna, Tanador-mor (Renter of customs), Locu, Gopu, important brahmins of this island ; and Madu Sinay Banuntacor, and Ralu Sinay, principal landholders of Great Neurá, and Bamu Camotym, landholder in the village of Gancim, and Mabel Parbu, and Locu Mungi, landholders of the village of Ellá, and Minguel Vaz, and Raulu Bandary of the village of Agaçayim, and Betu Parbu, and Locu Mungar, of the village of Carambolym, and Malu Camotym, and Ramu Camotym, of the village of Batym, and Ramu Neugy, and Betu Baguto, of the village of Calapor, and Madu Gar, and Santu Parto of the village of Great Morobym and Santu Camotym, of the village of Talaulym and Raulu Gar, and Beru Gar, of village of Taleigão, and Santu Naique of the village of Goally and Gorcá Naique of the village of Goa-Velha, and Malem Parubu, and Gondu Parbu, landholders of the village of Chorão, and Sapatu Camotym, and Ganapu Naique and Ralu Parbu, landholders of the island of Divar, and Sapur Sauntu, and Cuca Parbu, landholders of the island of Jua ; they were informed by the same Controller of Finances, that a few days earlier they were told that they should, with free will, be prepared to give and donate the income of the lands belonging to the temples and situated in this island, since these temples were entirely destroyed and there was no chance of their ever being built again and as previously they did not use this income fruitfully but spent all of it towards the same temples and its Gurous (ministers), dancing girls, brahmins, blacksmiths, carpenters, washermen, barbers, shoemakers, painters and other servants of the aforesaid temples...", it was resolved that the income should in future be applied towards and donated to the chapels built in this island, and also to defray the expenses of the confraternity of the converts to the faith.

A list[19] of the Hindu temples which existed in the island of Goa at this time is given hereunder :—

Names of Villages	*Names of the Hindu Deities*
Agaçaim	Somnath, Khetrapall.
Azossim	Malcumi (Maha-Lakshmi), Saptanath, Ravallnath, Narana, Sati, Bhumideutá, Vanadeutá, Grampurus and Ispor (Ishwar).
Bambolim	Santeri, Ravallnath.
Banguenim	Santeri.
Batim	Bauca-devi, Ravallnath, Santeri, Bhairão, Narana, Ramanath, Betall, Brahmann-purus.
Calapur	Santeri, Quellba-devi, Mayá, Betall, Ramnath, Ravallnath, Brahmann-purus, Panchedevatá.
Carambolim	Betall, Sidnath, Gram-purus, Khetrapall, Ravallnath, Santeri, Ganês, Vana-deutá, Butapiradar, Pondde-Gãoçaló-Purus, Curumbim-Purus, Brahmanna-Purus, Nirvãoci-Purus.
Chimbel	Bhagavati.
Daugim	Ravallnath, Narcinva, Sat-Purus, Barazann, Moqueá.
Chorão (*Choddné*)	Ganês, Ravallnath, Baucadevi, Mallnath, Bagavanti (Bhagavati), Deoqui, Santa-Purusha, Barazanna, Naraena, Cantacer (Kanteshwar), Chandeussor (Channddeshwar), Dadda-Sancol.
Caraim	Ravallnath, Vanadeutá.
Corlim	Sidhanath, Ravallnath, Santeri.
Cugirá	Ravallnath, Ramanath, Tornna-Vir.
Curcá	Santeri, Ravalnath.

[19] Francisco Pais, *Tombo da Ilha de Goa e das Terras de Salcete e Bardês*, (Annotated by P. S. S. Pissurlencar), Bastorá 1952, pp. 165-69.

Names of Villages	*Names of the Hindu Deities*
Divar	(At Malar) : Gram-Purus, Naranna, Bhairão, Ravallnath, Deutá, Saptanath, Satti, Bhagavati, Bauca-devi, Vãochanath, Vir.
	(At Goltim) : Khapri-deu, Gram-Purus, Ravallnath, Santeri.
	(At Navelim) : Ravallnath, Ganés.
	(At Diva) : Bhairão, Mascanaçani (Maskanashini), Mocheá (Moqueá), Nirgunna.
Durgavarim	Khetrapall, Ravallnath.
Elá	Drugadeu (Durgadevi), Ganês.
Gancim	Naranna, Durgadevi, Baunato (Bhavanath).
Goalim-Moulá	Khetrapall, Ravalnath, Santeri.
Goa-Velha (Goa-Old) :	(Kall) Bhairão, Chanddesvari, Ravallanath, Govanath our Govesvor, Gaddguesvar (Gallagueshwar).
Jua	Deutá, Ravalnath, Santeri, Khetrapall, Gram-Purus, Malanato (Mallanath).
Mandur	Ravallanath, Durgadevi, Naranna, Gram-Purus.
Mercurim	Khetrapall, Bhutnath.
Morombim (*Great*)	Madeu, Santeri, Malcumi, Ravallnath, Betall, Satti, Metragaddo. (?)
Morombim (*Small*)	Ravallnath, Khetrapoll, Vanadeutá,
Murdá	Khetrapall, Berma or Barma (Brahmá).
Neurá (*Great*)	Santeri, Ispor, Ravallnath, Baucadevi, Mayaquor, Bhavanath, Madeu, Gram-Purus.
Neurá (*Small*)	Ravallnath, Santeri, Gram-Purus.
Orara	Ravallnath.
Panelim	Bhavani, Santeri, Barazanno.
Siridão	Purush, Ramanath.
Talaulim	Gram-Purush, Ravallnath, Santeri, Bhavanath, Ispor (Ishwar), Narainna.
Taleigão	Ravallnath, Santeri, Betall, Ramanath.
Vanci	Baucadevi.

The destruction of the Hindu temples did not suffice to satisfy the fanatical zeal of the Portuguese rulers. Attempts continued to be made to convert the local population to Christianity and it was only natural that these should provoke stubborn resistance from their leaders. On November 6, 1541, Martin Afonso de Melo, a noble-man of the Royal family, wrote from Goa to the king of Portugal as follows :—

" In these islands of Goa many souls of Hindus and Muslims are converted to Christianity and many more would have been converted had it not been for some persons who support these Hindus, like Krishna, Luqu and Anu Sinai and some of their relatives who hold that all the Hindus should not be converted. Your Majesty, in the service of God, should provide in this matter that these principal leaders should be converted to Christianity and if they do not agree, order that they should be taken to Portugal, under the pretext that you wish to learn of certain matters relating to this territory from them. As a result of their being away from these islands for two years, I believe that all the people of these islands, or a major part of them, will become Christians. As regards the persons of whom I spoke, who would come there, if they do not become Christians before they return, it should be ordered that they should convert within the following six months and if they do not wish to do so that they should leave these islands. They would get converted in order to avoid banishment from the land of their birth and in this manner your Majesty shall be the cause of saving many souls and thereby render great service to God."[20]

Krishna, the Hindu leader mentioned in the above letter, has already been referred to in another passage quoted earlier. He held many important positions in Goa such as *Tanador-mor* (Renter of the Customs), captain of native troops, broker of horses of Goa, etc. He visited Portugal but did not embrace Christianity. He also worked as the representative of Portugal at the Court of Bijapur. He was arrested by the king of Bijapur and Professor Pissurlencar writes that it is exceedingly probable that he died in captivity in Bijapur.[21] His son Dadaji was appointed in his place in Goa. In the *Arquivo Nacional of Torre de Tombo* is preserved a letter written to the king of Portugal by Pedro Fernandes Sardinha, probably sometime in 1547, which refers to Dadaji as follows :

[20] J. Wicki, *op. cit.*, Vol. I, pp. 792-3.

[21] P. Pissurlencar, *Agentes de Diplomacia Portugueza na India*, Goa 1952, p. 14.

"The Brahman who is most prejudicial and opposed to Christianity in Goa is Dadaji, son of Krishna. Krishna came to Portugal and received many favours and honours from the king D. Manuel, your father, and promised to become Christian with his entire family as soon as he returned, in consideration of which he was favoured with the offices of *Tanador-mor* and official interpreter for life. He never became Christian. Formerly he was and now his son is the greatest enemy in Goa of our Holy Faith. From this it is clear that what Your Majesty ordered in the letter sent through Minguel Vaz should be complied with in its entirety."[22]

The letter referred to in the last sentence is one in which the king wrote to the Governor that Dadaji should be relieved of his office. I shall have occasion to refer to this letter later. (See p. 75). As Dadaji refused to become Christian, he was replaced by Loqu (Lakshman) in his official positions.

In a letter addressed to king D. João III on November 28,1548, bishop D. João de Albuquerque reports that Loqu was baptised on the preceding day, an event to which so much importance is attached that it arouses in his heart the hope that within a year or two he would succeed in converting the entire island to Christianity. The letter is reproduced hereunder :

" The fact is that yesterday, being Sunday, we baptised in the College of the Holy Faith, a Hindu who used to be called Loqu and is now given the name of Luquas de Saa. He ranked second among leaders who supported the Hindus of this island and favoured them in their faith. He was very rich, a great farmer of customs and other revenues of Your Majesty for a long time and a person who was very friendly with and had rendered great services to governors. He was very liberal and spent freely among the Hindus, giving money in charity and other favours to prevent them from being Christians. By so doing he sought to secure an advantage over Krishna, the *Tanador- mor* of this island, who used to have greater credit among the Hindus than he. With Loqu were also baptised five other persons, viz., his wife, two respected Gauncares, a nephew and another woman. Krishna s overthrown ; this Hindu *Tanador-mor* is under detention by Idalquão (Adilshah). His son has been carrying on his father's

[22] Silva Rego, *op. cit.*, vol. IV, Lisboa 1950, p. 560.

office till now. After removing this arrogant son from this position of authority, with the help of Christ, if we are permitted to give the offices to Christians and, with due discretion, to humble some of the honoured Hindus, the Fathers of the Society and I as their companion, within one year or at the latest in two, shall make this whole island Christian."[23]

The baptism of Loqu was celebrated with great eclat. The Archbishop officiated personally at the ceremony and the Governor acted as Godfather. Loqu, his wife and nephew were given the names of Lucas, Isabel and Antonio respectively. P. G. Barzaeus in a letter dated December 13, 1548 writes that the new converts were taken in procession on horse-back and that all notable persons and many Brahmins were present on the occasion.[24] Many other writers also have described this occasion with considerable enthusiasm.

The Vicar General Fr. Minguel Vaz and Diogo Borba struggled hard to bring about early Christianisation of the natives of Goa. St. Paul's College was started for imparting religious instruction to the new converts and it was maintained out of the income of the Hindu temples which had been destroyed.[25] The pace of proselytism, however, continued to be disappointingly slow and it was clear that unless recourse could be had to more drastic measures, it would not be possible to accelerate it. Consent of the king would be necessary before such measures could be adopted. To secure it, Minguel Vaz paid a visit to Portugal and in the *Archivo National of Torre de Tombo* is found a 41-point plan which he sent to the king from Evora in the month of November 1545. The origin of most of the harsh measures subsequently adopted to secure the conversion of the natives can be traced to this plan. Some of the suggestions contained in the plan are reproduced hereunder :

" 3. Since idolatry is so great an offence against God, as is manifest to all , it is just that Your Majesty should not permit it within your territories, and an order should be promulgated in Goa to the effect that in the whole island there should not be any temple public or secret, contravention whereof should entail

[23] Wicki, *op. cit.*, vol. I, pp. 325-7.
[24] *Ibid.*, p. 400.
[25] Silva Rego, *op. cit.*, vol. III, p. 14.

grave penalities; that no official should make idols in any form, neither of stone, nor of wood, nor of copper nor of any other metal; that no Hindu festival should be publicly celebrated in the whole island; that Brahmin preachers from the mainland should not gather in the houses of the Hindus; and that persons who are in charge of St. Paul's should have the power to search the houses of the Brahmins and other Hindus, in case there exists a presumption or suspicion of the existence of idols there.

4. Again, there exists in this island a caste of the people who call themselves *Synaes* Brahmins, who are much opposed to Christianity and not only do not convert themselves but also hinder the conversion of others whenever possible and support the error of heathenism...In times of trouble we cannot count upon their loyalty since they are loyal to the Moslems and treacherous to us, as experience showed during the wars with the mainland which took place in the times of Nuno de Cunha...These *Synaes*, who hinder conversions to Christianity, or at least their leaders, should be banished from the island. I know some who are awaiting such an order before they would convert themselves.

5. Also it will be in the interests of God and Your Majesty that in a city as noble as Goa, a Hindu Brahmin, by name Anu Synay, who is much opposed to Christianity, should not serve as the Broker of Merchandise (*Corrector das mercadorias*).

6. It will also be in the interests of God and Your Majesty that the governor should try to appoint as the official translator for dealing with incoming and outgoing correspondence a Portuguese or other Christian, so that all secrets and matters of importance might not pass through the hands of a Hindu, son of Krishna, who is held in great honour for not becoming a Christian. This action will redound in favour of Christianity and many will thereby be converted. And for the same reason, Krishna, his father should be excused from attending to our communications.

7. If Our Lord defend the lands of Salsete and Bardez, which he caused Idalcão (Adilshah) to give to Your Majesty, as it will please Him to do on account of your piety, it will be just and proper that in His interest and that of Your Majesty, you should, for commendation and honour of God, remove all traces of idolatry which exist therein and work for the conversion of these adjoining lands.

9. It is the custom in Goa that, when a native of the land dies without leaving male issue, even if he leaves daughters, all his estate passes to Your Majesty, which is very harsh. As this did not appear very reasonable to me, I suggested that it should be rectified. Recently Governor Martins Affonso, ordered that the movable estate may be retained by the daughters and the immovable pass to the king; this was however modified to provide that such movable estate should be limited to 50 *pardaos*. I feel it should at least be provided that, a daughter who becomes Christian, even though this occur after the death of the father, should get the entire estate, so that this should provide a motive for some of them to convert themselves."[26]

A letter of D. João III dated March 8, 1547, in which he has ordered that measures against idolatry and Brahmins on the lines recommended by Minguel Vaz be taken, has been published.

Minguel Vaz returned to India in 1546 with an order from the king to the governor to take stringent measures against Hinduism and soon died. In a letter addressed to the king on 30th November 1547, Cosme Anes refers to thick rumours that the death of Minguel Vaz during the preceding year was caused by poisoning. He adds :

" All this is accepted here as true, and I do believe that it is poison that caused the death of Minguel Vaz, which, as affirmed by many was given by Brahmins, who committed these betrayals and evils, for the very reason that they were convinced that Your Majesty had empowered Minguel Vaz to expatriate them from the island of Goa, and other things."[27]

There were also rumours that Bishop D. João de Albuquerque was implicated in the murder of Minguel Vaz. The Jesuit historian Francisco de Sousa writes :

" Minguel Vaz, was so much favoured by the king, and a man of such quick despatch and so much in a hurry that, having left India in January of 1545, he was back in Goa once again in October of 1546. He commenced to destroy Hindu temples and to suppress idolatry in accordance with the amplest provisions and

[26] Wicki, *op. cit.*, vol. I, pp. 66-72 ; Silva Rego, *op. cit*,. vol. III, pp. 203-8.

[27] Silva Rego, *op. cit.*, vol. III, p. 534.

powers which he had brought, and provoked against himself the odium of the Hindus to such an extent that they gave him poison, of which he came to die at Chaul as generously as he had lived. There were in India men who had the temerity to impute his death to the jealousy of Bishop D. João de Albuquerque and wrote to Portugal to that effect."[28]

The shock of the death of Minguel Vaz caused the death of his associate in proselytism Fr. Diogo Borba, Rector of the Seminary of Holy Faith (St. Paul's College) in 1548.

The territory conquered by Affonso de Albuquerque at the outset comprised the island of Goa and three adjacent islands of Divar, Chorão and Jua. The Hindu temples which existed in this territory were destroyed in 1540. In 1543 Ibrahim Adilkhan presented the sub-districts of Bardez and Salsete to the Portuguese. As stated earlier, Minguel Vaz suggested to the King that the temples in these areas should also be destroyed and accordingly in the letter addressed to the Governor of Goa in 1546, the king included the following directive :

" Since my principal aim in regard to matters relating to these parts, which I have in mind oftener than any other, is that our Lord should be served and His faith increased, to me it appears good that from the mainlands of Bardez and Salsete which Idalcão presented to me should be abolished all vestiges of idolatry which therein exist and that efforts should be made to effect the conversion of the Hindus living therein."[29]

Minguel Vaz died in 1547 before this royal order could be fully implemented. The order of D. Sebastião dated March 25, 1559 in which he had prohibited the existence of Hindu temples, private Hindu sanctuaries and images of Hindu gods as well as the celebration of Hindu festivals (this will be referred to in greater detail later), did not apply to Salsete and Bardez. On 29th August, 1566, however, vice-roy D. Antão de Noronha promulgated the following order which applied to the entire territory under Portuguese rule.

[28] Francisco de Souza, *Oriente Conquistado a Jesus Christo*, pt. I, (Conq. I., Div. I, § 31), p. 24.
[29] Silva Rego *op. cit.*, vol. III, pp. 324-5.

" I order that no Hindu temple be erected in any of the territories of my King, the lord of these parts, and that Hindu temples which already have been erected be not repaired without my special permission, contravention of which will entail the penalty of such temples being destroyed and their value applied towards the expenses of pious works. "[30]

The Portuguese rulers apparently hoped that the Hindu temples which would thus be left unrepaired would in the course of time fall into ruins and be extinct. The Hindus of Salsete approached the Viceroy and clamoured against this order but their appeals fell on deaf ears. They thereupon returned home " and placing in carriages the idols, whose temples were threatened with ruin, they moved to the other side where there were no Portuguese to persecute them. "[31] The image of Shri Mangesh was probably moved from Cortalim (Cudtthalla) at this time in 1566. The Jesuit historian Francisco de Souza gives the following interesting account of Shri Mangesh and his worshippers :

" Formerly the *Cortalôs* (the villagers of Cortalim) were greatly devoted to their idols as is seen from the fact that although Cortalim is not large it had many lands belonging to the temples. The reason of this was that they served the kings of the mainland in offices requiring penmanship ; and as this caste of people always find those whom they can exploit, they returned to their village rich, bought lands and offered them to the temples, in order to preserve the memory of their names. All of them bear the title " *Xenens* " (Shenvis), that is to say, teachers ; because in the region of Konkan they are the ones who teach the other Brahmins the three R's. There are other Brahmins in Salsete, who do not belong to Cortalim and yet take pride in the appelation *Xenens*... The Church of Cortalim is erected in the same site, where formerly the idol of Mangesh was worshipped. Mangesh is nothing but a stone and the reason which led the people of Cortalim to worship this stone is the following : The first *Cortalô* Brahmin who came to Salsete from Kashi-Pandharpur in the territory of Bengal, was wandering in search of a convenient place

[30] J. H. Cunha Rivara, *Archivo Portuguez Oriental*, Fasc. V, pt. II p. 613, (Doc. 576).

[31] Francisco de Souza, *op. cit.*, pt. II, (Conq. I, Div. I, § 15), p. 14.

in which to settle down with his family. He sought the advice of the Demon of this point who appeared before him and ordered him to build his home at the place where his cow would discharge her milk. The Brahmin kept his cow under observation while she left in the morning for grazing and saw that when she reached a certain stone, which adjoined the river, she poured her milk on it spontaneously. And here he built his home and adorned the stone as a precious treasure, in which had entered the god who had appeared before him and to whom the cow had made an offering of her milk... Cortalim is a place of Kashi-Pandharpur from which the Brahmin hailed and he gave the name to the new colony to conserve the memory of his land of birth."[32]

Kashi is Varanasi (Benares) which is in Uttar Pradesh, Pandharpur is in Sholapur district of Maharashtra, and neither of the places is in Bengal. Geographically, therefore, there is confusion in Father Souza's account. But, nevertheless, it may be taken as indicative of contemporary conceptions as regards the original home of the Shenvi Brahmins.

The missionary zeal of the rulers would not permit them to rest in patience until the Hindu temples fell into ruins for want of repairs. They also saw that the Hindus were migrating with their gods beyond the reach of their power. A pretext was therefore found in 1567 to destroy the temples of Salsete and break the images of gods found therein. The incident which provided the occasion for this action was as follows: Diogo Rodrigues, Captain of the fort of Rachol, had summoned some villagers of Loutolim, but they did not appear. He was advised to burn the houses of these villagers by way of punishment for their disobedience. Rodrigues felt that it would be a more effective punishment if the principal temple of the village was burnt down and he acted accordingly. The villagers sought redress from the "*Capitão às Justiças de sua Magestade*" in Goa who ordered that Rodrigues should make amends by rebuilding the temple which he had burnt. Rodrigues appealed against this decision and he received the powerful support of Archbishop Primaz and the Provincial who told the viceroy that the decision was deplorable. As a result the viceroy ordered Rodrigues to burn down as many temples of Salsete as possible. Elated at

[32] *Ibid.*, pt. II, (Conq. I., Div. I, § 13), p. 12.

his success, Rodrigues returned to Rachol and with the active assistance of the missionaries of Salsete strove day and night to burn down temples and break the images found therein. Francisco de Souza writes that the number of temples destroyed at this time was 280.[33]

In a report submitted by *Irmão* Gomes Vaz to the king on December 12, 1567, he gives extracts from some letters sent by the Captain of Rachol in which the latter gives particulars of his campaign of destruction of temples. In this we find a reference to " Malsa devi." In one of the extracts it is stated that on the preceding day the captain of Rachol broke the principal image of the temple of " Alardol " (Mardol ?) into pieces.[34] It is also stated that on March 15, 1567 the temples of Doro, Mando, Narana, Baguaonte and Hesporo (Ishwar) of Sancuale were burnt down and the images found therein destroyed. There is also a reference to the destruction of the temples of Cuncolim, Chinchinim and Ambelim. It is also stated that the images found in the destroyed temples were thrown into the rivers in the vicinity or melted to make candlesticks and other objects for use in the local churches.

On the basis of information available in the government archives of Goa Professor Pissurlencar has given the following list of the temples which existed in Salsete at this time :

Names of Villages	*Names of the Hindu Deities*
Adsulim	Khetrapall.
Ambelim	Madeu, Durgadevi, Bhairão, Purush.
Aquem	Sidnath, Gram-Purus, Marcadeu (Marcó-deu), Ecalavir.
Arossim	Boguespor (Bhogueshwar), Gão-Purush, Betall, Madeu, Satazanni (Sapta-matricá).
Assolná	Betall, Santeri, Purus Dequechó (Dekhecho).
Benaulim	Banespor (Baneshwar), Sanquespor (Shanqueshwar), Narainna, Bhairão, Cantarozadevi, Santeri, Deuna.
Betalbatim	Betal-aguió (Aguia-Vetall), Gorocó (Gorakh), Madeu, Ganês, Santeri, Gão-Purus, Quellevir, Barazann, Daro (Dadd), Gonu-gonichó.

[33] *Ibid.*, pt. II, (Conq. 1, Div. 1, § 16), p. 15.
[34] Silva Rego, *op. cit.*, vol X, p. 291.

Names of Villages	*Names of the Hindu Deities*
Calata	Santeri, Madei (Mahadevi),
Camorlim	Camequeá (Camakshá), Beirão (Bhairava), Camalespor (Camaleshwar), " Marcynquo "(?).
Caná	Khetrapall.
Cansaulim	Naganath, Santeri, Purus.
Carmoná	Madeu, Betall-aguió (Aguia-Vetall), Purush, Udió.
Cavelossim	Capellaspor (Capaleshwar), Khetrapall, Nanabai, Mandoli.
Cavorim	Naganath, Isvanath (Vishwanath).
Chandor	Vasouarazu (Bassavaraj).
Chicalim	Narainna, Ispor (Ishwar), Santeri, Barazann, Gãopurus, Chovisvir, Bodcó-Deu.
Chicolná	Santeri.
Chinchinim	Betall, Santeri, Baucadevi, Aguió-Betall.
Coelim	Ozinessor (Vazineshvar), Madeu Santeri, Gão-Purus, Oizari (Vaizari, that is Ganês).
Colvá	Malcumi (Mahalakshimi), Balespor (Baleshwar), Narainna, Vetall, Beirão (Bhairava), Ravallnath, Maculospor (Maculeshwar).
Cortalim	Manganath (Manguesh), Santeri, " Quemsooboo " (Keshav ?), Vir, Capilasor (Kapileshwar), Narainna, Bagonti (Bhagavati), Gopinath, Chandirnath.
Cuncolim	Santeri, Madeu.
Curtorim	Santeri, Narainna, Chandaspari (Chanddeshwari), Quetrapall, Santullió, Ravallnath, Chandranath, Durgadevi, Baguonto (Bhagavanta), Solebẽsor (Solvenshwar), Maiespor (Maheshwar), Ganês, Quẽsnanto.
Dabolim	Santeri, Ispor (Ishwar), Gãopurus, Khetrapall, Bagonti (Bhagavati), Barazann.
Davorlim	Bagavonti (Bhagavati), Barazan, Conti.
Deussua	Chinchininato (Chinchinni-nath), Beirão Locanato (Loknath), Purus.
Dicarpale	Santeri, Barazann.
Duncolim	Betall, Madeu.

Names of Villages	*Names of the Hindu Deities*
Dramapur	Madeu, Narainna, Betall, Beirão, Khetrapall, Durgadevi, Santeri, Gãopurus, Suntaparaulo.
Gandaulim	Durgadevi.
Gonsuá	Guotomosor (Gautameshwar).
Guirdolim	Ravalnath, Verbadeu, Ketrapall, Narainna.
Issorcim	Santeri, Barazann.
Loutulim	Ramunauto (Ramanath), Betall, Gram-Purus, Bagovonti (Bhagavati), Santeri, Naranna, Careá-Santeri (Karya-Santeri), Sidnath, Deiva, Vamonió.
Macazana	Ravallnath, Durgadevi, Narainna, Ispor (Ishwar), Ketrapall.
Majordá	Durgadevi, Soniser (Suvarneshwar), Purus, Vir (Virbhadra), Mamai (Maha-Mayá).
Margão	Damdor (Damodara), Chandenato (Chandranath), Narainna-Puturdev (Naraenna Paturdeu), Chamdeusery (Choundeshwari or Chamundeshwari), Santeri, Macazan, (Macagi), Mayasassor (Maixassur Mardini or Maheshvar), Vira (Mull Vir), Bagomte (Bhagavati), Gomespor (Goveshwar). Malcumi (Maha-Laxmi), Bhut (Bhutnath). Narainna, Ispor (Iswar), Gram-Purush.
Mormugão	Vagnath, Barazann.
Nagoá	Santeri, Bagonti, (Bhagavati), Ispor (Ishwar), Gão-Purus, Narainna, Ravallnath, Barazana.
Orlim	Gotimosor (Gautameshwar), Purus Cucumba. Vancadeu, Maisasor (Mhaixassur-mardini), Narainna.
Pale	Durgadevi, Ispor (Ishwar), Barazann, Gão-Purus, Adu-Purus (Adi-Purush), Daroo (Dhaddó, Dhareshwar), Vatachoru, Gorcharo.
Quelossim	Santeri, Naraina, Ispor (Ishwar), Gãopurus. *Ganês*. Baguonti (Bhagavati).
Raia	Raisvar, Camaquea (Camakshá), Bogvonti (Bhagavati), Narainna, Vatambi (Vattambi).
Raçaim	Trivicrama. Narainna, Ispor (Ishwar).

Names of Villages	*Names of the Hindu Deities*
Sancoale	Santeri, Ispor (Ishwar), Gão-Purus, Daroazoosini (?), Narainna, Bagonti (Bhagavti), Azossini, Narsu (Narcinha), Parmamedo.
Sarzorá	Naganath, Betall, Satteri, Durgadevi, Call-Purus.
Seraulim	Santeri, Madeu, Pavan-devi.
Sernabatim	Santeri, Sidhath
Teldulim	Sidnath, Cannó, Betall, Santeri, "Jogue Balgondar."
Vaddem	Santeri, Narainna, Ispor (Ishwar), Bandichó, Barazana, Chovis-Vir.
Vanelim	Goresnõr (Ghoddeshwar ?).
Varcá	Madeu, Purus, Beirão Santeri, Vir.
Velção	Madeu, Velbadevi, Gãopurus.
Velim	Santeri, Betall, Beirady.
Verná	Santeri, Malçadevi, Narainna, Bogonti (Bhagavati), Gram-Purus, Vernadevi, Lambesvor.
Utordá	Gram-Purus, Betall, Vaguiró, Madeu, Ekalla-vir (Kull-Vir ?).
Verodá	Durgadevi, Madeu.[35]

As was to be expected, soon after the campaign of the destruction of Hindu shrines had started in Salsete, similar activity was initiated in Bardez also. While the religious leaders of the missionary activity in Salsete were the Jesuits, those of the missionary activity in Bardez were the Franciscan friars. In 1567 the campaign of destruction of temples of Bardez was accomplished. Gomes de Vaz refers to it in his report in the following words :

"There also took place in this year the destruction of the Hindu temples which existed in these territories of Your Majesty, of which none remains, for the priests of St. Francis also razed out of memory all those which existed in Bardez."[36]

Records of the missionary activities of the Franciscans which are available are not as full and complete as those of the missionary activities of the Jesuits. In a report of the activities of the

[35] Pais, *Tombo da Ilha de Goa, op. cit.,* pp. 169-177.
[36] Silva Rego, *op. cit.,* vol. X, p. 298.

Franciscans which has been published under the title "*Noticia que obravão os frades de S. Francisco*," it is stated that they "destroyed 300 Hindu temples where false Gods were worshipped."[37]

The following is a list given by Professor Pissurlencar of the Hindu temples existing in Bardez at this time:

Bardez

Names of Villages	*Names of the Hindu Deities*
Aldoná	Bhagavati, Ravallnath, Narayann, Santeri, Sidnath, Bhut-nath, Dadda, Satti, Fulnath.
Anjuna	Vetall, Santeri, Bhagavati.
Arporá	Santeri, Vetall, Vanadeutá, Chourungó.
Assagão	Bhumicá (Bhumi-deutá), Bhagavati, Chava-teavoril Ravalnath, Devi Satti, Santeri, Khetrapall, Malicarjuna, Linga, Purvechó-Ravallnath.
Assonorá	Santeri, Ravallnath, Khetrapall, Vanadeutá, Purvachari.
Bastorá	Satmá (Sapta-Matricá), Naranna, Mailardeu (Malardeu ?), Ossolgaromba (?), Santeri.
Calangute	Santeri, Sitallnato, Saptanato, Brahmanath, Vetall.
Camorlim	Betall, Ajdevi, Mauli.
Candolim	Naranna, Santeri, Bhairão, Gagarespor (Gaddgueshwar), Rovolnato.
Cancá	Naranna, Khetrapall.
Colvale	Ravallnath, Bhairão, Ramanato, Dadd, Gautama.
Corlim	Santeri, Azonato (Ajnath).
Cunchelim	Barazann.
Guirim	Bhagavati, Naranna, Vanadeutá, Satti, Santeri.
Mapuçá	Santeri, Ganês.
Marna	Betall, Santeri, Ravallnath.
Moirá	Ravallnath, Santeri, Madeu, Rampurus, Vantipurus, Satpurus, Dadd.
Nachinolá	Ramnath, Malcumi (Mahalaxmi), Grampurus, Ravalnath, Vetal, Gopinath.
Nadorá	Khetrapall, Bhutnath, Dadd, Ghotteó.

[37] Silva Rego, *op. cit.*, vol. V., Lisboa 1951, p. 408.

Names of Villages	*Names of the Hindu Deities*
Nagoá	Vetal, Ravallnath, Naranna.
Nerul	Santeri, Khetrapall, Ravallnath, Vetall.
Olaulim	Naranna, Somanath, Santeri, Ganês, Ravallnath.
Ordá	Bhairão.
Oxel	Santeri.
Paliem	Santeri, Ramanath, Purus.
Parrá	Rampurus, Deu.
Pilerne	Santeri, Ravallnath, Ramnath, Bhairão, Baucadevi, Vetall, Hemanath.
Pirna	Santeri, Ravallanath, Linga, Calleadeutá (Calicadevi).
Pomburpá	Malicarjuna, Ravallanath, Grampurus, Santeri, Vanadeutà, Somanath, Ganês.
Punolá	Ganês, Capilesvor, Ravallnath, Vanadeutá, Vetall.
Revorá	Kellbadevi.
Saligão	Betall.
Sangoldá	Santeri, Narainna, Ganês, Ravallnath, Madeu, Satti.
Sinquerim	Gagresvor (Gaddgueshwar ?).
Siolim	Santeri, Satti, Ganês, Ravallnath, Kelbadevi, Vetall.
Sirçaim	Malcumi, Santeri, Vetall, Ravallnath, Kellbadevi.
Sirulá	Vetall, Naranna, Dhactti Vanadeutá, Ravallnath, Voddli Vanadeutá, Sidnath, Malcumi (Maha-Laxmi), Grampurus, Somnath, Vir, Caliapurus (Kall-Purus), Santeri, Khetrapall, Naganath, Mallanath, Bhagavati, Maha-Cali, Gopesvor.
Tivim	Ravallnath, Somnath, Vetall, Purvachari.
Ucassaim	Ravallnath.
Verlá	Santeri, Naranna, Ravallnath, Vardespor (Vardeshwar), Naganath, Bagavoti.[38]

Soon after the temples of Salsete had been destroyed a meeting of its inhabitants was convened through criers and they

[38] Pais, *Tombo da Ilha de Goa, op. cit.*, pp. 178-182.

were asked to disclose under oath information regarding the properties held by the Hindu temples which had been destroyed. The following gentlemen were present at one such meeting :

"Dama Parbu, and Gomu Parbu, Narse Parbu, another Damu Parbu, Chrisna Parbu, Vitoba Parbu, Ramu Parbu, other Ramu Parbu, another Gomu Parbu, Deuna Parbu, Damu Hegara, Anta Hegare, Azy Egoro, Chrisna Naique, Naru Ballo, Loqu Sinay, Ramu Sinay, Anta Synay, Mabolu Synay, Quensu Synay, Nargu Synay, Nagu Synay, another Quensu Synay, Chrisna Synay, Vitu Poy." At the meeting, the Indian Christians swore on the Bible and the Hindus took the oath by placing their hands on a wheel (*Roda*).[39]

Similar statements on oath were obtained from the villagers of Sancoalli on March 7, 1569 and from other villagers later. On March 21, 1569, D. Sebastião promulgated an order by which the income of the Hindu temples of Bardez and Salsete which had been destroyed was transferred to Christian Churches.

The campaign of the destruction of the Hindu temples existing in the Portuguese territories did not entirely succeed in its object as they were soon replaced by new temples in neighbouring territories. Whenever possible, the images of Gods worshipped in the temples which had been destroyed were smuggled outside the Portuguese territories and installed in new temples ; where this was not possible, new images were made and installed. For instance, Mangesh from Cortalim and Mhalasá from Vernem were installed at Priol ; Shantadurga from Cavelossim at Queulá and Ramnath of Loutulim and Mahalakshmi of Colvá at Bandorá. Hindus who had migrated to neighbouring territories also built new temples to their family Gods in those territories and many such temples are found to this day in the coastal districts upto South Kanara and Kerala. The Portuguese missionaries soon discovered that erection and maintenance of new temples outside Goa was being financed by the Hindu citizens in Portuguese territories and many new converts continued to remain attached to their old Gods. To put a stop to this, the third Concilio Provincial held in Goa in 1585 requested the King of Portugal by a resolution to pass a decree forbidding the Hindus from financing

[39] Cunha Rivara, *Archivo Portuguez Oriental*, Fasc. V, pt. II, p. 644, (Doc. 610).

the erection and maintenance of temples in neighbouring territories. This resolution ran as follows :

" It is known for certain that the Brahmins and other infidel subjects of Your Majesty have erected and are erecting in the lands of the neighbouring infidel chiefs, almost all the temples which in our territories had been pulled down and under the same names and titles as they previously had. The construction and maintenance of these temples as well as of the staff thereof are supported by moneys which are earned in our territories and taken out. This is a great offence against the laws of God and also has a deleterious effect on the New Christian converts as it weakens them in their faith, apart from the fact that it results in large sums being exported to foreign territories for being spent towards such idolatrous purposes. This Council prays Your Majesty to order under pain of grave punishments that no infidel subject of Your Majesty build temples or cause them to be built, nor reconstruct them nor finance at his cost their upkeep or maintenance of the staff therein nor give any assistance or gift for such purpose. Since Your Majesty prohibits the infidels from going on pilgrimage to or attending festivals held at such temples under pain of exile and fines, it is a much worse offence to build or maintain such temples at their cost. The *Concilio* begs Your Majesty that fines be imposed on such infidels, and such part thereof as he may consider appropriate be applied towards new Christian churches which may be erected in future or might already have been erected in the villages in which the said infidels reside, in case there is need for such assistance ; and in case the churches do not need the same, towards any other purpose which the Prelate may consider appropriate."[40]

The stages in the evolution of the policy of religious persecution so far traced, relate mainly to the period to the establishment of the Goa Inquisition. Thereafter the Inquisition played a major role in the formulation and implementation of the religious policies in Goa. Before proceeding to a review of the subsequent stages of the religious policy in chapter VIII, an idea of the organisation and procedures of the Goa Inquisition is, therefore, provided in Chapter VII.

[40] Cunha Rivara, *op. cit.*, Fasc. IV, p. 123.

CHAPTER VII

Organisation and Procedures of the Inquisition of Goa

A broad idea of the organisation and procedures of the Inquisition of Goa can be obtained from Dellon's *Account of Inquisition of Goa* which is reprinted in the second part of this book.

The Inquisition of Goa was modelled on the pattern of the Inquisition of Portugal and, broadly speaking, the working of these two tribunals was governed by similar rules and regulations. I have before me a copy of the *Regimento do Santo Officio da Inquisiçam dos Reynos de Portugal* (Manual of Rules and Regulations of the Holy Office of the Inquisition in the kingdoms of Portugal), which was published in 1640 by Bishop D. Francisco de Castro, Inquisitor General of the Kingdom and Dominions of Portugal. A prefatory note to this Manual makes clear that it was prepared on the basis of an earlier manual compiled in 1613 by Bishop D. Pedro de Castilho, then Inquisitor General, after incorporation of such amendments and alterations as were found necessary in the light of subsequent experience. This Manual consists of three volumes. The first volume, which is divided into 22 chapters and 75 folios, describes the functions and responsibilities of various officers of the Inquisition, as well as the qualifications which they were required to possess and the manner in which they were selected ; the second volume, divided into 28 chapters and 75 folios, outlines the procedures adopted in the trials of the Inquisition ; and the third volume divided into 27 chapters and 55 folios, sets forth the punishments and penalties imposed on those found guilty of various types of crimes of which the Inquisition took cognisance. From this Manual it is possible to obtain a fairly clear and complete idea of the manner in which the Inquisition of Goa must have functioned during the later stages of its career. An indication of the working of the Inquisition of Goa immediately following its establishment is provided by the following Draft Diploma on the basis of which it was established :

Diploma Establishing the Goa Inquisition

"We Cardinal Infant, Inquisitor General in these kingdoms and dependencies of Portugal, etc., make known to you the Very

Revd. Archbishop of the city of Goa, India, and thereby to the Inquisitors and officers of the Holy Inquisition which is now established, that being desirous of providing that the Holy Office of Inquisition should function in these parts in a manner that would best conduce to the glory and honour of Our Lord, and increase of the Holy Catholic Faith, and having consulted with persons of conscience, learning and experience in matters of the Holy Inquisition as to how best to achieve this, we have formulated the following articles, which we hereby order should be complied with and observed in their entirety, apart from the Manual of General Rules and Regulations which is sent herewith.

Before beginning to use the Holy Office of the Inquisition persons to hold the following posts should be found out and selected : First, an advocate to work as promotor ; and an apostolic notary, who should be a priest if one can conveniently be found, and, if not, a layman who should be an apostolic notary or a clerk of His Majesty or belong to the ecclesiastical auditorium, whosoever may appear best qualified and most suitable ; and also a *meyrinho* (officer to apprehend malefactors), who may be an ecclesiastic if one is available, and a solicitor who would also serve as gate-keeper and a jailor. All these officers should be Old Christians, god-fearing persons deserving of confidence who can keep secrets and having the other qualities required according to the Manual of Rules and Regulations. Before they begin to serve in their posts they should take the prescribed oath to serve truly and faithfully. It appears to us that more officers will not be necessary at present.

As regards a prison, for the present it may be in the part of the *aljube* (a prison for the ecclesiastic or other persons whose cause belongs to the ecclesiastical jurisdiction) attached to the Archbishop's house, which may be more convenient. If the *Aljube* is not available for this purpose some houses may be taken where the prisoners could be kept in such a manner that there would be no communication between those who have confessed and those who have not, or between those who have participated in the same crime and vigilance could be exercised to ensure that they do not receive messages from outside.

For the present it will suffice to publicise the Inquisition in the cities of Goa and Cochin—first in Goa and having done the visit there they shall proceed to publicise it in Cochin---since these two are the principal cities having the largest population. Thereafter in future if it appears necessary to publicise it in other parts, this should be done.

When the Holy Inquisition is to be publicised this should be done in the Cathedral Church or in the principal church and there should be preaching and proclamation of the Edicts of Faith and of Grace, in accordance with the Manual of Rules and Regulations. As to the period of grace, four months should be allowed within which the persons who come to confess their offences should not be imprisoned or given corporal punishment but only spiritual penances should be imposed.

There will be two registers with pages numbered and initialled. One will serve to take down the denunciations of those who come to denounce others and the other to write in it the confessions and reconciliations of those who come to confess their sins and ask for mercy.

The denunciations and reconciliations should be received by the Inquisitors in the presence of the Archbishop, when he can conveniently be present, and the same should be done when the parties are questioned. If the Archbishop cannot remain present, one of the Deputies and the Inquisitor should be present.

When a person is to be arrested this should always be done by a warrant signed by the Archbishop and the Inquisitors; if the person is of high status then this should be communicated to the Deputies and the Viceroy, if necessary, and in all the prisons great circumspection should be exercised before doing so.

If there exist two Inquisitors, one of them who is junior shall process the cases till the end and when parties appeal against any interlocutory order, the Archbishop with the other Inquisitor, if one exists, with the Deputies and such other advocates as they may consider necessary, shall decide the said appeals for which we grant them power and authority in conformity with the Bull of the Holy Office, notwithstanding anything to the contrary on this point in the Manual of Rules and Regulations. The Archbishop with the said Deputies with such other theologians and canonists as he may consider necessary, shall decide the final sentences and the interlocutory orders of torture.

If any person who is imprisoned by the Holy Office be so powerful and of such status that it is not possible to decide his case there, such prisoner should be sent here with the process and statement of offences of which he is accused. This should not be done except for adequate reasons and only when it is not possible to decide his case there and with him should be sent the witnesses and a summary of the process for final sentence.

It should be remembered in receiving denunciations, that denunciations of offences committed by New Christians other than those committed subsequent to the 10th of June, 1540 should not be accepted, since those committed upto that date have been forgiven by the Holy Father.

When a person is arrested for the crime of heresy, his entire property, whether moveable or immoveable, will be sequestrated and deposited in charge of persons of sound credit and an inventory thereof will be made ; and if he is condemned as a heretic such property will be confiscated for His Majesty's Municipality and the same will apply when such persons are reconciled for the crime of heresy after being imprisoned. This will not take place in the case of New Christians who will not lose their property as a result of an order of His Majesty who as an act of mercy has granted this favour to them during the ten years which commenced in 1559 ; nor will the property of the native Christians be confiscated during the period of the first five years following the publication of the Inquisition in these parts, since we consider this advisable in the service of God and His Majesty.

Although the New Christians were granted a papal brief in which His Holiness ordered that to them should be given the names of witnesses notwithstanding the common law, they should not be given since this brief has been revoked by an order of Pope Pius IV who presides in the Church of God, a copy of which the Archbishop possesses.

If those who have been recently converted to Christianity from the Muslim or Hindu sect commit the crime of heresy after becoming Christians and are imprisoned therefor, they should not, on confessing their crime, be immediately reconciled or made to abjure, but first they should be placed in the part of the prison where they could be instructed in matters of faith and well educated in all that pertains to their salvation and all that is important from the point of view of their falling into similar errors; and thereafter they should be reconciled and made to abjure in the form prescribed by law. Except when the Inquisitors think otherwise, this should be done only after they are satisfied that there would be no relapse.

After the Inquisition is publicised there should not be *Auto de Fé* with the solemnity of the scaffold for execution of criminals until we order to the contrary; but, as the cases of the prisoners are decided they should be taken to a church where their sentences should be read out and they should make their abjurations.

We direct that, in view of the great distance between those parts and this Kingdom, the Archbishop of Goa and the Inquisitors with the opinion of the Deputies, if these can be present, may commute the penances of those who are reconciled and those on whom penances have been imposed by the Holy Office notwithstanding anything to the contrary in the Manual of Rules and Regulations on this point.

The Inquisitors and Deputies should in the manner prescribed by law take the oath to keep secret all matters pertaining to the Holy Office and to well and faithfully administer justice in these parts, which will be registered and duly signed by them, and the other advocates who may be called upon to engage in the affairs of the Holy Office should at the outset take the oath of secrecy.

If any of the parties comes out with the plea of suspicion against the Archbishop (disqualifying the latter from trying his case) the Inquisitor or Inquisitors with the Deputies or every one of them should hear the same and should they wish to recuse any of the Inquisitors the plea should be heard by the Archbishop with the other Inquisitors with the Deputies in the same manner and should they wish to recuse any of the Deputies the plea should be heard by the Archbishop with the Inquisitors. Having regard to the great distance which exists between India and this kingdom, this should be complied with notwithstanding any directions to the contrary in the Manual of Rules and Regulations.

The procurators who act on behalf of the parties in the

trials of the Holy Inquisition should be Old Christians who are persons of learning and good conscience and should be selected by the Archbishop for the purpose, nothwithstanding anything to the contrary in the Manual of Rules and Regulations.

These articles and the Manual of Rules and Regulations and other papers relating to the Inquisition should not be taken out of the house of the Holy Inquisition where cases are tried, as this will conduce to the service of God and secrecy of the Holy Office."[1]

The types of offences of which the Inquisition of Portugal took congnisance are enumerated in the Edict of Faith which is appended to the Manual of Rules and Regulations referred to above. This edict is reproduced hereunder :—

The Edict of Faith

"The Apostolic Inquisitors against the wickedness of heresy and apostasy, in this City and Archdiocese of...and its district etc...

Be it known to those, who may see this Edict or may acquire knowledge thereof in any way, that in pursuance of the obligation which we have of searching for, repressing and extirpating every offence and crime of heresy and apostasy, for better preservation of the good customs and purity of our Holy Catholic Faith ; and being informed that some persons not having perfect understanding of the cases which fall within the province of the Holy Office, do not come to denouce some of them ; and as sufficient provision against the resulting inconvenience has not been made, for the reason that the edict in which these cases are specified is publicised only on the occasions on which *Autos de Fé* are held and is on that occasion heard with little attention ; and being desirous of providing a means by which the faithful Christians may not remain with their consciences burdened with guilt and exposed to the terrible punishment of excommunication which is laid down in the said edict ; we have considered it advisable to order that all the said cases should be published once again through this monitory letter. Through this, by our Apostolic authority

[1] Antonio Baião, *A Inquisição de Goa*, Vol. I, pp. 80-85.

we order all persons, ecclesiastical, secular and regular ; of whatever grade, status, preeminence, order or condition they may be and whether exempt or not ; by virtue of holy obedience and under pain of major excommunication, to be incurred *ipso facto*, absolution of which we reserve to ourselves ; that within the precise and unalterable period of the next thirty days, which we fix by three canonical admonitions, giving ten days by each admonition, they should come to denounce and declare before us what they know of the cases which are specified hereunder.

If they know or have heard that any baptised Christian has said or done anything against the Holy Catholic Faith and against what the Roman Catholic Church holds, believes and teaches, even though they might know this by natural secret.

That any person after receiving baptism has had belief in the Mosaic law, subsequent to the last general pardon which was published on the 5th of January 1605 ; not acknowledging Jesus Christ, our Redeemer, as true God and Messias, promised to the Patriarchs and prophesied by the Prophets ; performing Jewish rites and ceremonies, namely : not working on Saturday but remaining dressed on that day as on a feast day, commencing the observance on Friday evening ; always abstaining from the flesh of pig, hare and rabbit and scaleless fish and other things prohibited in the old law ; fasting on the great day that comes in the month of September, and on other days on which Jews are accustomed to fast ; solemnising their Passover ; saying Jewish prayers ; bathing their dead, dressing them in a long shirt made of new cloth, covering them with a folded sheet, putting on them linen pants, burying them in virgin soil and in very deep graves, weeping before their litters, singing as the Jews do and placing in their mouths *aljofar* (seed-pearls) and gold and silver coins, cutting their nails and preserving them; eating on low tables; placing themselves behind doors for mourning; or performing any other act which appears to be done in observance of the said Mosaic law.

That any Christian after being baptised, follows or has at any time followed the abominable sect of Mahomed and observed any of the precepts of his Koran ; or

Holds or has held as good the sects of Luther or Calvin or

any other heresiarch whether old or modern, which are condemned by the Holy See ; or

Has denied or doubted that the body of Our Lord is really and truly present in the Holy Sacrament of the Eucharist and should be venerated with the same adoration as is due to God; or

Has denied or doubted that there is Heaven for the good, Hell for the wicked and Purgatory in which the souls of persons who die without having fully expiated their offences are purged before they proceed to enjoy perfect bliss ; or

Has denied or doubted that men are by divine command required to confess their sins to the priests and affirms that it is sufficient to confess them to God alone ; or

Has estimated falsely or doubted any of the Articles of Faith ; or

Has denied or estimated falsely the Sacraments of Holy Mother Church such as those of Holy Order and Matrimony ; by celebrating or hearing confessions without having received the Holy Order or publicly receiving the Sacrament of Marriage after having taken the solemn vow of chastity or receiving Holy Orders, or marrying again whilst the first husband or wife is living ; or

Has said or affirmed that man does not have the liberty to freely do or not do good or evil ; or

Has said that faith without good works is sufficient to save one's soul and that no baptised Christian who has faith can be lost ; or

Has said or affirmed that man is not responsible for his acts between birth and death ; or

Has denied that Saints should be venerated and considered as our intercessors before God ; or

Has denied veneration and reverence to the relics of the Saints ; or

Has falsely estimated vows, religion and ceremonies approved by the Holy Mother Church ; or

Has denied to the Pope authority over the other Bishops, and that he has authority to grant indulgences and their efficacy to the souls ; or

Has denied the duty of fasting at the times ordered by the Church ; or

Has affirmed that *onzena* (usury) and simple fornication are not mortal sins ; or

Has thought adversely of the purity of the Blessed Virgin Mary and does not believe that she was virgin before, in and after child-birth.

That any person practises Jewish astrology or possesses or reads books thereon or on any other art of prophesying.

That any person possesses or reads forbidden books even though under the pretext of permissions which have been secured for the purpose ; since all such permissions have been revoked by His Holiness the Pope upto the 7th June, 1633.

That any confessor, diocesan or regular, of whatever dignity, order, condition and preeminence he may be, solicited or in any way provoked either men or women to commit with himself or others any illicit or dishonest acts, either during, before or immediately after the act of sacramental confession, or on the occasion and under the pretext of hearing confession, even though such confession did not take place ; or outside the confession but in the confessional, or at an alternative place fixed for hearing confessions or any other place selected under the pretence of hearing confession.

That any person punished by the Holy Office for offences of which he has confessed before it, says subsequently that he confessed falsely of what he had not committed ; or discloses the secret of what transpired at the Inquisition ; or slanders or gives a false idea of the procedures and lawful ministry of the Holy Office.

All those who know that any or all of the offences mentioned above have been committed or will be committed in future should come personally to the Holy Office for denouncing them. And in places where there is a Commissary of the Holy Office denunciation should be made before him ; and where there is no Commissary, every one should give the information to his own Confessor, who has the obligation to make it known to the Holy Office within the same period. On the expiry of the said period of thirty days, if such persons should not come forth to make denunciations of what they know (which God forbid) by these presents we place on the persons of those whose names and surnames we have here stated and declared major excommunication and we shall apply for further proceedings to be taken against them in conformity with the Bull of Holy Inquisition, and such persons will in addition incur the malediction of omnipotent God and the blessed St. Peter and St. Paul, the chief Apostles. And under the same pain we order that no person should be so bold as to impede denunciations or to advise others not to denounce by threatening, suborning or doing some harm to those who wish to denounce or are known to have denounced.

In the same manner they should also denounce if they know of any person or persons who have committed the nefarious and abominable sin of sodomy.

And with the same Apostolic authority and under pain of major excommunication and payment of 50 *crusados*, to be applied towards the expenses of the Holy Office, we order all Priors, Vicars, Rectors, Curates and other ecclesiastical persons, to whom this our Edict may be presented that on the day and at the hour which may be fixed, they should read it or have it read in their churches, in a loud and intelligible voice, so that it should come to the notice of all and there should be not one who could allege ignorance thereof.

Given at in the Office of the Inquisition under our signature and seal......on day of the month......of........."[2]

It will be seen that the offences referred to in the above edict are mainly those which the New Christians converted from the Jewish and Muslim religions were liable to commit. As seen earlier, it was this class of converts with whom the Inquisition in Portugal was primarily intended to deal. The Inquisition of Goa had also to deal with the offences committed by the new converts from Hinduism. These are enumerated in a remarkably comprehensive Edict published in Goa in 1736.

The aims and objects of the edict are set forth in its preamble. It is pointed out that the native Christians in the island of Goa

[2] *Regimento do Santo Officio da Inquisiçam*, ff. 207-210.

and adjoining islands and the sub-districts of Salsete and Bardez, since the time when they were converted to Christianity from Hinduism, have continued to practise certain customs which they had practised when they were Hindus. They were permitted to do so as these appeared to be merely civil and political in nature, the fact that their very similarity to the customs observed by Hindus should suffice to consider their observance by Christians inexpedient not having been appreciated. The Inquisitors consider it necessary that these customs, as they are associated with rites of Hindu faith and as under the pretext of observing them, idolatry is being practised by the Christians, should be abolished and that all the people generally should be forbidden to continue to observe them. This will ensure that no occasion exists for idolatrous practices among native Christians who would, as a consequence, in all their behaviour lose all resemblance to the Hindus and conform to that of the Portuguese, from whom they receive the incomparable benefit of conversion. There are also other customs which are observed not only by the natives of these territories, but also by some of the other residents therein, without realising that such observance shows lack of reverence to religion and disrespect to the clergy. The object of the edict is to prevent the pernicious damage to the consciences of the faithful Roman Catholics which results from such customs and to preserve the purity of the Catholic faith.

The main body of the edict is given hereunder :

Edict of the Goa Inquisition

" By virtue of Holy Obedience and under the sanction of spiritual and temporal punishments incurred by those who disobey Apostolic Mandates, we order all persons, both natives of India as well as of any other nation, who are resident in the island of Goa and the adjoining islands or the sub-districts of Salsete and Bardez, both ecclesiastic and lay people, whatever their grade, order, status, condition, dignity or pre-eminence, exempt or not exempt,.........that they faithfully and fully comply with and conform to all that we by this edict resolve with the object of condemning and prohibiting for all time the customs referred to in the preamble, in the manner undermentioned.

All the natives of India, resident in the island of Goa and

other adjacent islands and in the sub-districts of Salsete and Bardez, are hereby ordered that during the celebration of their marriages, before or after it or on occasions connected therewith, they should not use *Gaitas*, or other Hindu musical instruments, as they have been accustomed to do till now.

The said natives of India are hereby ordered that they should not invite, at the time of fixing their weddings, making payment of dowry, or giving wedding presents, relatives of the bridegroom and bride, whether male or female, who commonly are known as *Daijis* or *Gotris*, to attend such functions ; and should any of them happen to be present uninvited, he should not be the one who receives in the name of the bridegroom dowry or wedding presents from the bride, but this work should be done by the parents or guardians of the bridegroom or, if desired, by any other respectable person, whether ecclesiastic or secular, who may be authorised for the purpose by the bridegroom or bride.

The said natives of India are hereby ordered that when dowry is taken to the house of the bridegroom, wedding presents are handed, or bethrothals are celebrated and in any other functions pertaining to weddings whether held on, before or after the wedding day, they should not send from the house of the bridegroom to that of the bride, or vice-versa, flowers of any kind, betel-leaves, areca-nuts or any other things which could be substituted in the absence of these prohibited objects.

The said natives of India are hereby ordered that at the functions of their marriages, and all other functions related thereto, they should not distribute "*virós*" (*viddas*) of betel-leaves and areca-nuts to those present at the house of the bridegroom or bride, publicly or in private ; and if they wish to use these things, they should be placed on a table without being individually distributed and the persons present should not take them in any order of honour or pre-eminence but each person should take them as his turn happens to come.

The same natives of India are hereby ordered that at the functions of their marriages or other related occasions they should not send from the house of the bride or bride-groom any gift of flowers, betel-leaves, areca-nuts or *fugueos* (fried cakes) or any of these things, to the houses of the *Daijis*, *Gotris* or relatives or the houses of any other persons.

The same natives of India are hereby ordered that on the occasions of their marriages and all other functions which they might order or direct to take place for solemnising marriages, either in the house of the bridegroom or of the bride, songs, which it is customary to sing in the language of the land and are commonly known as "*vovios*", should not be sung, either publicly or in private ; and when they desire to hold celebrations in demonstration of their joy, this should not be done with songs which may have a resemblance with the said *vovios* ; and female relatives or *Daijis* of the bridegroom should never sing in such functions.

The same natives of India are hereby ordered that in their houses should not be sung on any occasion and under any pretext, songs called "*vovios*", either in public or in private so that the use of these songs among the faithful Christians would thereby effectively cease.

The said natives of India are hereby ordered that on the occasion of their marriages, whether in the house of the bridegroom or bride or at any other place, they should not commence on fixed days preceding the marriages, to crush rice, grind condiments or flour, fry cakes and prepare other things necessary for wedding feasts ; nor should these services be carried out in the first place by any particular relative or *Daiji* of the bridegroom or bride. These preparations should be started at such opportune time as may be convenient to expedite things and with the participation therein simultaneously of as many persons as may be necessary, without any order of preference, or respect for any custom so far observed.

The same natives are hereby ordered that in the functions of their marriages or other functions which may be ordered or directed to take place in connection therewith, they should not anoint the bridegroom or bride, either together or separately, with a mixture of ground saffron, milk, cocoanut oil, rice powder, crushed leaves of "*abolim*" or any other things, especially on the day of the betrothal, the eighth day preceding marriage, the day preceding marriage, the day of marriage, the day following marriage or the third, fifth or eighth day following marriage.

The same natives are hereby ordered that on the occasion of their marriages or any functions ordered or directed in connection therewith, and especially on the days mentioned above, the bridegroom and bride, either jointly or separately, should not be bathed in the presence of other persons; and when they find necessary to bathe they should do so by themselves and in the presence of only one other person to help them to draw water, who should not be a relative or *Daiji* of either the bridegroom or the bride.

The same natives of India are hereby ordered that they should not erect pandals with festoons of leaves at the gates of the houses of the bridegroom and bride.

The said natives of India are hereby ordered that, on the day of the wedding when the bride and the bridegroom return from the church to the house of the bride, and on the following day when they go from the house of the bride to that of the bridegroom they should not be received at the said houses by the relatives of the bride or bride-groom nor be seated under a canopy built for the purpose, but should be conducted immediately to such apartment as may be convenient; the relatives and *Daijis* of the bride and the bridegroom should not strew flowers, or sprinkle scented water on the married couple or the guests who accompany them.

The said natives of India are hereby ordered that their weddings should be celebrated at such hours that the married couple can reach home before sunset; and under no pretext should they be delayed on the way so that they may reach home after sunset.

The said natives of India are hereby ordered that under the oed on which the married couple would sleep, they should not place betel-leaves, areca-nuts or any other edible thing.

The said natives of India are hereby ordered that, on the day of the marriage or the following day, when the married couple enters the house of either the bride or the bridegroom, they should not be conducted immediately to the place where they would sleep by any person of their lineage, nor should any person cover them with a cloth, nor ask them both to drink from the same cup, or to share the same fruit or dish.

The said natives of India are hereby ordered that at the wedding feasts food should not be served by relatives of the bride or bridegroom who are known as *Daijis* or *Gotris*–these will not be taken to include persons who live in the same house as the bride or bridegroom or those who are related to them in the first grade of consanguinity in a straight and transversal line; and if the persons who serve food at these functions are of such status that they are habituated to use foot-wear, they should not remove the foot-wear before serving.

The said natives of India are hereby ordered that on the wedding day, after returning from church where they were married, the bride should not wear the clothes or ornaments which on the said wedding day were sent for her from the bridegroom's house; nor when it is necessary to change her apparel should the bridegroom hand her the clothes; in the same manner, the bridegroom on the same day should not change his apparel by discarding the clothes in which he was married, and wearing others which are given him at the bride's house; nor should the bridegroom at the time of going to bed remove his inner garments in the presence of other persons, and particularly women, as preliminary to wearing others.

The said natives of India are hereby ordered that on the day of wedding or any subsequent day, whether in the house of the bridegroom or the bride, no person should touch their foreheads with grains of raw rice or perform any other similar ceremony.

The said natives of India are hereby ordered that on the occasion of their marriages, from the day of betrothal, inclusive, until the expiry of one month from the day of marriage, neither the bridegroom nor the bride, jointly or separately, should visit, by day or by night, the house of the *Daiji* who is the head of their families.

The said natives of India are hereby ordered that if the married couple go to the house of the bridegroom according to custom on the day following the wedding day, they should not return to the bride's house within a period of one month; and if they do not go on that day to the bridegroom's house, they should remain for the same period of one month at the bride's house; and invitations should not be extended or gifts sent in any form for the purpose of the married couple moving from one house to the other.

The said natives of India are hereby ordered that when the married couple go from the house of the bride to that of the bridegroom, or from that of the bridegroom to that of the bride, neither they nor any persons who accompany them should take paddy, areca-nuts, cakes, cocoanuts, rice or any other edible thing.

The said natives of India are hereby ordered that the persons who take some clothes or ornaments or any other things from the house of the bridegroom to that of the bride during the functions of their marriages, should not go adorned nor clothed in gay attire nor should they take with them clothes other than the usual.

The said natives of India are hereby ordered that, neither before or after the marriage nor in connection therewith, they should offer anything to the person who has served in the office of *Mully* of any village, ward or district.

The said natives of India are hereby ordered that any person, whether male or female, who has exercised the office of *Mully* in any district, or worked as substitute in that office, should not attend any marriage ceremony except only those of their own sons and daughters.

The said natives of India are hereby ordered that of the edible things out of which feasts were prepared on the occasions of their marriages, they should not preserve a portion for being cooked and eaten on a specified day.

The said natives of India are hereby ordered that during the functions of their marriages, whether in the house of the bridegroom or that of the bride, they should not place in any basket, *supa* (a suttleform basket for sifting corn), earthen pot or any other place, rice, beans, cocoanuts, betel-leaves, areca-nuts or other edible things, for being preserved at an assigned spot for being cooked and eaten on a fixed day.

The said natives of India are hereby ordered that when on the occasion of their marriages it becomes necessary to make new *choolas* for cooking food, they should not place under the said *choolas* betel-leaves, areca-nuts or any other things which are not necessary for making the said *choolas*.

The said natives of India are hereby ordered that when their sons and daughters are born, they should not be received at birth or placed after they are born on raw rice.

The said natives of India are hereby ordered that on the sixth day of the birth of their sons and daughters, they should not celebrate the function of keeping vigil with banquets, public or private, or gathering of many persons at their houses. When they believe that special care of children is necessary against the risk which children run on that day, they should not perform any act or ceremony which would exceed the requirements of such care. And since not only the natives of India but also many other residents of the island of Goa and other adjacent islands, as well as of the sub-districts of Salsete and Bardez and even the Portuguese to this day celebrate the sixth day of the birth of their sons and daughters with banquets and other festive demonstrations, we hereby forbid the continuation of this custom in the form described above.

The said natives of India are hereby ordered that on the days of the confinement of their wives, neither before nor after such confinement, they should coat with cow-dung the place in the house where the confinement has taken or is to take place.

The wives of the said natives of India are hereby ordered that within a period of two months after the confinement they should not wash their bodies near any well ; and when they find it necessary to wash themselves in another place, they should not place thereon betel-leaves, areca-nuts or any other edible things.

The said natives of India are hereby ordered that within the period of one year after the birth of their sons and daughters, they should not take or send the child to the house of the oldest *Daiji* or *Gotri* of their lineage.

The said natives of India are hereby ordered that on the day on which a married woman commences her first menstrual period, they should not arrange a banquet or any other festive demonstrations or send gifts of bananas, flowers or any other things on account of the said occurrence.

The said natives of India are hereby ordered that when some person dies, they should not coat with cow-dung the place or the house where he dies, as a condition for such place or house being habitable; and if it becomes necessary to clean the said place, this should be done in a manner other than that of coating it with cow-dung.

The said natives of India are hereby ordered that they should not throw the clothes used by the deceased person or his bed into the sea or river; and when it is necessary to avoid contagion, these things should be burnt.

The said natives of India are hereby ordered that they should not invite the poor for giving them feasts for the souls of one or many of their deceased relatives. When they wish to give alms to the poor with the said object, they can do so in any other manner but never by giving feasts.

The said natives of India are hereby ordered that neither during the season when functions in memory of the deceased are held nor after the death of any person nor on any other occasion, they should arrange feasts in their houses in memory of their deceased relations.

The said natives of India are hereby ordered that during the season of appearance of new crops (*Novidade*) they should not arrange feasts in their houses.

The said natives of India are hereby ordered that in their houses cooking of food should not be done by the principal woman or women wearing wet cloth nor should they bathe in their clothes before entering kitchen for cooking food, in the manner which is customary among the Hindus.

The said natives of India are hereby ordered that they should not use in their meals rice cooked without salt, adding salt subsequently according to taste. as the Hindus are accustomed to do.

The said natives of India are hereby ordered that they should not observe fasts on the eleventh day of the new moon or full moon, nor on any other days on which the Hindus are accustomed to fast in observance of their sect, and when it happens that on such days they have the duty to fast according to the teachings of the Church, they should do so in conformity with the said teaching, but the fast should be observed in the manner of the Christians and not in the manner in which the Hindus are accustomed to fast, not eating or drinking anything except at night and using only dry food and fruit.

The said natives of India are hereby ordered that they should not observe as feast days Wednesdays, days of the new moon or full moon, or the twelfth days following the new moon or full moon, nor any other days which according to the Hindu custom are so observed ; and when on any such day falls one which is to be so observed according to the teachings of the Church, it should be observed merely in conformity with such teaching.

The said natives of India are nereby ordered that on the days of the new moon or full moon or on the twelfth days following these days they should not hold banquets or any solemnity.

The said natives of India are hereby ordered that on the days of the eclipses of moon they should not observe fast until the eclipse ends nor hold banquets or any other solemnity.

The said natives of India are hereby ordered that men should not either in public or at home wear *purvem* (*dhoti*) as it is the custom of Hindu men to do, and that women should not wear *cholis*, as it is the custom of Hindu women to do.

The said natives of India, as well as all residents of the aforesaid districts including the Portuguese, are hereby ordered that they should not have in their home gardens, *anganas* (house-yards), cocoanut gardens, or other properties, the plant known as *Tulosi*, and if it exists in any place it should be uprooted immediately.

The said natives of India and all residents of the said districts, even the Portuguese, are hereby ordered that they should not refer to or address any Christian person by the name or surname of a Hindu.

The said natives of India are hereby ordered that no one should exercise the office of a *Mully* nor should any one be considered or recognised as such.

The said natives of India are hereby order that on no occasion and under no pretext, they should give anything to any person who exercises the office of *Mully*, or is acting in that office.

The said natives of India are hereby ordered that they should not treat with respect due to honour and pre-eminence any person who exercises the office of *Mully* or is acting in that office, nor should such persons be the first to start the work of cultivation in the hills and in the fields and other tillage, nor that of covering the roofs of the houses before the rainy season, but these things should be done without distinction, according to the convenience of the persons concerned.

The said natives of India are hereby ordered that during the period of three days commonly known as "*Entrudo*" men and boys of any village or ward should not move dancing and singing in groups from door to door and should they do so without forming such groups, they should not be offered food, coins or anything else.

The said natives of India and all the residents of the said districts, even the Portuguese, are hereby ordered that in the processions, *camisades* or any other festivals which they may hold in praise of God or His saints, no Christian individual should go clothed in Hindu apparel, nor should Hindus be admitted in the said functions for dancing or participating in any entertainment nor should in these be used *robanas*, *gaitas* or any other Hindu musical instruments which the Hindus are accustomed to use in the solemnities of their temples. Christians may use Hindu apparel only in the dance which it is the custom to present on the day of the conversion of St. Paul, or in any other similar genuine representation.

The said natives of India and other residents of the said districts, even the Portuguese, are hereby ordered that in the processions, *camisades* or any other festivals, no individual in jest or in the course of a burlesque representation should disguise himself in the clerical dress or dress worn by the Religious, nor should indulge in any acts of mimicking the ceremonies and rites of the Church.

It is ordered that in the *Passos* held during Lent, in which is represented the story of the Passion of our Lord Jesus Christ, in the churches of the clergy as also in those of the Regulars, there should not be figures living or dead, other than those which represent the said Lord, or an image of Our Lady or some Saints, which would conduce to make the representation realistic, and there may also be some figures of Angels, in accordance with the concessions of the Archbishop Primaz but in no form should there be the figures of Pilatos, Judas, Anaz, Caifax, Herodes or of the Pharisees, nor any others except those mentioned above, from which result not only scandalous indecencies but also much material idolatries.

It is ordered that in the processions which are arranged during the period of Lent for representing the Passion of our Lord Jesus Christ, both in diocesan as well as in religious churches, should not be presented the figures of Centurion and Pharisees, from which result the same scandals and perils.

All the residents of the said districts of the island of Goa and other adjacent islands, and subdistricts Bardez and Salsete, whatever may be their condition or status, are hereby ordered that they should not help, attend, or in any other manner cooperate in any of the forbidden actions enumerated above".[3]

From the Edict of Faith given above, as also from what Dellon writes, it will be clear that any person who knew or had heard that another individual had committed any offence of which the Inquisition took cognisance, was required to apprise the Inquisition of this information within a period of thirty days and failure to do so attracted dire punishments. The rules of the Inquisition provided that if the denunciation was made after a considerable period after the offence was committed, the accusers would have to explain the reason for the delay. It was mainly on the basis of these denunciations as well as those made by the accused themselves against their accomplices that the proceedings of the Inquisition were initiated. The distinction between "the Inquisitorial Procedure" adopted by the Holy Office and the normal procedures followed in criminal courts is clearly brought out in the following passage from "*Malleus Maleficarum.*"

'There are two forms of criminal procedure : (1) the old legal or *accusatorial* form where the prosecutor offers to prove his charge and to accept the consequences of failure, which must

[3] Cunha Rivara, *Ensaio Historico da Lingua Concani*, Goa 1858, pp. 370-380, (Doc. 59).

be carefully avoided as being dangerous and litigious ; and (2) the *inquisitorial*, where a man denounces another either from zeal for the faith, or because called upon to do so, but takes no further part nor offers to prove his charge, or where a man is suspected by common report and the judge makes inquiry, and this method must always be preferred."[4]

Dellon discusses at length the manner in which this Inquisitorial Procedure operated in actual practice and the iniquities resulting therefrom.[5]

As the witnesses were neither required to substantiate the charges nor confronted with the accused, the trade of giving false testimony out of malice or for gain prospered. The possibility of such abuse is inherent in " the Inquisitorial Procedure " and in the following passage H. C. Lea describes the abuses to which it led in Spain.

" The trade of false witness was a thriving one, both for gain and the gratification of enmity. There were regular associations of perjurers, who made a living by levying black-mail on rich New Christians, accusing those who refused their demands, so that the unfortunate class lived in perpetual terror and purchased temporary safety by compliance. The matter was reduced to a fine art. The accusing witness would give a fictitious name and address, so that the accused could never recognise and disable him. Sometimes, indeed, when additional evidence was necessary, a witness would change his name and garments and give the required corroborative testimony. (Bibl. Nationale de France fonds italien, 1241, fol. 8,9, 23)."[6]

There is evidence to show that the same infamous trade flourished in Goa also. For instance, in a letter addressed by the king of Portugal to the vice-roy of India on March 24, 1702, we find a reference to the arrest of six recent Indian converts who moved from door to door demanding money from the Hindu residents under the threat that if the latter refused they would be falsely denounced to the Inquisitor Frei Manoel de Assumpção

[4] Charles Singer, *Studies in the History and Method of Science*, Oxford 1917, p. 201.

[5] *Vide* part II, pp. 28-36.

[6] H. C. Lea, *A History of the Inquisition of Spain*, Vol. III, p. 287.

as having hidden away Hindu orphans to prevent their being baptised.[7]

It was to be expected that Christians would denounce Hindus in this manner to the Inquisitors. But there were cases where Hindus accused other Hindus out of malice. We reproduce hereunder a petition addressed by the Hindu residents to the king of Portugal in which one of the requests made is that the Holy Office should be ordered not to take cognisance of accusations against Hindus for which the sole evidence was the denunciation made by their correligionists. The petition also provides an idea of the extent of harassment to which the Holy Office subjected the Hindu population :

"Sir, the Hindus, who with their homes, families and friends live in the territories in India which are Your Majesty's royal dominion, by birth and domicile receive the favours of Your Majesty and the privilege of being recognised as your Majesty's subjects, serve Your Majesty both in the island of Goa and the adjoining islands as well in the territories to the North, carry on their occupations and have won the confidence of Your Majesty's representatives the Viceroys of India and have shown their zeal in the royal service by complying with all the obligations as regards donations, taxes and pensions which are imposed on them ; which facts being well-known speak for themselves and require no document to support them, state that as residents of the territories under the Royal Crown of Your Majesty, they are oppressed by certain procedures of the Holy Office, in the undernoted cases.

" Sir, the supplicants do not seek exemption from the punishments which deserves the performance of rites which are intrinsically related to the Hindu sect, when these are against natural law, and even of those which are merely of the nature of ceremonies, when they are performed with such publicity as to cause offence to the Christian population, or in association with or company of Christians. They are well aware that in these two cases they can hope for no favour from His Majesty, since as a Christian prince His Majesty can make no concessions in respect of ceremonies intrinsically related to the Hindu sect which are specified in the

[7] Cunha Rivara, *Archivo Portuguez Oriental*, Fasc, VI, suppl. ii, p. 1. (Doc. 1).

Bull of Gregory XIII ; nor in respect of those which are public and offensive to the Christians or performed in association with Christians, for these impede the propagation of Christianity which His Majesty greatly desires to promote in his dominions. The request which they wish to submit to His Majesty is the following :

" In their homes and in association solely of the Hindu members of their families, in secret, and without any communication with Christian persons, they may be permitted to perform the rites and ceremonies ordered by their ancestors, which are neither contrary to natural law or offensive in any manner to Christianity.

" Sir, it happens that some Hindus who have themselves attended or heard that others have attended such ceremonies, denounce to the Holy Office that such ceremonies have been practised in the lands of Your Majesty, and on this evidence of the Hindus alone, and without any indication that they were public or offensive or that Christians were present at them, the Holy Office proceeds to arrest, prosecute and sentence the accused. In the sentences are publicly expressed the punishments of whipping and transportation to the *Casa de Polvora* (Gunpowder factory), which is a common feature of most of the sentences, the only difference being the longer or shorter duration of the transportation. This is proved by the sentences which are published at the *Auto de Fé* against the Hindus who are found guilty. The harassment begins with imprisonment in the *Aljube* or the prison of the Holy Office, which leads to the death of a majority of the prisoners, as according to their custom they cannot eat food unless it is cooked by persons of their own caste......only dry food. From such food spring mortal diseases which end their lives either before they are sentenced or soon after the sentences are passed and they are in exile. This causes great distress among the Hindus, and being naturally timid they leave the territories even when there exists the slightest fear of being denounced. In such cases we feel the proceedings against the Hindus are illegal, since there is no law neither divine, nor human, nor any made by Your Majesty, which forbids them to practise their rites behind closed doors of their houses, without publicity and without causing offence to the Christian population. We feel, therefore, that Your Majesty, having regard to the fact that the Hindu population are your subjects and residents with permanent domicile and zealous in your Royal service, may grant them the following favour, which the Hindu population relying on your generosity and munificence hopes to receive.

" That the Hindus should be allowed to perform the rites of their sect provided this is done in their homes, with the attendance of Hindu persons only, without the presence of any Christian individual, and not in a public place.

" That they should be permitted to teach in their homes their sons and other Hindu individuals the diversity of languages which are current in Asia, so that they may be able to communicate through such languages with the Hindus who inhabit other territories, and who do not understand either the language of the natives of Your Majesty's territories nor the literature therein, as well as the sciences communicated through the books which exist in their languages and which are taught only by teachers who are known as *Botos*. This name has been made odious and for that reason the Hindus who appear to be *Botos* are prohibited from entering Your Majesty's territories by the new edict of the Holy Office. However, they are not all teachers of law but only persons learned in sciences and languages which they teach other Hindus; and in their absence the Hindus of this land cannot communicate with other Hindus of Asia and without such communication trade and commerce which depends on writings cannot be carried on.

" When the Hindus denounce the crimes of other Hindus to the Holy Office it is obvious that they cannot have been prompted by zeal for the Christian faith but only by private hatred and anger, since had the motive been zeal they would have converted themselves to Christianity, and as they are motivated by hatred they cannot be legitimate witnesses in the matters which they denounce. Having regard to this fact, we beg that the Holy Office should not take cognisance of any crime of which one Hindu is denounced by other Hindus, unless it is proved that the crime of which information is given was offensive for having been committed in public where the Christians could watch it, or Christians were associates or accomplices therein......it is desired that what Your Majesty has ordered in the matter should be observed wholly and completely, viz. that if the Hindus are guilty of performing their ceremonies in public and thereby causing offence, or even if performing them in secret associate Christians therein, they should be punished by the Holy Office. From this prohibition, it is clear that those who perform such ceremonies in secret, without attendance of Christians and without such publicity as to enable Christians to see them, are exempted from the said punishment, since such performance is neither offensive nor likely to prevent the increase of Christianity.

" In view of this we pray Your Majesty that having regard to the justice of their petition, he may be pleased to order :

" That the Holy office do not take cognisance of any crime by denunciation and proof furnished by Hindus alone, and unless it is proved that in the crimes of which information is given Christians were associated or that they were performed with such publicity as to by itself cause offence to Christianity ; and

" that they be permitted to have their schools in their homes to enable them to teach their sons the languages and sciences by the use of books which teach them and through teachers appointed for that purpose.

" As Your Majesty has granted to the Hindus in the fortress of Diu favours in this matter greater than those for which the supplicants pray similar concessions may be granted to the Hindu population of Goa, adjacent islands and the northern territories who are more deserving of the same and zealous in the service of Your Majesty and we pray that after Your Majesty has generously granted the concessions, Your Majesty's Viceroy may see that they are observed in their entirety."[8]

The foregoing petition shows how insecure the life of the Hindus had become as a result of the activities of the Inquisition. Earlier in this chapter we have reproduced in full the Edict of April 1736 which prohibits the performance of a large number of Hindu practices. It will be seen that these embrace every phase of the existence of an individual in Indian society. The natives were subjected to perpetual espionage and slightest suspicion that a native had been guilty of adhering to customs, which for generations had formed part of daily life would render him liable to arrest

[8] *Ibid.*, p. 292, (Doc. 105).

or prosecution by the Inquisition. It was pointed out by the *Chanceler do Estado da India* that many of the practices banned in the edict were not properly speaking against religion and hence it would be oppression if the Inquisition punished those who practised them since the cases could not be counted among those which pertained to the Holy Office. Notwithstanding this, the edict was supported by the viceroy Conde de Sandomil.[9] In chapter X, is quoted a letter of viceroy João Saldanha da Gama dated December 19, 1729 in which he reports that the effect of the harassment by the Inquisition was a large-scale migration of the Hindus to the neighbouring territories of Asiatic and other European rulers, where they were allowed liberty of conscience, and the consequent ruin of commerce within the Portuguese territories. It will be seen that viceroy Gama also expresses doubt whether the Inquisition could legitimately take cognisance of the actions of those who were never Catholics.

[9] Baiào, *op.cit.*, Vol. I, p. 322.

CHAPTER VIII

ANTI-HINDU LAWS IN GOA

TOMÉ Pires, a Portuguese apothecary, came to India in 1511. Later he went to China as the Portuguese ambassador and died there sometime about 1540. He gives a description of the parts of India visited by him in a book called *Suma Oriental*, which was published in 1944 by the Hakluyt Society with an English translation and notes. According to the editor, Armando Cortesão, the greater part of the book was written in Malacca and the rest in Cochin, during the period 1512-1515. Tomé Pires gives the following account of the Hindus of Goa :

" There are a great many heathens in this kingdom of Goa, more than in the kingdom of the Deccan. Some of them are very honoured men with large fortunes ; and almost the whole kingdom lies in their hands, because they are natives and possess the land and they pay the taxes. Some of them are noblemen with many followers and lands of their own, and are persons of great repute, and wealthy, and they live on their estates, which are very gay and fresh. The heathens of the kingdom of Goa surpass those of Cambay. They have beautiful temples of their own in this kingdom ; they have priests or Brahmans of many kinds. There are some very honoured stocks among these Brahmans. Some of them will not eat anything which has contained blood or anything prepared by the hand of another. These Brahmans are greatly revered throughout the country, particularly among the heathen. Like those of Cambay, the poor ones serve to take merchandise and letters safely through the land, because the rich ones rank as great lords. They are clever, prudent, learned in their religion. A Brahman would not become a Mahommedan (even) if he were made a king."[1]

As stated above the book was written before the death of Albuquerque, which occurred on December 16, 1515, and the Hindus of Goa had not till then been subjected to cruel pressures intended to convert them to Christianity. Tomé Pires, who did not visualise this possibility, asserted merely that " a Brahman

[1] *The Suma Oriental of Tomé Pires* (Translated and edited by Armando Cortesão), London 1944, pp. 58-59.

would not become a Mahomedan if he were made a king." Subsequent history demonstrated that the Hindus of Goa remained faithful to their religion in the face of temptations and threats of a varied nature intended to convert them to Christianity and many of them preferred exile to conversion.

In the present chapter it is proposed to review in brief various measures taken by the Portuguese rulers in India with the object of converting the natives to Christianity. The measures fall into two broad categories. Firstly, there were those the object of which was to make it difficult for the natives to continue to retain their old religion. The temples and shrines of the Hindus were destroyed and they were forbidden to erect or maintain new ones even outside the Portuguese territories; practice of Hindu rites and ceremonies such as the marriage ceremony, the ceremony of wearing the sacred thread, ceremony performed at the birth of a child, was banned; priests and teachers of the Hindus were banished; Hindus whose presence was considered as undersirable from the point of view of propagation of Christianity were sent into exile; those who remained were deprived of their means of subsistence and ancestral rights in village communities; they were also subjected to various humiliations, indignities and disabilities; "orphan" children of the Hindus were snatched away from their families for being baptised; and men and women were compelled to listen to the preaching of Christian doctrine. In the second category can be classed the measures intended to provide positive incentives for conversion to Christianity, such as, those which sought to give the Christians a monopoly of public posts, altered the laws of inheritance in favour of persons who changed their religion, discriminated in favour of Christian converts in the matter of the rights and privileges in the village community. As would be expected, the Inquisition played a prominent role both in bringing pressure on the secular authorities to pass discriminatory legislation and in enforcing the measures with characteristic sternness and severity. In the following paragraphs measures having a similar purpose are dealt with together under appropriate headings, as it is felt that this manner of presentation would help the reader to obtain a clearer picture.

Banishment of the Hindus

On April 2, 1560, the vice-roy D. Constantino de Bragança ordered that a large number of Brahmins, whose names were included in the rolls appended to the order should be thrown out of the island of Goa and the lands and fortresses of the Portuguese king. Only those who were natives of Salsete and Bardez were permitted to return to their villages. Others were banished under pain of their being made prisoners on the galleys without remission and losing all their property, one half to the accuser and the other to whatever purpose the viceroy may consider appropriate. They were given one month within which to dispose of their property.[2] On 8th June of the same year was issued a similar order banishing persons of the Goldsmith caste who had their families and properties outside the Portuguese territories unless they brought back their families and property within a period of 10 days.[3]

The result of such orders was that the Hindus migrated to the neighbouring lands *en masse*, business establishments were closed down, and there was an acute dearth of agricultural labour, artisans and mechanics. Faced with this economic crisis, viceroy Conde de Redondo D. Francisco Coutinho published the following order on December 3, 1561 with the object of inviting the Hindus back home :

" On my arrival I found that this island of Goa and other islands annexed thereto were much depopulated, the villages therein deserted and fields overflown with water of the rivers, and that the Hindu residents thereof were absent and did not wish to return to reside therein as their properties and goods had been given to other persons by virtue of an order passed by viceroy D. Constantino, which provided that the Hindus who had left these lands on the alleged ground that they were being made Christians by force, should lose their estates if they did not return within a specified period. Having regard to the great harm which I saw had resulted from this state of things to the interest of my king and the welfare of this land, and having taken the opinion of the Archbishop and lawyers, both jurists and theologians, with

[2] Cunha Rivara, *Archivo Portuguez Oriental*, Fasc. V, Part i, Goa 1865, p. 451, (Doc. 344).

[3] *Ibid.*, p. 454, (Doc. 349).

whom the matter was discussed and who agreed that the law made by D. Constantino was very harsh and should not be enforced; I hereby order that any infidel who may return should be handed over his estate and that he should hold and possess the same as before..."[4]

It is possible that this order would have attracted some of the Hindus back to their homes. However, the fanatics soon succeeded in bringing sufficient pressure on the king to secure a reversal of this policy, and on November 27, 1563, viceroy D. Francisco Coutinho promulgated another order which required that the *Ouvidor Geral* of India should notify all Brahmins whose names appeared in the rolls given to him by the Archbishop, the Provincial of the Company of Jesus, Vicar General of S. Domingo and the Wardens of S. Francisco, that within the period of one month from the date of such notification they should leave the island. These rolls included all Brahmin residents of the islands with the exception of those who tilled land with their own hands, physicians, carpenters, blacksmiths, shopkeepers or collectors of the royal revenues. Those to be exiled were required to sell their property within one month and if this was not possible within one year through persons empowered on their behalf. If they entered Portuguese territory after the expiry of the prescribed period they would be imprisoned on the galleys for all time and their estates confiscated.[5]

On February 7, 1575, governor Antonio Moniz Barreto ordered that if any of the Brahmins who had been expelled on the ground that their presence was prejudicial to the interests of Christianity made an unauthorised entry into the Portuguese territory, his estate should be confiscated and used to provide clothes to the New Christians.[6]

The Third *Concilio Provincial* which met in 1585 passed the following resolution:

"His Majesty the king has on occasions ordered the viceroys and governors of India that there should be no Brahmins in his lands, and that they should be banished therefrom together

[4] Cunha Rivara, *op. cit.* Fasc. V, pt. ii, Goa 1865, p. 488, (Doc. 391).
[5] *Ibid.*, p. 544, (Doc. 472).
[6] *Ibid.*, p. 902, (Doc. 776).

with the physicians and other infidels who are prejudicial to Christianity, after taking the opinion of the Archbishop and other religious persons who have experience in the matter. As the orders of His Majesty in this regard have not been executed, great impediments in the way of conversion and the community of New Christians have followed and continue to follow. Having regard to this, this *Concilio* orders that from now onwards at certain times in each year the Archbishop should obtain information regarding Brahmins, physicians and any other infidels who might be prejudicial to the conversion to Christianity, and in consultation with the Christian priests prepare a roll of their names which should be signed by him. This should be presented to the viceroy or the governor in order that the latter might issue orders for banishing them from the lands of the king, as His Majesty has ordered. The Prelates should do the same in their respective bishoprics as well as their ministers in consultation with the captains of the fortresses, and in case the local secular authorities do not comply with their requests, as His Majesty has ordered, they should send the rolls of the prejudicial infidels to the Archbishop in order that he may secure orders for the banishment of such infidels from the viceroy or the governor."[7]

Ban against the performance of Hindu rites and ceremonies

On March 13, 1613 the viceroy D. Hyeronimo de Azevedo issued an order that no infidel should marry during the times forbidden by the Church and during other times of the year they could do so only outside their villages and observing all that the *Concilio Provincial* had laid down and other relevant laws, under pain of a fine of 1000 *Xerafins*, of which one-third would be paid to the accuser and two-thirds applied towards the expenses of the High Court.[8] A still more draconian order promulgated on January 31, 1620 ran as follows :

" In the name of His Majesty I order that as from the date of publication of this order, no Hindu, of whatever nationality or status he may be, can or shall perform marriages in this city of Goa, nor in the islands or adjacent territories of His Majesty, under pain of a fine of 1000 *Xerafins*, one-third of which would

[7] Cunha Rivara, *op. cit.*, Fasc. IV, pp. 124-5.
[8] Cunha Rivara, *op. cit.*, Fasc. VI, Goa, 1875, p. 965, (Doc. 242).

be paid to the accuser and two-thirds applied towards the expenses of His Majesty's navy ".[9]

Viceroy Conde de Linhares in a note addressed to the king on December 6, 1630 has made certain interesting suggestions in this regard. He refers to a payment of 32,000 *Xerafins* made by the Hindus during the viceroyalty of Conde de Vidigueira in consideration of which they were given permission to celebrate their marriages in the city of Goa. The permission was however subsequently withdrawn. He points out that in the vicinity of the island of Goa there are many islands which are uninhabited and in which there are no Churches. If permission to celebrate marriages in these islands was granted no offence to the Christian community or their Churches could result, and at the same time this would yield considerable revenue to the royal treasury, which he estimated at 6000 *Xerafins* per annum. He goes on to add that the *Concilio* had also forbidden the Hindus to anoint their foreheads with sandalwood paste and rice. He was of the opinion that it would be convenient if the Hindus did so, just as the Jews in Portugal and Spain were directed to wear yellow hats in order that they might be easily identified. This concession could also yield an annual revenue of 2000 *Xerafins* to the royal treasury. He added that if these suggestions were approved, the collection of the revenues might be entrusted to the officials of the Inquisition, just as in Lisbon they held the monopoly of playing cards, or to the chapter of the Cathedral.[10]

As marriages were forbidden in Portuguese territories, Hindus had to go to neighbouring territories under Muslim rule for celebrating them and the marriage parties were frequently waylaid by robbers. The viceroy D. Pedro de Almeida in 1679 permitted the Hindus to celebrate marriages in their houses behind closed doors, provided outside the houses were present an armed guard appointed by appropriate authorities who would prevent *Bottos* (Hindu priests) and other ministers of the Hindu temples from entering the houses for performing sacrifices or other Hindu rites and ceremonies as was customary. The Inquisition took over the duty of policing such marriages by sending parties of the notorious *Naiques* of the Holy Office. It was, however, pointed

[9] *Ibid.*, p. 1201, (Doc. 511).
[10] *Ibid.*, p. 1255, (Doc. 568).

out that "the order made performance of marriages totally impossible, because, according to the custom of the Hindus, marriages could not be valid without the presence of *Bottos* and performance of Hindu ceremonies, and if performed otherwise they would be null and void, the wives taken by such marriages only concubines and the children born of such marriages illegitimate and deprived of the social status of their fathers." The order was accordingly revoked and replaced by the decree of king D. Pedro dated August 29, 1679 which permitted the Hindus to perform marriages in ships or barges in the rivers which separate the Portuguese territories from the territories ruled by Muslims, provided no Christians were present.[11]

The Hindus continued to represent to the king that the law prohibiting them to perform marriages in their own houses caused great hardship. As a result, the king decided on March 4, 1701 that the Hindus should be permitted to perform marriages in the customary form in their own houses behind closed doors but that Christians who attended or watched such marriages as well as the Hindus who agreed to their doing so would be liable to punishment. The viceroy informed the king on December 5, 1704 that the Holy office had protested against this decision and the king thereupon withdrew it by his letter of September 22, 1705.[12] The views of the Holy Office on the representation of the Hindus are given hereunder :

"The marriages of the supplicants are superstitious acts or functions which include Hindu rites and ceremonies as well as cult, adoration and prayers of Hindu temples ; in case the supplicants deny this, they may agree that a *Naique* or other person nominated by the tribunal of the Holy Office may attend these functions and examine the ceremonies which the *Botto* performs in the houses of the bride and bridegroom during the five days and nights of his stay. If it is found that it is true that the rites and ceremonies referred to above are not practised, I shall agree willingly to their petition and express the view that, subject to the said condition, they may be permitted to do all that they ask for and much more if they so desire."[13]

[11] *Ibid.*, pp. 1286-9, (Doc. 595).
[12] Cunha Rivara, *op. cit.*, Fasc. VI, supplement ii, p. 181. (Doc. 42)
[13] *Ibid.*, p. 505, (Doc. 185).

The severity with which the Inquisition enforced the law banning marriages of Hindus in their own homes led to migration of the Hindu population outside the Portuguese territories. Refering to this, king D. João wrote to the viceroy on March 8, 1715 as follows :

" I am informed that when the Hindus who live in my dominions marry, they perform certain Hindu ceremonies and that as a result, inspite of such ceremonies being performed in secret and without causing offence to the Catholics, they are imprisoned and punished by the Inquisition. This leads to their leaving our villages which are thereby ruined and many villages are found deserted for this reason. As this and other similar proceedings lead to this and other consequences equally detrimental to the state, I desire that after ascertaining all that takes place in this matter, you give me an account of your findings together with your own views. "

The viceroy replied that he did not find any excesses on the part of the Inquisition.[14]

The thread ceremony of young sons of the Hindus had also to be performed outside the Portuguese territories. Having regard to the inconvenience which this caused both to the people and the government, on October 25, 1726 viceroy João Saldanha de Gama issued the following order :

" I hereby order that no Hindu subject proceed beyond the borders of the state to celebrate the thread ceremony, and in order to enable them to do so at their convenience and that of the state, I fix for the Hindu subjects of Goa the island of Cumbarjua, for those of Salsete the village of Cuncolim and for those of Bardez the island of Corjuem, and in these parts they may invite their *Bottos* according to usage for a period of five days, provided they first obtain my permission and inform the captains of fortresses and officers of the boats of the arrival and departure of the said *Bottos*, and perform the said celebrations behind closed doors in the form laid down in the orders of His Majesty in respect of marriages and other ceremonies. In the event of their proceeding to the neighbouring lands to perform the said celebrations or performing them in a form other than that hereby permitted,

[14] *Ibid.*, pp. 18-9, (Doc. 11).

they shall incur the penalty of deportation to the lands of the North for a period of two years and a fine of 500 *xerafins* for the expenses of the docks."[15]

There is evidence to show that in 1640 the Jesuits had forbidden the Hindus to wear the sacred thread.[16] The Third *Concilio Provincial* which met in 1585, recommended to the king that Hindus who wore sacred threads should be forbidden to do so or to initiate their sons in wearing sacred threads.[17]

In 1680, at the instance of the *Conselho Ultramarino* the ceremony of keeping vigil and giving feasts at the birth of children was forbidden. It is interesting to note that the practice was observed not only by the new converts but also by the Portuguese residents. The representation made by the *Conselho Ultramarino* in this regard is as follows:

" In this Council was seen a paper in which it was represented to His Majesty that the residents of the State of India practised a great abuse when sons were born to them by imitating the Hindus among whom it was the custom to hold great celebrations for eight days at the birth of sons and give banquets to all those who attend; and although the number of the Hindu community is considerably reduced owing to many having been baptized, the converts inspite of their being Christians continue to do what they did as Hindus, and the bad example is so powerful that it has infected even the Portuguese in such a form that there is no person whether rich or poor who does not practise these celebrations which are known as the vigil."[18]

Viceroy João Saldanha de Gama declared on March 22, 1729 that those who practised such celebrations would incur the following penalties: If they were Portuguese a fine of 500 *xerafins*, one half to be applied towards the expenses of the royal navy and the other to be paid to the accuser; and if they were Christians who were natives of the land, for the first offence a fine of 100 *xerafins* to be used as above; and for the second offence imprisonment and deportation for two years to China or Mombaça.[19]

[15] *Ibid.*, p. 285, (Doc. 101).
[16] Cunha Rivara, *op. cit.*, Fasc. VI, p. 1268, (Doc. 580).
[17] Cunha Rivara, *op. cit.*, Fasc. IV, p. 124, (Decreto 5),
[18] Cunha Rivara, *op. cit.*, Fasc. VI, pp. 1290-3, (Doc. 596-8).
[19] Cunha Rivara, *op. cit.*, Fasc. VI, suppl. ii, pp. 313-5, (Doc. 123).

Ban on the Hindu priests

One of the provisions of the law passed by king D. Sebastião on December 4, 1567 was to the effect that in his dominions there should not exist any Muslim *kajis* or Hindu preachers, *Joshis*, *Joguis*, Sorcerers, *Gurous* of temples or any other person who held a religious office among the Hindus or were the heads or supporters of the religions of the Hindus; he ordered that they should leave his dominions within one month; failing which they would be held as captives for service in the docks.[20]

On June 28, 1727 viceroy João Saldanha de Gama issued the following order :

" It has been brought to my notice that various Hindus who are by profession *Bottos*, have under false names and pretexts, secured permission for living in this land, which is against the practice observed by us. I hereby order that all those who being *Bottos* by profession, have obtained permission by pretending to be something else, leave immediately the lands of this state, notwithstanding the orders which they might have secured. I permit them to be present within the dominions of the king only if they have obtained permission of the Tribunal of the Holy Office."[21]

Orders compelling Hindus to listen to the Christian doctrine

The law promulgated by D. Sebastião on December 4, 1567 provided, *inter alia*, that the Hindu residents of the city of Goa and certain other cities should compulsorily attend preaching of the Christian doctrine by a priest deputed for the purpose.[22] This was, however, one of the provisions of this law which was not put into execution for some time. In 1715, Padre Ignacio de Almeida, Principal of the Company of Jesus and Padre Affonso de Costa, Father of Christians, secured an order of the chapter of the Cathedral, based on the said law of 1567, which required that " all Hindus should come with their families to places assigned for the purpose to listen to the preaching of the Holy Gospel."[23]

[20] Cunha Rivara, *op. cit.*, Fasc. IV, p. 69.
[21] Cunha Rivara, *op. cit.*, Fasc. VI, suppl. ii, p. 300, (Doc. 109).
[22] Cunha Rivara, *op. cit.*, Fasc. IV, pp. 68-9.
[23] Cunha Rivara, *op. cit.*, Fasc. VI, suppl. ii, pp. 19-66, (Doc. 12).

The law led to a mass exodus of the Hindu residents of the city and as a result trade and commerce were paralysed and the royal treasury was depleted. The magnitude of the exodus caused general consternation and the senate of the Municipal Corporation had to represent about the ruinous consequences of the measure. Viceroy Vasco Fernandes thereupon suspended the order and the suspension was confirmed by the king on January 14, 1717. Some of the emigrants returned to the city but many others preferred to remain in the lands to which they had migrated.[24]

Laws depriving Hindus of their means of subsistence

Repeated attempts were made to make it impossible for the Hindus to live in the Portuguese territories by depriving them of the means of subsistence. The following order in the name of king D. João was published by the governor Francisco Barreto on June 25, 1557 :

" I make it known to those who see this letter, that having regard to the great disadvantage to the service of God and my service which can result and to the inconvenience which can arise, from my officers in these parts, those of justice as well as of revenue, utilising the services of Brahmins and other Hindus, and being desirous of taking steps in that regard I hereby order that, as from the notification hereof, no officials of mine, controllers of revenues, commissioners of customs, treasurers, receivers of customs, accountants, lessees of my customs or other revenues, judges, scriveners and notaries and other officials of revenue and justice should utilise the services in any way whatsoever of any Brahmin or other infidel in matters of his office ; and any of such officials who do the contrary shall incur the penalty of losing his office, and the said Brahmins shall become captive, and lose all their property one half to me and the other to the person who denounces them, and this should be so understood in my city of Goa as well as other cities and forts of those parts. Also as I hold it a great disservice to God and to me that in the said cities and fortresses the said Brahmins and Hindus should exercise the offices which are given them by my governors, captains and

[24] *A India Portuguesa*, vol. II, Nova Goa, 1923, pp. 297-300.

officials, I hereby order that from now onwards they should not serve in those offices and that such offices should not be given them ; and that all the offices which it is customary to give to the natives of the land should be given to the Christians and not to the Hindus, as stated above ; and I also order that all *Mucadams* of all offices in the land shall be Christians and this work should be given to Christians and not to any Hindus or infidels."[25]

The same order was repeated by D. Sebastião in his decree of March 28, 1559.[26]

On April, 8, 1582, the following royal decree was issued :

" Being informed that Brahmins and Hindus of these parts of India are collectors and contractors of my revenues and also serve my officials in matters relating to their offices, which is greatly detrimental to Christianity and contrary to canonical law, and although the governor had provided against this by his order of the year 1557 the same was not being executed, and being desirous of providing in this matter in pursuance of my duty to propagate our Holy Catholic Faith in the said parts, I hereby order that from now onwards no Hindu, whatever be his status or condition, should hold public office."[27]

On January 12, 1591 while reiterating this order the king emphasised that no officials should utilise the services of Brahmins or other Hindus, nor enter the houses of the latter nor speak or have dealings with the latter directly or through third parties, under pain of being suspended from their offices.[28]

Measures depriving Hindus of rights and privileges in village communities

By an order of December 11, 1578 governor Antonio Moniz Barreto deprived the Hindus of Salsete of their rights an privileges as *Gauncares* (original members of the village communities) :

" From now onwards the *Gauncares* of the lands of Salsete shall not meet in assembly nor pass resolutions without the

[25] Cunha Rivara, *op. cit.*, Fasc. V, pt. i, p. 310, (Doc. 195).
[26] *Ibid.*, p. 388, (Doc. 286).
[27] Cunha Rivara, *op. cit.*, Fasc. V. pt. iii, p. 980, (Doc. 821).
[28] *Ibid.*, p. 1277, (Doc. 954).

Christian *Gauncares* being present, under pain of each one of them paying in respect of each such occasion 20 *pardaos* towards the clothing of Christians, and the resolutions passed shall be null and void. Also in the villages where there are more Christian *Gauncares* than Hindu *Gauncares*, the Hindus should not enter into *Gauncarias* and when assemblies are held the names of the Christians should be written first and only when the number of Christians is not sufficient to form the quorum according to the custom of the respective village, the names of so many Hindus as are required to make up the quorum should be entered."[29]

Each *Gauncar* was entitled to receive annually a share in the income of the village community which was known as *Jono*. On March 7, 1634, Francisco de Tavora ordered that the Hindu natives of Salsete who migrated to neighbouring territories to escape religious persecution would lose the right to *Jono* :

" I am informed that many natives of the territories of Salsete absent themselves with their families and households to Canara and other territories of the infidels, so as to enjoy greater liberty of conscience, thereby causing the lands of His Majesty to be depopulated ; but come back on the occasion of the payment of the *Jonos* and having received the same return to the said lands of the infidels. As it is necessary to put a stop to this, as a convenient remedy, I hereby order that the natives of Salsete who absent themselves with or without their families and households in order to live in Canara and other lands of the infidels should not be admitted to recover the *Jonos* to which they might be entitled, and should lose the same to the royal treasury."[30]

On November 21, 1573, king D. João issued an order that the villagers of Bardez who had migrated outside the Portuguese territories should not be paid *Jonos*.[31]

There is evidence to show that even the New Christians took up domicile outside the Portuguese territories, probably with the intention of escaping the attentions of the Inquisition. In a letter dated January 4, 1715 addressed to the king, the viceroy refers, *inter alia*, to " the great harm which may be caused to the souls

[29] Cunha Rivara, *op. cit.*, Fasc. V, pt. ii, p. 891. (Doc. 768).
[30] Cunha Rivara, *op. cit.*, Fasc. VI, p. 1295, (Doc. 600).
[31] Cunha Rivara, *op. cit.*, Fasc. VI, suppl. ii. pp. 6-9, (Doc.4-5).

of those who take up domicile in the lands of the infidels from the liberty of conscience in which they live there, forgetting their duties as Christians."[32]

Forcible conversion of the Hindu Orphans

On March 23, 1559 D. Sebastião issued the following order, which struck terror in the hearts of the Hindus :

"...I order that as from the date hereof, the children of Hindus, who in this city of the island of Goa in the territory of India, are left without father, mother, grandfather, grandmother or other ascendant lineals and are not of an age at which they can have understanding and judgment, as soon as the last of such relatives is dead, the Judge of Orphans who has jurisdiction, should cause to be taken immediately and handed over to the College of St. Paul of the Society of Jesus of the said city of Goa, for being baptised, educated and indoctrinated by the Fathers of the said College and being directed by them and placed in positions according to their respective aptitudes and abilities."[33]

The royal order was endorsed by viceroy D. Antão de Noronha in 1564[34] and by Governor Antonio Moniz Barreto in 1575.[35] There is another royal decree to the same effect dated April 3, 1582.[36]

As originally intended the decree applied to orphans who had neither parents or grandparents or other elderly relatives. But there were frequent complaints that even children whose mother and grandparents were living were being snatched away from their families for being baptized. We find that in 1546, while considering a complaint of Recumeny (Rukmini), widow of Beru Chatim, D. Philippe Mascarenhas of the Council of State of His Majesty, agreed that in that case and in similar cases which might arise in future, wherein the son of an infidel became orphan by the death of his father but had his grandparents and other ascendant lineals living, he could be given a Christian tutor.[37]

[32] *Ibid.*, p. 9, (Doc. 5).
[33] Cunha Rivara, *op. cit.*, Fasc. V, pt i, p. 385, (Doc. 287).
[34] Cunha Rivara, *op. cit.*, Fasc. V, pt. ii, p. 577, (Doc. 523).
[35] *Ibid.*, p. 904, (Doc. 778).
[36] Cunha Rivara, *op. cit.*, Fasc. V, pt. iii, p. 989, (Doc. 821).
[37] Cunha Rivara, *op. cit.*, Fasc. VI, p. 1265,(Doc. 584).

The Inquisitors also complained that cases of orphans were not reported to them promptly and that orphans were being hidden away or removed to neighbouring territories to prevent their being baptised. The following is an edict of the Inquisition on this subject, dated December 11, 1616.

" As we are informed that there is considerable omission in making reports to the Father of Orphans (*Padre Pae dos Orphãos*) about orphan sons of Hindu subjects of His Majesty in order that they might be baptized, in conformity with our duty to take steps in this matter in the interests of greater increase of our Holy Catholic faith and extirpation of idolatry, we hereby order all Mucadams of chawls (*Mocadões dos chales*) of this city and other persons concerned who are herein declared, under pain of excommunication, absolution from which we reserve for ourselves, and such other proceedings against them as we may consider appropriate, that within a period of six days they report to the Father of Orphans for being baptized all the orphans of whom they have knowledge as well as other persons who are known to have hidden away orphans or removed them to the mainland to prevent their receiving Holy Baptism."[38]

There is reason to believe that the zeal to snatch away orphans was inspired not only by desire to save their souls but also by anxiety to take charge of their estates. On March 31, 1677 the King of Portugal wrote to the viceroy, enclosing a petition addressed to him by the Hindu people of the community of Brahmins, high officials and artisans residing in the city of Goa and neighbouring villages, in which they complained that contrary to the law on the subject, the Father of Orphans takes away from the charge of their living mothers sons who had lost their fathers, *together with the estates which had passed to them upon the deaths of the fathers*, to compel them by force to receive baptism.[39] In the Orme Manuscripts (Vol. 114, Sect.4, p.164), it is stated that disputes arose continuously between Shivaji and the Portuguese in regard to orphans and their estates:

"Sevagee and they (the Portuguese) daily quarrell, the chiefest cause of his hatred to them being for forcing orphans of his

[38] *Ibid.*, p. 1281, (Doc. 592).
[39] *Ibid.*, p. 1281, (Doc. 593).

cast to turn Roman Catholicks. There has also of late happened some disputes among them in the same account, the Captain General of Busseen taking the part of some orphans, against the Jesuits, and forcing the said Jesuits to restore the said orphans a considerable estate, which they had been possessed of many years, which they highly resented. One dispute brought on another, and these quarrels increased daily."[40] (dated Nov. 26, 1675.)

There were cases where orphans who had been taken away from the families were returned on receiving money. Unscrupulous persons also extorted money from Hindu families by threatening to report orphans to the Inquisitors. In a letter dated March 24, 1702 addressed by the King to the viceroy he refers to certain incidents of this type. He writes :

" Having seen the account given by you of the procedure adopted by the Inquisitor Frei Manoel da Assumpção in taking away sons of Hindus even when their mothers were living, which was illegal, and in this connection having imprisoned in the prisons of Holy Office certain Hindus, contractors of my revenues, who had approached him with a request to conform to the laws which had been passed on the subject, without consent or any order of the Tribunal other than his own word ; and that as a result many Hindus have migrated to the mainland and contracts have been discontinued ; that to avoid the great harm which would result from such procedures and the loss to the State which would ensue, you used the most suave methods you could think of, without raising issues of conflict of jurisdictions, having called the Inquisitors to your presence and shown them the law which I had ordered to be passed in the matter ; and that having seen the same they replied uniformly that they had not concurred in the procedures which the Inquisitor Frei Manoel de Assumpção had adopted, and that earlier they had always expressed the contrary view ; upon which you decided to order the said Inquisitor to release the prisoners, which he promptly obeyed and did not interfere further with the said boys ; that, however, after the said Hindus had been released, they complained that a broker of the said Frei Manuel had asked their wives to pay 6000 *Xerafins* in order to secure their release ;

[40] *English Records on Sivagy*, vol. II, Poona 1931, p. 74, (Doc. 131).

that, when you ordered the said Hindu broker to be arrested he confessed having received the said sum of 6000 *Xerafins* but that it was by way of alms to N. Senhora do Monte, of the hermitage in which the said Inquisitor lived;...and that in the same manner were arrested six Christians recently converted for having moved from house to house of the Hindus demanding money, threatening that if they did not pay they would be denounced to Frei Manoel for having hidden away children..."[41]

There were also cases where children were removed from their families even during the lifetime of their fathers. The king in a letter addressed to the viceroy on March 21, 1709 refers to a representation of the Hindus complaining of such excesses:

"I have seen a representation made by the Hindu people of this city in regard to the excess of zeal shown by the Father of Christians in taking account of the orphans who are placed in his charge, by attempting to take away even those who have fathers and other ascendant lineals;...they represent that when they seek to demonstrate that some of the children who are taken away have fathers, they are faced with the difficulty that the official concerned does not admit Hindus as witnesses and those who are Christians fear to come and declare the truth owing to the fear and respect which they entertain for the Father of Christians. They request me to order it to be declared that only those who come to the house of the Father of Christians asking to be indoctrinated or state that they wish to be Christians should be converted, and that he should not convert by force any Hindu, even if he does not have father and mother, nor enter the houses of the Hindus, nor interfere with them..."[42]

The Hindus when they felt their days were numbered arranged to send their children outside the Portuguese territories to prevent their being baptised. On July 11, 1718 the viceroy issued the following order with the object of putting a stop to this practice:

"I hereby order and declare that from now onwards no Hindu man or woman, resident of or present in the territories of this State, and having sons or grandsons aged less than 14 years or daughters or granddaughters aged less than 12 years should

[41] Cunha Rivara, *op. cit.*, Fasc. VI, suppl. ii, p. 1, (Doc. 1).
[42] Cunha Rivara, *Ibid.*, p. 3, (Doc. 3).

when his life is in danger and in case such minors have no other ascendant lineals, take them or send them to the mainland. Nor should this be done by any other Hindu, even if he is a relative of such minors, on the death of their fathers or grandfathers. Those who contravene this order shall incur the penalty of the loss of their estate which would be confiscated to the Royal Exchequer, and those who do not possess any estate, shall incur the penalty of whipping and banishment to the rivers of Guama for a period of ten years, from which penalties they can be released only if they hand over the orphans for whose removal to the mainland they have been responsible."[43]

There is evidence to show that a law of this nature existed even prior to the date mentioned above. It is recorded, for instance, that the Inquisitor instituted proceedings against one Mangugy Sinay Quencró of Cortalim (Salsete), a contractor of tobacco, for having sent three orphan grandchildren outside Portuguese territories and that at the *Auto de Fé* of 1662 he was sentenced to deportation to Rio de Guama (Mozambique) for six years. While he was awaiting execution of this sentence in a prison in Goa known as *Tronco*, viceroy Antonio de Mello de Castro, at the instance of Ramogy Sinay Cottary, a diplomatic agent of the Portuguese government, pleaded with the Inquisitor Paulo Castellino de Freitas that he might be pardoned. As the Inquisitor refused to do so, the viceroy ordered the jailor not to permit the prisoner to be removed from the prison, and eventually he died in the prison before the sentence of banishment could be carried out. The Inquisitor thereupon strongly complained to the king that the viceroy was hindering his work.[44]

Ramogy Sinay Cottary, the diplomatic agent mentioned above, was himself exempted from the application of this law. He was a native of Quelossim (Salsete), but in order to escape the oppressive law, had chosen to live at Bicholim, which was then under Muslim rule. However, in recognition of his political services, governors Francisco de Melo e Castro and Antonio Souza Coutinho secured a royal decree on January 3, 1659 exempting him from the application of the law. The order ran as follows :

[43] *Ibid.*, p. 104, (Doc. 25).
[44] P. Pissurlencar, *Agentes Hindus da Diplomacia Portuguesa na India, I Cothari*, Nova Goa 1933, p. 35.

" The said Ramogy Sinay and his family are permitted to live in my lands and on his death and that of any of his descendants, children major or minor should not be taken away for being made Christians nor should their estates be taken away nor should such children be removed from the protection of their mothers nor should any relative be harassed to hand over such children and they may continue to live freely without any disability. And in the same manner, their estates should not be confiscated to the Royal treasury on the ground that they died without living male heirs, notwithstanding any provisions to the contrary in the revenue codes, laws or charters."[45]

It may be mentioned, however, that while agreeing to exempt Ramogy Sinay, the king ordered that no such exemptions should in future be granted, " in view of the greatest impediments which could result therefrom in the propagation of Christianity."

It should be remembered that when children were snatched away from their families for being baptized, their share of the estates went with them. Further, when children were baptized, frequently mothers and other near relatives were tempted to embrace Christianity in order that they might not lose their children. These were substantial advantages involved in the conversion of children and there was therefore a tendency to apply the provision for the conversion of Hindu orphans in cases where it obviously did not apply. The Holy Office assisted in this abuse of law. The only remedy left to the unfortunate Hindus was to appeal to the king against the excesses and it must be said to the credit of the king that he did take preventive measures. The effect of these was however short-lived as is evidenced by the repeated complaints on this score made by the Hindus. Referring to one such complaint the king wrote on February 28, 1704 to the viceroy as follows :—

" The Hindu population of this city has complained to me, that although I have by my letter of March 24, 1681 addressed to vice-roy Conde de Alvor decided that the law passed in the year 1556 shall be conformed with...the Father of Christians (*Pae dos Christãos*) has been abusing the said order and entering

[45] P. Pissurlencar, *Agentes da Diplomacia Portuguesa na India*, Bastorá 1952, p. 61.

the houses of Hindus and taking away the children found therein, even when they have mothers, and ascendant lineals, on the ground that they are orphans. And when they wish to have recourse to the Judge of Orphans, who is the appropriate authority in the matter according to my laws, for showing the justice of their case and proving that the said Father could not use such violence in respect of such children, they are prevented from doing so by being dragged before the tribunal of Holy Office, which on no justifiable grounds can concern itself with hearing cases relating to orders passed by me."[46]

Another letter addressed by the king to the viceroy on March 21, 1709 also refers to a representation addressed to him by the Hindu people in regard to the excesses committed by the Father of Christians in "attempting to take away even such children as have fathers and other ascendant lineals living."[47]

In yet another letter dated March 28, 1726 the king, referring to a representation of the Hindus, pointed out to the viceroy that the Father of Christians removed from paternal protection, children who had reached the age of reason and had their fathers living, admitted them to the house of Cathecumens, and whether by their consent or by force baptized them and placed them in the Colleges and Convents of the Fathers of the Company without admitting the applications made by their fathers or executing the orders passed by the viceroy or the decisions of the *Juiz Conservador*.[48]

A remarkable incident, illustrating how conversion of children led to the conversion of their families, is narrated by Padre Francisco de Souza, celebrated historian of the Society of Jesus :

"The Brahmins of superior understanding and authority of Divar, finding themselves surrounded on all sides by Christians, convened their assembly and proposed that as the law of Christ had reached their very gates, it would be advisable either to receive the same or to migrate to other lands. The proposal caused perplexity. Some judged, and rightly so, that it was the will of God that they should also become Christians ; and that the time

[46] Cunha Rivara, *op. cit.*, Fasc. VI, suppl. ii, p. 155, (Doc. 48),
[47] *Ibid.*, p. 216, (Doc. 68).
[48] *Ibid.*, p. 281, (Doc. 98).

fixed by Heaven for change of their religion had arrived. Others, however, could not bring themselves to give up their ancient superstitions and were prepared to abandon the land of their birth rather than the religion of their forefathers. The more devout in the assembly pacified the discord by advising that counsel might be taken of God Ganessa, an idol with a human body and the head of an elephant, which was very famous and held in great reverence in a village in the mainland called Malar, which is in front of Divar. The suggestion was agreed t and for carrying gifts to the idol were selected a band of boys from the noblest and richest families of the area. While they were passing through the river between the island and the mainland they fell into the hands of Portuguese soldiers who, without discriminating between the mainland where Portuguese subjects could practise their rites and the Portuguese territories where they were prohibited from doing so, seized them and took them to Goa. The viceroy ordered that the children should be lodged in the house of Cathecumens while he investigated the offence. The priests proceeded immediately with the utmost care to catechise the boys and all of them promised to be Christians. On receiving their promise, the fathers who were demanding their sons back were given permission to speak to their sons so that they might enquire whether the latter were embracing the faith of Christ of their free will. They put the questions, as was often allowed to satisfy the complaints of the Hindus, and the replies were such that, either because they were convinced of the truth or being carried away by the love for their children, they let themselves remain with the children and sent for their wives in order that all of them might be instructed and baptised."[49]

Another case in which an entire Hindu family became Christian out of love for a child who had been baptized is mentioned by Padre Francisco Cabral in a letter dated December 10, 1563 addressed to his colleagues in Portugal :

" The captain resolved that this young Hindu should become Christian, and having become one he remained in this house. When his father came sometimes to see the son, I used to speak to him that he should become Christian. He used to reply :

[49] Francisco de Souza, *Oriente Conquistado a Jesus Christo*, Part I (Conq. 1, Div. 11, § 50), p. 98.

'Leave me alone. Be satisfied with having taken my son, because I am now old.' Nevertheless, after I had lost hopes of his conversion, God moved him without my having spok en to him further, and he came here with his wife and three or four sons to ask that they should all be made Christians and they are now good Christians."[50]

Interesting human dramas were occasionally enacted in the process of the enforcement of the law relating to orphans. Chrishna Naique of St. Mathews was married to a minor girl. She was taken away by the Father of Christians on the ground that she was an orphan aged under 10 years, baptized and given the name of Maria Anna. Chrishna demanded that his wife be restored to him. The case was heard by Dr. Pedro Pinheiro de Souza, Judge Conservator of the new converts on November 27, 1710, and, as would be expected, the husband's demand was refused ![51]

On April 3, 1720 king D. João, in response to complaints made by the Father of Christians, directed that a law may be promulgated to the effect that persons who removed children outside Portuguese territories, should lose their estates, a penalty to which Hindus were most sensitive, and in addition should be awarded some corporal punishment.[52]

Fathers of Christians frequently complained to the king that laws intended to promote propagation of Christianity were not properly enforced. In a letter dated March 15, 1714 the king advised the viceroy that he should remind the Inquisitors to proceed severely against those who impeded conversions of Hindus and to see that the law requiring orphans to be taken as Cathecumens was observed.[53]

Viceroy Aires de Saldanha ordered on March 28, 1604, that no person should remove boys and girls aged upto 18 years outside the Portuguese territories, and passage should not be allowed to such boys and girls by the *Capitães dos Passos*, under

[50] Silva Rego, *op cit.*, Vol. IX, 1953, p. 226.
[51] Cunha Rivara, *op. cit.*, Fasc. VI, suppl. ii, p. 5, (Doc. 3).
[52] *Ibid.*, p. 11, (Doc. 31).
[53] *Ibid.*, p. 18, (Doc. 10).

pain of a fine of 100 *pardaos* and deportation to galleys for two years.[54]

The following extract from a letter addressed by viceroy João Saldanha de Gama to the king on January 24, 1728 illustrates another ruse adopted by Fathers of Christians to effect conversions of children:

" By the indiscreet zeal and imprudence of some Fathers of Christians the government is many times embarrassed by complaints and mutinies of the Hindus on the ground that orders of His Majesty are not observed. The Father of Christians takes away their children and servants, without awaiting orders from the Judge Conservator and proceeds immediately to cut their *Sendies* (tufts of hair at the back of heads), in order that when they are ordered to be released, they should be considered as unfit for being admitted within their castes. "[55]

Role of the Father of Christians in enforcing measures against the Hindus

In Chapter V we have had occasion to refer to the main function of the Father of Christians (*Pae dos Christãos*). An idea of the important role which was assigned to him in the missionary work can be obtained from the following specific instructions issued to him:

" He should obtain knowledge of the times and days when the festivals of the infidels, such as that of areca-tree, *Setim* and others, came, in order that persons may be prevented from participating therein and those guilty of participating may be punished. The same would apply to the times of the pilgrimages to the temples; they should ascertain whether any of our infidel subjects go on such pilgrimages and whether, others who are not our subjects pass through our lands for that purpose, in order to prevent their doing so and punish those who do so, as His Majesty has ordered. The same would apply to the times when the Hindus customarily celebrate their marriages with Hindu ceremonies and festivities, in order to prevent them and punish those who perform them, although Hindu marriages performed without ceremonies and festivities cannot be prevented.

[54] Cunha Rivara, *op. cit.*, Fasc. VI, p. 768, (Doc. 30).
[55] Cunha Rivara, *op. cit.*, Fasc. VI, suppl. ii, p. 305, (Doc. 114).

" He should ascertain whether in the parts where the infidels live there are any orphans who are without father, mother and grandparents and are aged under 14 years, so that they may be sent to the College, as the king has ordered, educated and baptised ; they should also ascertain whether any infidels have removed the said orphans to the mainland for being kept until they cross the said age, so that they may not be baptised, and in the meanwhile enjoy the income of their estates, in order that such persons might be punished as the king has ordered ; and the said estates sequestrated in the hands of Christians of sound credit, as the viceroy has ordered. And through his own efforts and those of the secular *Pae dos Christãos*, the solicitor and the procurator, he should see that this is put fully into execution and that Christian tutors are given to as many orphans of the infidels as may be possible, in conformity with the relevant provision as the king has ordered."[56]

Pressure from Fathers of Christians and others for greater discrimination against the Hindus

Although the Hindus continued to groan under various oppressive laws. the Father of Christians persisted in his complaints that the favourable treatment accorded to the Hindus prevented them from embracing Christianity. The king sent to viceroy Conde de Villa Verde on January 30, 1698 a letter from Padre Ignacio Martins, Father of Christians, in which the latter represented " that the Hindus were treated better than the Christians, that they were not only held in greater esteem but also more trusted than persons who had converted themselves and this was the reason why many did not embrace Christian religion."[57]

In his reply dated December 14, 1698 the viceroy wrote :

" I discussed with Archbishop Primaz and found that the good treatment given to the Hindus, was born of no other motive than that it is they who manage the entire business by correspondence which they have with others of their calling. As the converts lack this means, they are thereby deprived of the mutual relationship and esteem which business helps to cultivate with

[56] Cunha Rivara, *op. cit.*, Fasc. V, pt. iii, pp. 1432-9, (Doc. 1022).
[57] Cunha Rivara, *op. cit.*, Fasc. VI, p. 1299, (Doc. 603).

those who manage it by the dependence which many people have in their interests. As a result, in these parts there are difficulties in reducing the friendship, but all that can help to profit the Christians in securing greater esteem in comparison with the Hindus, I shall do with the attention and care which this matter calls for. "[58]

In a letter addressed to the king on January 21, 1735 Manoel de Abreu, Father of Christians, enumerated the reasons why propagation of Christianity in India did not proceed at a faster pace. Among these he included the following :

First, the great esteem accorded to the Hindus and none to the New Christians.

Second, the great liberty with which the Hindus live in the state.

Last, briefly stated, the omission to observe the laws and charters passed in favour of the increase of Christianity.[59]

The Procurator of the Crown, who was asked to comment on these views wrote on January 20, 1738 as follows :

" I am persuaded that the zeal with which the Father of Christians desires to bring our Holy Faith to the Hindus, moved him to give an alarming account to His Majesty. Referring to the first complaint, I find no basis therefor, since *I have not yet seen a Hindu converted to our Holy Faith who did not come to it for his convenience, to enjoy the privileges of the Cathecumen, or in order that his debts may be paid.* I never saw among these Cathecumens good Christians or persons with ability who could be entrusted with any duties, and it is hence that offices which are customarily given to the natives are not bestowed upon them. It is certain that jobs must be given to those who have the capacity to serve therein, and I have many times informed Your Majesty that I wished to give them to the Cathecumens, but on enquiries it was found that they did not have the capacity.'[60]

The viceroy while forwarding the reply of the Procurator of the Crown, endorsed on January 21, 1738 the latter's views. He wrote :

[58] *Ibid.*, p. 1303, (Doc. 603).
[59] Cunha Rivara, *op. cit.*, Fasc. VI, suppl. ii, pp. 445-6, (Doc. 162).
[60] *Ibid.*, p. 448.

"Sir, I heard the Procurator of the Crown whose reply is enclosed. I am in entire agreement with what he states and wish to add that the esteem which the Father of Christians says is accorded to the Hindus, does not arise from their being Hindus but from being men of worth such as are wanting among the Christians. This is what happens in all parts of the world, in that it is always the men of worth who win esteem. In matters of commerce the Christians cannot have the same means as the Hindus, since the main commerce of this land is wholly dominated by the Hindus. The Christians cannot carry on correspondence in these matters, nor easily learn to do so, because of the difference of languages and of scripts with characters so diverse that no Christian understands them. It is inevitable that the said commerce should be appropriated by the Hindus and that by the means acquired by them they should win the esteem of rich persons."[61]

The Municipal Corporation of Bardez complained to the king on December 10, 1741 that the Hindus harassed people in collecting revenues and that the work should, therefore, be entrusted to Christians. Viceroy Marquez do Louriçal in his letter dated December 10, 1741 defended the prevailing practice in the following words :

"The Hindus of good credit are the better collectors of revenues, principally of the customs, because having an interest in profiting therefrom, they seek to attract the commerce of the mainland where they have greater credit and greater correspondence than the Christians. Recently the revenue from customs in Salsete and Bardez which was leased to two Hindus increased to a figure which could not be hoped for in the times of distress and neither the Municipal Corporation nor any Christian appeared on the day of the auction. From which, I am of the opinion that His Majesty in order that he may be best served should leave this matter to the Council of Revenues, where great attention is paid to secure proper administration thereof."[62]

An idea of the relative numbers of Hindus and Christians in Portuguese territories at the beginning of the 18th century

[61] *Ibid.*, p. 447.
[62] *Ibid.*, p. 457, (Doc. 166).

can be had from the comments submitted to the king by the viceroy on December 22, 1705, in connection with two plans for Christianisation of the Hindus of Goa placed before the king by *Desembargador* Domingos Dourado de Oliveira :

"The first plan starts by exaggerating so excessively the number of the Hindus living in the dominions of the king, that to a person who has no other information about India, it would give the impression that in the territories subject to the Crown, Christianity is totally extinct or that till now not more than a small fraction of the subjects have been converted to it. On the contrary, the fact is that the Hindus are few and Christians many and the latter so well indoctrinated that they can serve as examples to those in Europe. Beginning with districts annexed to Goa, where the said plan starts, in Salsete there will be, 1,00,000 Christian souls and the Hindus 3000 and these latter not in the interior of the peninsula but in the villages which border on the mainland, where few of them are born and many casual visitors who are present only as residents for the conduct of their contracts. Almost the same proportion is witnessed in Bardez and specially in the islands adjacent to Goa where Hindus are rare as they are also in the villages of the island of Goa. It is only in the city of Goa that the number is larger, but much less than the total to which the figures given in the plan add up which would increase it to 30,000 or 40,000, being little more than 12,000. This should not appear large since Goa is a port which is free and open where all the nations of Asia gather with their contracts."[63]

Measures intended to Humiliate the Hindus

On December 15, 1572 the viceroy ordered that Hindu Pandits and physicians should not move in the city on horse-back or in *andores* (a kind of sedan-chair) or *palanquins* under pain of a fine of 10 *crusados* on the first occasion; a fine of 20 *crusados* and loss of the horse, *andor* or *palanquin* on the second ; and imprisonment on the galleys of the king on the third. The Pandit who was the physician of the viceroy's household was exempted from this order.[64]

The same order was repeated on December, 14, 1575.[65]

[63] *Ibid.*, p. 185, (Doc. 57).
[64] Cunha Rivara, *op. cit.*, Fasc, V, pt. ii, p. 899. (Doc. 738).
[65] *Ibid.*, p. 910, (Doc. 781).

In 1731 viceroy Conde de Sandomil ordered that Christian *bois* or *boias* (bearers of *palanquins, andores,* etc.) should not carry Hindus. On March 6, 1733 the captain of Cuncolim and Rachol was ordered not to agree to any Hindu being carried by Christian *bois*, even though he might have obtained permission for being so carried, as such permits had been cancelled.[66] The Archbishop excommunicated Christian *bois* who had carried two famous businessmen of Goa, Roulu Camotim and Chrishna Camotim. These gentlemen requested the viceroy that they may be exempted from the law but their request was turned down on March 5, 1744.[67]

Christian agricultural labourers were forbidden to work in the lands owned by the Hindus and the Hindu landowners were prohibitted to employ Christian labourers. Lists of persons punished by the Inquisition for these offences are available.[68]

Other Privileges available on conversion

On September 22, 1570 it was decreed that the Hindus who embraced Christianity would be exempted from the payment of the *Dizimos* land-tax for a period of fifteen years.[69]

On November 3, 1592 viceroy Mathias de Albuquerque proclaimed that slaves of infidels who converted themselves to Christianity would be freed.[70]

Alteration in the laws of inheritance of the Hindus intended to benefit the converts

According to the Hindu law, if a person died without leaving male children, his wife and daughters did not inherit his property. King D. João, acting on the suggestion of the Fathers of St. Paul decreed that in such cases the widow and daughters would inherit the estate if they became Christians, and if they did not, the nearest relatives who became Christians would do so. This law was published by the governor Francisco de Barreto on

[66] Cunha Rivara, *op. cit.*, Fasc. VI, suppl. ii, p. 399, (Doc. 148).
[67] *Ibid.*, p. 462, (Doc. 169).
[68] Antonio Baião, *A Inquisição de Goa*, Vol. I, Lisboa 1949, pp. 279-83.
[69] Cunha Rivara, *op. cit.*, Fasc. V, pt. ii, pp. 733, 786, (Doc. 684, 718); pt. iii pp. 965, 976, (Doc. 801, 809).
[70] *Ibid.*, Fasc. V, pt. iii, p. 1300, (Doc. 983).

June 15, 1557.[71] D. Sebastião endorsed the same provision by his decree of March 22, 1559 :

" I decree that as from the date of the publication hereof the estate left on death of a Hindu person in this city and island of Goa in my Indian dominions, who does not leave surviving male children as heirs, can and shall be inherited by his wife and female children who survive the deceased, provided they become Christians ; and if they do not wish to become Christians, the surviving relative who is the nearest of kin to the deceased, if he becomes a Christian shall inherit and succeed to the estate ; although other relatives of the deceased become Christians, they shall not be his heirs nor inherit anything out of his estate, except the relative who is the nearest of kin and becomes Christian, as provided above."[72]

There is a decree of March 26, 1559 of D. Sebastião which provides that sons, grandsons and other relatives of a Hindu individual will inherit his estate on his death only if they become Christians.[73] It was declared on July 27, 1559 that although in accordance with the Hindu custom, daughters could not inherit the property of the deceased father, they would do so if they became Christians and no other relative would in that event do so.[74] A decree similar to that of June 15, 1557, which has been reproduced above, was again passed by the king in March 1583.[75] If a Hindu died without leaving heirs or making a will his estate passed to the king.[76]

It was provided that the wife of a Hindu individual who became Christian and separated from her husband on the ground that he adhered to his old religion, should get a part of the husband's estate during his lifetime. A decree promulgated by D. Sebastião in 1562 ran as follows :

" I order and decree that as from the publication hereof, any Hindu wife who becomes Christian, and who does not wish to live with her husband and separates from him on the ground that he continues to be an infidel, shall have all the ornaments

[71] Cunha Rivara, *op. cit.*, Fasc. V, pt. iii, p. 1570, (Doc. 1095).
[72] Cunha Rivara, *op. cit.* Fasc. V, pt. i, p. 381, (Doc. 285).
[73] *Ibid.*, p. 392, (Doc. 292).
[74] *Ibid.*, p. 410, (Doc. 304).
[75] Cunha Rivara, *op. cit.*, Fasc, V, pt. iii, p. 995, (Doc. 826).
[76] Cunha Rivara, *op. cit.*, Fasc, V. pt. ii, p. 522, (Doc. 435).

and personal clothes which she might have at the time of conversion, as well as one half of the husband's estate, movable or immovable, which might have been acquired after their marriage, and in compliance herewith this much should be handed to her when she becomes Christian."[77] It may be doubted if there was any Hindu wife who claimed the benefit of this provision.

In a letter dated August 12, 1557 D. João provided that if a son or daughter of a Hindu father became Christian, they would be entitled to one-third of the father's estate, even during his lifetime and would inherit further portions thereof on the father's death. The letter is reproduced hereunder:

"In the interests of Christianity and increase of our Holy Faith and in order that the newly converted should have a remedy against the harm which might be caused to their legitimate interests by fathers, who continue to be infidels, on seeing their children converted, squandering away their estates, I hereby order that when any such person, whether male or female, converts himself or herself to our Holy Faith, he or she should receive as the legitimate share one third of the estate, movable as well as immovable, of his or her father and mother, who continue to be infidels, provided they have no other brother, and this would not prevent them from inheriting further estate on the death of the parents."[78]

Racial discrimination between the Indian Christians and the Portuguese

It is interesting to note that although the New Christians were preferred to the Hindus, the racial distinction between the Indian Christians and the Portuguese was scrupulously maintained. In a letter dated February 19, 1718 the king impressed on the viceroy that while the laws in regard to giving preference to New Christians in appointments to Government jobs should be carefully observed, greatest care should be taken to see that the *Canarins* (Indian Christians) were not given preference over or equalised with the Portuguese in any manner, "as this is necessary in the interests of my service and authority and respect of the nation." The letter also lays down that in the

[77] *Ibid.*, pp. 514-5, (Doc. 427).
[78] Cunha Rivara, *op. cit.*, Fasc. V, pt. iii, p. 1572, (Doc. 1096).

posts to which the Portuguese are considered as qualified after eight years the *Canarins* should not be considered as qualified in less than twelve years, "as it is reasonable that there should be a difference between them and the Portuguese."[79]

There was a remarkable incident which showed vividly how the distinction between the Indians and the Portuguese was one of the essential principles of the Portuguese administration in India. In 1736 the king decided to confer on an Indian Christian, João Menezes de Aguiar by name, the honour of the *Habito de Nosso Senhor Jesus Christo.* The viceroy Conde de Sandomil in his letter dated January 24, 1736 pointed out to the king that he found it necessary to suspend the execution of this order, as until then it had been the invariable practice to give that honour only to the Portuguese, and when natives had to be honoured on account of distinguished services to the State Secretariat or Revenue Tribunal or in military posts the honour of *Habito de S. Thiago* was conferred on them. The viceroy added that the distinction which existed between the natives and the Portuguese was manifest and had been observed at all times. He pointed out that as a result of the decision of the king, the Portuguese could not but feel greatly perturbed in being equalised with the natives, from whom they at all times had been considered as totally different and that he was informed that the decision had caused great commotion among the Portuguese who had served His Majesty with honour and distinction.[80] The king informed the viceroy on April 12, 1737 that after consulting the *Conselho Ultramarino* he had decided to confer on João Menezes de Aguiar only the *Habito de S. Thiago.*[81]

One of the instances mentioned by viceroy Conde de Sandomil in his letter to the king to illustrate his contention that a distinction between the natives and the Europeans had always been observed is that of Lucas de Lima, whom he describes as a secular priest of great reputation for learning and virtue. The viceroy points out that he was appointed as a *Qualificador* (Censor) in the Inquisition of Goa, a post of comparatively minor importance, but the ministers of the Inquisition did not allow

[79] Cunha Rivara, *op. cit.*, Fasc. VI, suppl. ii, p. 102, (Doc. 24).
[80] *Ibid.*, p. 440, (Doc. 158).
[81] *Ibid.*, p. 455, (Doc. 164).

him to take charge of it. The Inquisitors represented the matter to the General Council and in consequence the appointment was cancelled. Some biographical details of Lucas de Lima are given in the *Biographia Goana.* He was a native and *Gauncar* of the island of Chorão (Goa) where he was born in 1654. He died in 1717. Diogo Barbosa Machado in his *Bibliotheca Lusitana* writes that " he studied the sacred and profane sciences, and in all of them became eminently learned, being endowed with great talents and a perspicacious comprehension. He was not only a consummate theologian but also an excellent canonist, being consulted in the greatest controversies, in which his opinion was decisive."[82] He worked as Vicar of the Churches of Panelim, Talaulim and Chorão and also held the appointments of Promotor of the Ecclesiastical Court, Procurator of the Primatial Mitre of Goa and Syndic of the Senate of the city of Goa. That a divine of such eminence should have been considered as unworthy of holding a minor post in the Inquisition because of his Indian origin shows how deep-rooted racial prejudice was.

Other evidence of racial discrimination in various fields is found in the writings of contemporary travellers. For instance, François Pyrard states that Indian Christians were not admitted to the Royal Hospital of Goa, which he describes as "finest in the world." He writes :

" The sick are sometimes very numerous, and while I was there, there were as many as 1500 all of them either Portuguese soldiers or men of other Christian races of Europe, of every profession and quality who are all received ; for the Indians are not taken in these, having a hospital apart, endowed by the townspeople, wherein are received only Christian Indians. There is still another hospital for the women of Christian Indians, also endowed by the town, to which women only may go."[83]

The English traveller John Fryer, referring to conditions in Goa in 1675, writes as follows :

" The Mass of the People are *Canorein* though *Portuguezed* in Speech and Manners; paying great Observance to a White Man,

[82] *Biographia Goana*, p. 20.
[83] *The Voyage of François Pyrard*, Vol. II, pt. i, London 1888, p. 7.

whom when they meet they must give him the Way with a Cringe and Civil Salute, for fear of a *stochado*."[84]

There is evidence to show that the new converts were required to adopt European dress and habits and the policy of proselytism was thus based on an implicit assumption of the superiority of European culture. In a letter dated July 7, 1569, viceroy D. Luiz de Atayde lays down that import duties should not be charged on clothes given to new converts.[85] From a letter of the king dated January 25, 1571 it also appears that new converts were required to appear at Baptism in a suit of western clothes which was given free to them. It will be clear, however, that even though those who adopted Christian religion had perforce to adopt the western way of life, they were not considered as equals of the Christians of European origin and the distinction between them and the latter was rigorously observed.

Communal dissensions among the Indians

We have referred in the last chapter to a petition of the Hindus of Goa one of the demands made in which was that the Inquisition should not take cognisance of denunciations made against them by other Hindus. The extent to which this practice prevailed is indicated by the fact that viceroy João Saldanha da Gama reported to the king that this would be one of the conditions which the Hindu business-men who had migrated to neighbouring territories would insist on being fulfilled before agreeing to return to Goa. The methods of the Inquisition provided splendid opportunities for the black-mailer to exercise his vile art. In addition, such denunciations must have had their origin not only in purely personal enmity, anger, rivalry and malice but also in communal antagonisms and passions between various groups. The presence of deep-rooted communal antagonisms and rivalries also explains the inability of the Indians to present a united front to the common oppressor.

In the contemporary literature we come across references to two major instances of such group antagonisms, viz., the dissensions between the Brahmins and *Charado's* among the new converts

[84] John Fryer, *A New Account of East-India and Persia, London* 1698, p. 156.

[85] Cunha Rivara, *op. cit.*, Fasc. V, pt. ii, p. 710, (Doc. 674).

and those between the *Smarta* and *Vaishnava* sects of the *Saraswata* Brahmins.

Brahmins and *Charadós* (or *charodós*) were the two more advanced castes among the Indians in Goa at this time. The attachment of their members to their castes was so deep that even after their conversion to Christianity they continued to mention their castes after their new Christian names and surnames in all documents. We find this practice adopted even in the contemporary lists of the prisoners of the Inquisition which are available.[86] The term *Brahman* was applied at this time only to the *Saraswata* or *Shenvi* Brahmins and the *Karhadás*, another Brahmin sub-caste which has lived in Goa from ancient times, were generally known as *Karhadás* or *Bhats*. The same practice is current in Goa and the neighbouring territories to this day. There are, however, no Hindu communities in Goa or in its vicinity today who are called *Charadós*. It has been suggested that the *Charadós* belonged to the Kshatriya caste, but it appears surprising that the appellation should have fallen into total disuse among the Hindus today. Another theory, which appears comparatively more worthy of credence, has been advanced by Dr. Luis Cunha Gonsalves in his book *O Direito Hindu e Mahometano* (Hindu and Mahomedan Laws).[87] He identifies the word *Charadó* with *Caradó* (Karhada Brahman) and suggests that this word, which was pronounced as "Charadó" (as in the word *character*) originally, in course of time came to be pronounced as "Charadó" (as in the word *Charm*). It appears curious, however, that members of the community themselves should have cherished their Brahmin origin so little that they themselves came to believe that they were Kshatriyas and that their true caste name should have been completely obliterated even amongst them.

There were quarrels among the Brahmin and *Charadó* converts regarding pre-eminence of their communities in local affairs, which occasionally assumed a violent form. The viceroy in a letter addressed to the king on January 15, 1714 reports such an incident which took place at the Church of *Nossa Senhora de Belem* at Chandor. He writes :

86 Baião, *op. cit.*, Vol. 1, pp. 279-83.
87 A. K. Priolkar, *op. cit.*, p. 151, (F. N. 4).

"Among three villages of Salsete, which border on the mainland, there was recently a feud between the Brahmins and the *Charadós*, over their respective pre-eminence. They waited for a decision until a feast-day when the Blessed Sacrament was exposed, for which they showed so little respect and veneration that either side called armed soldiers to fight on its behalf and there was so much blood-shed that the tabernacle in which the Lord was exposed came to be stained."[88]

An investigation into this faction-fight was carried out and the list of persons punished as a result is available.[89]

Another major communal feud was that between the *Smarta* and *Vaishnava* sects of the *Saraswata* Brahmins. The former sect was popularly known as Kelashikar or Kutthalkars. There is a letter of the king dated April 5, 1727 in which he refers to a petition addressed to him by the *Vaishnavas* of Salsette and Bardez against the *Smartas*. A petition addressed by the *Smartas* to the king against the *Vaishnavas* and some other related correspondence are also extant.[90] The *Vaishnavas* claimed that the rites and customs of the two sects were totally dissimilar and co-existence between them was impossible.[91] The viceroy on the plea that the bickerings and controversies between the two sects had reached such lengths that unless Government intervened both of them would be ruined, ordered that the two sects should live in complete segregation. Individuals born in one sect who wished to adopt the customs and rites of the other and live with the latter were, however, allowed to make the choice within one month. This would mean their total and permanent isolation thereafter from their own sect. As marriages between the two sects had been common, the order meant that women of one sect who were married into another had to choose between their parents and brothers or husband and children. The choice was in some cases difficult and three women are stated to have killed themselves with their own hands as a consequence.[92] The *Vaishnavas* supported the vice-regal order and prayed for its confirmation by the king while the *Smartas* prayed that it be

88 Cunha Rivara, *op. cit.*, Fasè, VI, suppl. ii, p. 13, (Doc. 7).
89 *Ibid.*, pp. 13-14, (Doc. 8).
90 *Ibid.*, pp. 299-300, (Doc. 108).
91 *Ibid.*, pp. 376-7, (Doc. 142).
92 *Ibid.*, p. 373, (Doc. 142).

rescinded as instead of ending the controversies between the two sects it had accentuated and multiplied them and had meant " great oppression, and inexplicable confusion and perturbation." The *Vaishnavas* were led by Nillea Camotim, Rama Sinay, Gunea Camotim, and others. The names of the leaders of the *Smartas* are not known.

It is sad to note that while some Hindus were making heroic sacrifices out of love for their religion, others, at the same time, utterly oblivious to the common peril, were bent on magnifying petty differences, fomenting internal discord and inviting the intervention of the foreign rulers in their family bickerings, thereby impairing the capacity of the Hindus to resist the foreign onslaught against their religion and culture.

CHAPTER IX

Use of torture by the Inquisition and the Palace of the Goa Inquisition

(1) *Judicial use of Torture by the Inquisition* :

WHILST Dellon's account provides a fairly complete and accurate picture of the working of the Inquisition, there is one aspect thereof, viz. the use of torture in its judicial proceedings, to which he makes only passing reference. This may be attributed to the fact that Dellon himself was not put to torture at any stage of his trial. Also it may be presumed that his fellow-victims who had undergone that experience were reluctant to recall it to their minds or afraid to break the oath of secrecy administered to them. It is therefore proposed, in the interest of completeness, to supplement Dellon's account with some information on this point. That torture was used freely and with all severity by the Inquisition in Goa may be inferred from the following passage in Dellon's account :

"During the month of November and December, I every morning heard the cries of those to whom the torture was administered, and which was inflicted so severely, that I have seen many persons of both sexes who have been crippled by it, and, amongst others, the first companion allotted to me in my prison."[1]

Torture was used by the Inquisition as an expedient to obtain a confession where the evidence against the accused was incomplete, defective or conflicting. As is well-known, the Inquisition, through whose agency unrepentant or relapsed heretics were consigned to the stake, did not itself condemn them to it, but merely pronounced them to be heretics of whose conversion no hope was entertained, cut them off from the Church and abandoned or "relaxed" them to the secular arm for punishment. The secular arm was bound to sentence and execute them. The *negativo*, a person who denied his heresy, was classed as an impenitent heretic and doomed to relexation, if there was sufficient evidence of his guilt. In such cases torture was considered necessary only where the offence was of sufficient gravity but the evidence was insufficient or not wholly conclusive. Of course,

[1] *Vide* Part II, Chapt. XXIX, p. 48.

in actual practice what was conclusive evidence it was difficult to decide and the matter had to be left to the discretion of the judges in a large measure.[2] In the case of the *Diminuto*, a person who made a confession which " did not satisfy the evidence" and was therefore held to be imperfect, torture was necessary in order to account for the deficiency. No confession was accepted as complete unless it revealed the names of those whom the penitent knew to be guilty of heretical acts, and if there was reason to suspect that he was not fully discharging his conscience in this respect, torture was the natural resort. Even a person against whom sufficient evidence existed and who was condemned to relaxation, could be tortured *in caput alienum*, for eliciting information about his accomplices. It was made clear in the sentence passed in such cases that the accused was to be tortured only as a witness and not as a party and that he should be questioned only in respect to what concerned his accomplices. In the Manual of the Regulations a warning is given to the Inquisitors that such sentences should be passed only in very serious cases and when from them " great fruits can be hoped for " ; and it is laid down that before their execution all such sentences should be sent to the *Conselho Geral* for confirmation. Retraction or vacillation of confession necessarily required torture to reconcile the contradiction. Torture of witnesses, who were themselves not under trial, was permitted when they varied or retracted or so contradicted other witnesses that torture was considered necessary to ascertain the truth.[3]

Torture was preceded and accompanied by formalities which were intended to prevent its abuse. These are set forth in great detail in the Manual of Regulations of the Inquisition in a chapter entitled " How to proceed with the accused who have to be put to torture and in the execution of the sentence of torture."[4] After the prosecution and defence had closed if the judges found that the evidence was inconclusive they adopted a vote to torture the accused and postponed the decision to await the outcome. A sentence to the effect that the accused be put to torture so that he might reveal the truth about himself and about other persons

[2] Lea, *op.cit.*, pt. III, p. 198.
[3] *Ibid.*, pp. 10-12.
[4] *Regimento do Santo Officio da Inquisiçam*, Livro, II, Titulo XIV, ff. 119-124.

with whom he committed the crime or who were known to him to have committed the crime, was thereupon drafted. In the case of a *diminuto* the nature of the deficiencies in his confession was indicated and it was made clear that the sentence would be without prejudice to what was proved against him and what he had already confessed. Similarly, in the case of a *negativo*, it was made clear that the sentence would be without prejudice to what was proved against him. The accused was then brought before the judges and without informing him of the decision he was asked whether he wanted to confess or to complete his confession. If he said 'yes', the case was examined afresh in the light of his confession. If he said 'no', he was informed that a stern decision had been arrived at in his case, and that it would be better for him to confess his guilt before its execution. If he did not change his mind, the sentence was read out to him. If he did not confess even then, the Inquisitors ordered the *alcaide* to take him to the chamber of torture. The accused had the right to appeal against the sentence to the *Conselho Geral* at this stage.

At the chamber of torture while the sentence was being executed the episcopal ordinary or the person acting in his place was requested to attend. If he came, two other persons, viz. either two Inquisitors or one Inquisitor and one Deputy also attended; if he did not come, two Inquisitors and one Deputy or one Inquisitor and two Deputies attended; so that in all cases there would be three votes for arriving at decisions during the administration of torture. The accused was adjured in their presence to tell the truth and to unburden his conscience and thereby to avoid the trouble and difficulty in which he found himself. If he did not confess even then, the executioner, a physician and a surgeon were called and sworn to do their work truly and well and to keep the secret. A notary, who was also present, kept a record of the proceedings. The accused was taken to the place of torture, and while he was being tied up for the purpose, the notary declared in the name of the Inquisitors and other judges that if in the course of the torture the accused died, broke a limb or lost his senses, the responsibility would be his as he voluntarily exposed himself to that risk, which he could avoid by confessing his guilt.

Ill. No. 2. Hall of the Inquisition.

ll. No 8
rture by fire.

ILL. No. 4.
Torture of *Potro*
or Water torture.
(See pt. I,
pp. 154-8).

ILL. No. 5. Water-torture and torture of pulleys. (See pt. I, pp. 153-4).

During the torture the only words to be addressed to the accused were "Tell the truth." "The notary faithfully recorded all that passed, even to the shrieks of the victim, his despairing ejaculations and his piteous appeals for mercy or to be put to death, nor would it be easy to conceive anything more fitted to excite the deepest compassion than these cold-blooded matter of fact reports."[5]

It was a rule that torture could be applied only once unless new evidence against the accused supervened. The Manual of Regulations also provides that the same accused should not be put to torture more than twice ; and in case fresh evidence came to light after it had been administered twice, the case should be referred to the *Conselho Geral*. H. C. Lea points out, that such humane rules could easily be evaded. "Though torture could not be repeated, it could be continued and when it was over the patient was told that the Inquisitors were not satisfied but were obliged to suspend it for the present and that it would be resumed at another time, if he did not tell the whole truth. Thus it could be repeated from time to time as often as the *Consulta de Fé* deemed expedient."[6]

The Manual of Regulations provides that ordinarily the "torture of *polé*" (pulleys) should be administered but where the physician or surgeon feels that on account of weakness or indisposition the accused could not stand it, "the torture of *potro*" may be given. It lays down that women should never be given the "torture of *potro*", and where it was found that they could not stand the "torture of *polé*", the case should be referred to the *Conselho Geral*.[7]

An idea of these forms of torture may be obtained from the illustrations Nos. 3–5 and the following description given by H. C. Lea :

"The former (i.e. the torture of *polé*), known in Italy as the *strappado*, consisted in tying the patient's hands behind his back and then, with a cord around his wrists, hoisting him from the floor, with or without weights to his feet, keeping him suspended

[5] Lea. *op. cit.*, Vol. III, p. 18.
[6] *Ibid.*
[7] *Regimento do Santo Officio da Inquisiçam*, f. 121.

as long as was desired and perhaps occasionally letting him fall a short distance with a jerk. About 1620 a writer prescribes that the elevating movement should be slow for if it is rapid the pain is not lasting; for a time the patient should be kept at tiptoe, so that his feet scarce touch the floor; when hoisted he should be held there while the psalm *Miserere* is thrice repeated slowly in silence, and he is to be repeatedly admonished to tell the truth. If this fail he is to be lowered, one of the weights is to be attached to his feet and he is to be hoisted for the space of two *Misereres*, the process being repeated with increasing weights as often and as long as may be judged expedient."[8]

"The water-torture (i.e. the torture of *potro*) was more complicated. The patient was placed on an *escalera* or *potro* a kind of trestle, with sharpedged rungs across it like a ladder. It slanted so that the head was lower than the feet and, at the lower end was a depression in which the head sank, while an iron band around the forehead or throat kept it immovable. Sharp cords, called *cordeles* which cut into the flesh, attached the arms and legs to the side of the trestle and others, known as *garrotes*, from sticks thrust in them and twisted around like a tourniquet till the cords cut more or less deeply into the flesh, were twined around the upper and lower arms, the thighs and the calves; a *bostezo*, or iron prong, distended the mouth, a *toca*, or strip of linen, was thrust down the throat to conduct water trickling slowly from a *jarra* or jar, holding usually a little more than a quart. The patient strangled and gasped and suffocated and, at intervals, the *toca* was withdrawn and he was adjured to tell the truth. The severity of the infliction was measured by the number of jars consumed sometimes reaching to six or eight."[9]

The Inquisition at different times and places made use of a variety of other forms of torture also. Referring to the forms of torture used by the Inquisition, E.T. Whittington writes as follows :

"As to the torture itself, it combined all that the ferocity of savages and the ingenuity of civilized man had till then invented. Besides the ordinary rack, thumb-screws, and leg-crushers or Spanish boots, there were spiked wheels over which the victims

[8] Lea, *op. cit.*, Vol. III, p. 19.
[9] *Ibid.*

were drawn with weights on their feet; boiling oil was poured on their legs, burning sulphur dropped on their bodies, and lighted candles held beneath their armpits. At Bamberg they were fed on salt fish and allowed no water, and then bathed in scalding water and quicklime. At Lindheim they were fixed to a revolving table and whirled round till they vomited and became unconscious, and on recovery remained in so dazed a state that they were ready to confess anything. At Neisse they were fastened naked in a chair, 'with 150 finger-long spikes in it' and kept there for hours. And so effective were these tortures that nine out of ten innocent persons preferred to die as confessed sorcerers rather than undergo a repetition of them."[10]

To illustrate the process of torture and its effects on the accused H. C. Lea reproduces a notary's record of "a very moderate case" of water torture, carried only to a single *Jarra*, administered in 1568 by the Tribunal of Toledo to Elvira del Campo, accused of "not eating pork and of putting on clean linen on Saturdays." The record is reproduced hereunder in its entirety:

"She was carried to the torture-chamber and told to tell the truth, when she said that she had nothing to say. She was ordered to be stripped and again admonished, but was silent. When stripped, she said "Señores, I have done all that is said of me and I bear false witness against myself, for I do not want to see myself in such trouble; please God, I have done nothing." She was told not to bring false testimony against herself but to tell the truth. The tying of the arms was commenced; she said "I have told the truth; what have I to tell?" She was told to tell the truth and replied "I have told the truth and have nothing to tell." One cord was applied to the arms and twisted and she was admonished to tell the truth but said she had nothing to tell. Then she screamed and said "I have done all they say." Told to tell in detail what she had done she replied "I have already told the truth." Then she screamed and said "Tell me what you want for I don't know what to say." She was told to tell what she had done, for she was tortured because she had not done so, and another turn of the cord was ordered. She cried "Loosen me, Señores and tell me what I have to say:

[10] Charles Singer, *op. cit.*, pp. 203-4.

I do not know what I have done, O Lord have mercy on me, a sinner!" Another turn was given and she said "Loosen me a little that I may remember what I have to tell; I don't know what I have done; I did not eat pork for it made me sick; I have done everything; loosen me and I will tell the truth." Another turn of the cord was ordered, when she said "Loosen me and I will tell the truth; I don't know what I have to tell—loosen me for the sake of God--tell me what I have to say—I did it, I did it—they hurt me Señor—loosen me, loosen me and I will tell it." She was told to tell it and said "I don't know what I have to tell —Señor I did it—I have nothing to tell—Oh my arms! release me and I will tell it." She was asked to tell what she did and said "I don't know, I did not eat because I did not wish to." She was asked why she did not wish to and replied "Ay! loosen me, loosen me—take me from here and I will tell it when I am taken away—I say that I did not eat it." She was told to speak and said "I did not eat it, I don't know why." Another turn was ordered and she said "Señor I did not eat it because I did not wish to—release me and I will tell it." She was told to tell what she had done contrary to our holy Catholic faith. She said "Take me from here and tell me what I have to say—they hurt me—Oh my arms, my arms!" which she repeated many times and went on "I don't remember —tell me what I have to say—O wretched me!—I will tell all that is wanted, Señores—they are breaking my arms—loosen me a little—I did everything that is said of me." She was told to tell in detail truly what she did. She said "What am I wanted to tell? I did everything—loosen me for I don't remember what I have to tell—don't you see what a weak woman I am?—Oh! Oh! my arms are breaking." More turns were ordered and as they were given she cried "Oh! Oh! loosen me for I don't know what I have to say—Oh my arms! I don't know what I have to say—If I did I would tell it." The cords were ordered to be tightened when she said "Señores have you no pity on a sinful woman?" She was told, yes, if she would tell the truth. She said, "Señor tell me, tell me it." The cords were tightened again, and she said "I have already said that I did it." She was ordered to tell it in detail, to which she said "I don't know how to tell it señor, I don't know." Then the cords were separated and counted, and there were sixteen turns, and in giving the last turn the cord broke.

She was then ordered to be placed on the potro. She said "Señores, why will you not tell me what I have to say? Señor, put me on the ground—have I not said that I did it all?" She was told to tell it. She said "I don't remember—take me away—I did what the witnesses say." She was told to tell in detail what the witnesses said. She said "Señor, as I have told you, I do not know for certain. I have said that I did all that the witnesses say. Señores, release me, for I do not remember it." She was told to tell it. She said "I do not know it. Oh! Oh! they are tearing me to pieces.—I have said that I did it—let me go." She was told to tell it. She said "Señores, it does not help me to say that I did it and I have admitted that what I have done has brought me to this suffering—Señor, you know the truth—Señores, for God's sake have mercy on me. Oh Señor, take these things from my arms—Señor release me, they are killing me." She was tied on the potro with the cords, she was admonished to tell the truth and the garrotes were ordered to be tightened. She said "Señor do you not see how these people are killing me? Señor, I did it—for God's sake let me go." She was told to tell it. She said "Señor, remind me of what I did not know—Señores have mercy upon me—let me go for God's sake—they have no pity on me—I did it—take me from here and I will remember what I cannot here." She was told to tell the truth, or the cords would be tightened. She said "Remind me of what I have to say for I don't know it—I said that I did not want to eat it—I know only that I did not want to eat it," and this she repeated many times. She was told to tell why she did not want to eat it. She said, "For the reason that the witnesses say—I don't know how to tell it—miserable that I am that I don't know how to tell it—I say I did it and my God how can I tell it?" Then she said that, as she did not do it, how could she tell it—Then she said that, as she did not do it, how could she tell it—"They will not listen to me—these people want to kill me—release me and I will tell the truth." She was again admonished to tell the truth. She said, "I did it, I don't know how I did it—I did it for what the witnesses say—let me go—I have lost my senses and I don't know how to tell it—loosen me and I will tell the truth." Then she said "Señor, I did it, I don't know how I have to tell it, but I tell it as the witnesses say—I wish to tell it--take me from here—Señor as the witnesses say, so I say and confess it." She was told to declare it. She said " I don't know how to say it—I have no memory—Lord, you are witness that if I knew how to say anything, else I would say it. I know nothing more to say than that I did it and God knows it." She said many times, " Señores, Señores, nothing helps me. You, Lord, hear that I tell the truth and can say no more—they are tearing out my soul—order them to loosen me." Then she said, " I do not say that I did it—I said no more." Then she said, " Señor, I did it to observe that Law ." She was asked what Law. She said, " The Law that the witnesses say—I declare it all Señor, and don't remember what Law it was—O, wretched was the mother that bore me." She was asked what was the Law she meant and what was the Law that she said the witnesses say. This was asked repeatedly, but she was silent and at last said that she did not know. She was told to tell the truth or the garrotes would be tightened but she did not answer. Another turn was ordered on the garrotes and she was admonished to say what Law it was. She said " If I knew what to say I would say it. Oh Señor, I don't know what I have to say—Oh !. Oh ! they are killing me—if they would tell me what—Oh, Señores, ! Oh, my heart !" Then she asked why they wished her to tell what she could not tell and cried repeatedly O, miserable me !" Then she said " Lord bear witness that they are killing me without my being able to confess." She was told that if she wished to tell the truth before the water was poured she should do so and discharge her conscience. She said that she could not speak and that she was a sinner. Then the linen toca was placed (in her throat) and she said " Take it away, I am strangling and am sick in the stomach." A jar of water was then poured down, after which she was told to tell the truth. She clamored for confession, saying that she was dying. She was told that the torture would be continued till she told the truth and was admonished to tell it, but though she was questioned repeatedly she remained silent. Then the inquisitor, seeing her exhausted by the torture, ordered it to be suspended."[11]

As Dellon has stated, in the procession of the Act of Faith each prisoner was placed in charge of a godfather. Whittington

[11] Lea, *op. cit.*, Vol. III, pp. 24-6.

recounts in the following passage the experiences of Father Spee, a Jesuit, who had to serve as a godfather on numerous occasions :

"Why do we search so diligently for sorcerers? I will show you at once where they are. Take the Capuchins, the Jesuits, all the religious orders, and torture them—they will confess. If some deny, repeat it a few times—they will confess. Should a few still be obstinate, exorcise them, shave them : they use sorcery, the devil hardens them, only keep on torturing— they will give in. If you want more, take the Canons, the Doctors, the Bishops of the Church— they will confess. How should the poor delicate creatures hold out? If you want still more, I will torture you and then you me. I will confess the crimes you will have confessed, and so we shall all be sorcerers together."[12]

Scholars are generally agreed that the Inquisition of Goa had earned "a sinister renown as the most pitiless in Christendom." From the foregoing account of the use of torture by its counterparts in Europe it should be possible to imagine the cruel excesses which the Inquisition of Goa must have practised to have merited such notoriety.

It will be seen from the preceding chapters that the Inquisition of Goa punished not only Christians who were suspected of heresy but also Hindus and other non-Christians who were accused of obstructing conversion or infringing some of the laws directed against their religions. As Dellon points out, the Inquisition never punished non-Christians with death, but generally sentenced them to "banishments, corporal correction or the galleys." Their estates were also confiscated and they were probably liable to be tortured in the course of their trials. In ChapterVII, we have reproduced a petition addressed to the king by the Hindus of Goa in which they state that those denounced for performing Hindu ceremonies were generally sentenced to lashes and deportation, the only difference being the longer or shorter period of deportation. It may be expected that during the period of deportation or enslavement on the galleys the Hindus would be forced to eat food forbidden by their religion and custom, just for keeping their bodies and souls together; and there would be also

[12] Charles Singer, *op.cit.*, p. 204.

serious doubt whether on their return after expiry of their sentences they would be admitted within their families and castes. In these circumstances, embracing Christianity would be an easy way of escape from their predicament and it may be expected that this must have proved an effective way of propagation of Christianity.

(2) *The Palace of the Inquisition at Goa*

The palace in which the Inquisition of Goa was housed stood to the South of the Cathedral Square in front of the Townhall. Before the Portuguese conquest of Goa it used to be the residence of Adilshah and during the early days of Portuguese regime the governor and the viceroy lived therein. In 1554, as vice-roy D. Pedro Mascarenhas, who was an old man of seventy, found it inconvenient to climb the stairs of this two-storeyed building, he decided to change his residence to a house within the fort which was previously occupied by the captain of the ships and the viceroys who succeeded him continued to live in the same house.[13] Minguel Vicente Abreu writes :

" As the palace of Sambaio was untenanted, the tribunal of the Inquisition, the establishment in India of which was decreed in 1560, was accommodated therein. With the march of time, the Inquisition made such alterations in its interior as were required for its functioning—a chapel, an entrance hall, an audience hall, a hall where trials were held, residence of the first Inquisitor, secret house, house of doctrine, and innumerable other prisons and houses some ordinary and others intended for special secret purposes, such as the house of penitence, perpetual prison, the house of torture, etc.—all these within one large edifice the outer wall of which was seven palms thick."[14]

Dellon, who describes the palace of the Inquisition in the 15th chapter of his account, states that it contained about 200 prison cells. Some of these were dark and window-less but it appears that there were no underground dungeons similar to those contained in some of the houses of Inquisition in Europe.

[13] Diogo de Couto, *Da Asia*, Decada VII, Livro I, Capitulo III. Lisboa 1782, p. 37

[14] M. V. Abreo, *Narração da Inquisição de Goa*, Goa 1866, p. 57.

A description of the latter is given by Pretorius, an eye-witness, in the following words :

" Some (of the dungeons) are holes like cellars or wells, fifteen to thirty fathoms (?) deep with openings above, through which they let down the prisoners with ropes and draw them up when they will. Such prisons I have seen myself. Some sit in great cold, so that their feet are frost-bitten or frozen off, and after-wards, if they escape, they are crippled for life. Some lie in continual darkness, so that they never see a ray of sunlight, and know not whether it be night or day. All of them have their limbs confined so that they can hardly move, and are in continual unrest, and lie in their own refuse, far more filthy and wretched than cattle. They are badly fed, cannot sleep in peace, have much anxiety, heavy thoughts, bad dreams. And since they cannot move hands or feet, they are plagued and bitten by lice, rats, and other vermin, besides being daily abused and threatened by gaolers and executioners. And since all this sometimes lasts months or years, such persons, though at first they be courageous, rational, strong, and patient, at length become weak, timid, hopeless, and if not quite, at least half idiotic and desperate."[15]

At the time when the Inquisition of Goa was suspended, Marquez de Pombal, by a letter dated February 10, 1774, ordered that the palace of Inquisition should again be used as the residence of the viceroy.[16] The contemporary viceroy D. José Pedro de Camara, however, pointed out that the changes made by the Inquisition were so extensive, that considerable expenditure would have to be incurred in making alterations if it were to be used again as the viceregal residence. The idea was therefore abandoned and when the Inquisition was reinstated in 1778 in the reign of D. Maria I, it was housed in the same building. A passage in which Dr. Buchanan describes the palace as he saw it in 1808, is reproduced in Part II of this book.[17]

Dr. Buchanan's account of the Inquisition was instrumental in causing the British government to bring pressure on the Portuguese government to abolish the Inquisition of Goa. It will be

[15] Charles Singer, *op. cit.*, p. 203.
[16] Abreo, *op. cit.*, pp. 62-3.
[17] *Vide* Part II, p. 97.

seen from the following passage from the writings of the Abbe Cottineau who visited Goa in 1821, that the palace was then already in a condition of decay :

" At present the whole is fast decaying : there are no doors nor window-cases now existing ; shrubs, thorns, and rubbishes chock up the entrance, and the interior must be filled with serpents and other reptiles. It was in 1812, at the time that the British Government had a garrison in Goa, that orders came from Court of Rio Janeiro, at the recommendation of that of London for the suppression of the inquisition."[18]

Sometime during 1828 to 1830, the government of Goa ordered that the palace of Goa should be demolished so that the materials could be used for the construction of another edifice at Panjim. Referring to its subsequent history, J. N. Fonseca writes :

" The *debris* was suffered to remain on the spot till it was removed in 1859, on the occasion of the exposition of the body of St. Francis Xavier. The labourers who were employed in its removal discovered a subterraneous staircase, and human bones buried under a thick piece of lead of the shape of a whale or a boat."[19]

The information given by Fonseca lends support to the surmise that an underground dungeon might have existed in the palace of the Inquisition of Goa also.

[18] Cottineau de Kloguen, *An Historical Sketch of Goa*, Bombay 1922, p. 78.

[19] J. N. Fonseca, *An Historical and Archaelogical Sketch of the City of Goa*, Bombay 1878, p. 216.

CHAPTER X

THE JURISDICTION AND AUTHORITY OF THE INQUISITION OF GOA

IN matters which fell within its purview the powers of the Inquisition were unlimited and its jurisdiction extended to the mightiest in the land. Lea writes :

" Over the laity the jurisdiction of the Inquisition was complete. No one was so high-placed as to be exempt, for heresy was a universal leveller. Theoretically the king himself was subject to it, for it was based on the principle of the supremacy of the spiritual over the temporal power."[1]

Dellon explains in the following passage the scope of the authority of the Inquisition of Goa :

" At Goa, the Grand Inquisitor alone, has, or claims the privilege of a carriage, and receives more respect than the Archbishop or the Viceroy. His authority extends over all descriptions of persons as well lay, as Ecclesiastic ; except the Archbishop, his Grand Vicar (who is generally a bishop), the Viceroy, and the Governors in case of the Viceroy's decease ; but he can cause any of these to be arrested, after previously informing the court of Portugal, and receiving secret orders from the Sovereign Council of the Inquisition of Lisbon, called, " *Conselho Supremo.*"[2]

In the working of the Inquisition of Goa the Archbishop of Goa participated actively during the early years ; but later he played only a minor role. There were also frequent occasions when Inquisition came into conflict with viceroys and governors. A number of such incidents are recorded in the correspondence of the Inquisitor of Goa published by Antonio Baião;[3] and Baião discusses these at some length in the second chapter of the introductory volume to the correspondence which he recently brought out.[4] Limitations of space do not permit a detailed review of such incidents here : but as an interesting illustration I would like to mention a case in which the Inquisitors found it necessary to

[1] H. C. Lea, *A History of the Inquisition of Spain,* Vol. II, New York 106, p. 29.

[2] *Vide* Part II, *Dellon's Account,* chap. XXIII, p. 37.

[3] Antonio Baião, *A Inquisição de Goa,* Vol. II, Correspondencia dos Inquisidores da India (1569-1630), Coimbra 1930.

[4] Baião, *op.cit.,* Vol. I, p. 53.

proceed against a governor and members of his family. In a letter dated November 20, 1589 written from Goa the Inquisitors Rui Sadrinho and Thomas Pinto report to the king that there was much laxity in the land especially at the time when ships from Europe were expected to arrive, when recourse was had to oracles in the temples of the mainland; and that it is common knowledge that even the governor Manuel de Souza Coutinho and his wife participated in such practices and had mystic dealings with Hindu sorcerers.[5] They also complain that the governor looks with little favour on matters relating to the Inquisition. In a subsequent letter to the king written on December 12, 1591, after the said governor had left India, it is stated that Diogo Lobo de Souza, Captain of Bardez and cousin of Manuel de Souza, had been arrested during the latter's tenure as governor, for consulting temples, sending them gifts and offering money and other assistance to enable their being housed on the mainland, for persuading and obliging Christians of the land to make contributions for the same purpose and for agreeing to and helping the performance of many Hindu ceremonies and sacrifices. The same letter also contains the information that Dona Ana Espanholim, wife of the said former governor, confessed at the monastery of S. Domingos before the Inquisitor Fr. Thomas Pinto that she had been very lax in seeking to foretell the future, consulting sorcerers and ordering magic practices. As punishment for these offences she was made to abjure *de levi* and fined 1000 *pardaos*. With the same letter two processes, one relating to the case against the said governor himself and the other to that against his son Heronimo de Souza, were sent to Portugal for final sentence, as it was felt that since they related to a person of noble family who had returned home after serving as governor, it would be better that the case should be decided in Portugal.[6]

Another remarkable incident of this nature was the conflict between viceroy D. Luis Mascarenhas, Conde de Alva, and Inquisitor Manoel Marques de Azevedo which arose sometime about 1755. The reasons for the differences were that the viceroy ordered that one Agostinho Ribeiro de Costa who had been arrested at the instance of the Inquisition should be released from

[5] Baião, *op. cit.*, Vol. II, p. 127.
[6] *Ibid.*, p. 186.

the prison *Tronco*, and that he permitted the celebration of the Hindu festival of *Shimagó* and allowed in the territories newly conquered by the Portuguese, erection of Hindu temples and open performance of Hindu rites and ceremonies. The conflict was resolved in an unexpected manner as a result of the murder of Conde de Alva in June1756 at Ponda, during a war with the Marathas. It was rumoured that the murder was committed by Portuguese soldiers.[7] It is not possible to say whether the differences of the viceroy with the Inquisitor directly or indirectly contributed to the murder.

Even members of religious orders renowned for their piety occasionally incurred the wrath of the Inquisition. A notable instance was the imprisonment by the Portuguese Inquisition of Padre Antonio de Vieira, a distinguished Jesuit who had the courage to espouse the cause of the New Christians and had earned the name of the Apostle of Brazil. H. C. Lea describes in the following passage the treatment meted out to him by the Portuguese Inquisition :

" Few members of the Society of Jesus at that time, were more distinguished than Antonio Vieira, who had earned the name of the Apostle of Brazil. He had long regarded the New Christians with compassion and had urged João IV not only to abolish confiscation but to remove the distinctions between them and the Old Christians. He had made enemies and the Inquisition readily undertook his punishment, his writings in favour of the oppressed were condemned as rash, scandalous, erroneous, savouring of heresy and well adapted to pervert the ignorant. After three years of incarceration, he was penanced in the audience-chamber of Coimbra, December 28, 1667, and his sympathy for the victims of the Holy Office was sharpened by his experience of its unwholesome prisons, where he tells us that five unfortunates were not uncommonly herded in a cell nine feet by eleven, where the only light came from a narrow opening near the ceiling, where the vessels were changed only once a week, and all spiritual consolation was denied."[8]

Another outstanding case is that of Father Ephraim of Nevers

[7] M. J. Gabriel de Saldanha, *Historia de Goa*, Vol. I, Bastorá 1925, p. 216.
[8] Lea, *op. cit.*, Vol. III, p. 284.

who was imprisoned by the Inquisition of Goa. Father Ephraim was a Frenchman who belonged to the order of Capuchins, a reform of the order of St. Francis, living in greater poverty and austerity than the others and going barefoot. Dellon in chapter XXXVII of his account,[9] describes how during one of the audiences the Inquisitors tried to lay a snare for him by asking him whether he defended the errors of Father Ephraim of Nevers, who, he well knew, had been arrested from invidious motives. The interesting case of father Ephraim has been described by Tavernier, renowned French Traveller of the 17th century, who devotes to it an entire chapter of his *Travels of India.* This chapter, which bears the caption " History of Father Ephraim, Capuchin, and how he was cast into the Inquisition of Goa ", is reproduced hereunder :

The case of Fr. Ephraim of Nevers

The Shaikh (the son-in-law of the king of Golkonda) was unable to induce the Rev. Father Ephraim to stay at Bhāgnagar... But the English managed so well that they attracted him to Madras... Madras is only half a league from St. Thomé, a small maritime town on the Coromandel coast fairly well built, and belonging at that time to the Portuguese.

Its trade was considerable, especially in cottons, and many artisans and merchants dwelt there, the majority of whom would have been very glad to settle with the English at Madras, but for the fact that there were opportunities at that time for the exercise of their religion in that place. But since the English built this Church and kept Father Ephraim, many of the Portuguese left St. Thome, attracted principally by the great care which this devout man took to instruct the people, preaching to them every Sunday and on all festivals, both in Portuguese and in the language of the country a thing which was very unusual while they dwelt at St. Thomé. Father Ephraim came from Auxerre, and was a brother of M. de Château des Bois, Counsellor of the Parliament of Paris, and he possessed a happy genius for all kinds of languages, so that in a short time he acquired both English and Portuguese in perfection. The ecclesiastics of St. Thomé, oberving that Father Ephraim enjoyed a high reputation, and attracted by his

[9] *Vide* Part II, p. 65.

teaching large numbers of their flock to Madras, conceived so much jealousy of him that they resolved to ruin him; and they made use of the following means to accomplish their object:— English and Portuguese being such close neighbours, they naturally had occasional differences, and generally both nations employed Father Ephraim to settle these, because he was a man of peace and of good sense, and knew both languages perfectly. One day the Portuguese purposely picked a quarrel and beat some English sailors, whose ship was in the St. Thomé roads. The English President thereupon demanding satisfaction for this insult, strife began to kindle between the two nations, and would have ruined all the trade of the country if the merchants on both sides had not set themselves to arrange the affairs, knowing nothing of the vile plot which certain persons were weaving to catch Father Ephraim. But all the mediation of these merchants availed nothing, and by the intrigues of the Portuguese ecclesiastics, it was so managed that the Father got mixed up in the matter, became the mediator, and undertook to conduct the negotiations between both sides a part which he very readily undertook. But he had no sooner entered St. Thomé than he was seized by ten or twelve officers of the Inquisition, who placed him in a small armed frigate, which at once set sail for Goa. They put irons on his feet and hands, and during a voyage of twenty-two days they never permitted him to land, although the majority of those on the frigate slept on shore nearly every night, it being the custom to sail from place to place along these coasts. On arrival at Goa,, they waited till dark to land Father Ephraim and conduct him to the house of the Inquisition, for they feared lest by landing him in the daytime the people might have wind of it, and make an attempt to release a person so venerated in all that part of India. The report spread however in many directions that Father Ephraim the Capuchin was in the hands of the Inquisition and as many people arrived daily at Surat from the Portuguese territories, we were among the first to receive the news, which amazed all the Franks residing there. Father Zenon, the Capuchin, who had formerly been a companion of Father Ephraim, was most surprised and most specially annoyed; and after consulting with his friends regarding the affair, he resolved to go to Goa at the risk of himself falling into the hands of the Inquisition. It was in truth a risk; for after a man is shut up in the Inquisition, if any one has the hardihood to speak for him to the Inquisitor, or to any member of his Council he is himself immediately placed in the Inquisition, and is regarded as more criminal than the person on whose behalf he desired to speak. Neither the Archbishop of Goa nor the Viceroy himself dare interpose, they being the only persons over whom the Inquisition has no power. But even should they do anything which gives offence, the Inquisitor and his Council write to Portugal, and if it be so ordered by the King and the Inquisitor General, when the answers arrive, proceedings are taken against these dignitaries, and they are remanded to Portugal.

On his arrival at Goa, Father Zenon was at first visited by some friends there, who, knowing the object of his journey advised him to be careful not to open his mouth on behalf of Father Ephraim, unless he wished to be sent to keep him company in the Inquisition. Every one knows the strictness of this tribunal and not only is it forbidden, as I have said, to speak for a prisoner, but moreover the accused is never confronted with those who give evidence against him, nor even allowed to know their names. Father Zenon perceiving that he was unable to accomplish anything at Goa, advised M. de la Boullaye to return to Surat, and entrusted to him 50 *écus* which he was to give at Paris to the widow of M. Forest who had died in India. Accordingly, he left for Surat by the first opportunity, and Father Zenon went straight to Madras to find out more exactly all that had passed in connexion with the arrest of Father Ephraim. When he had ascertained the treachery practised upon Father Ephraim at St. Thomé, he resolved to get to the bottom of it, and without the knowledge of the English President confided his plan to the captain in command of the fort, who, like the soldiers, was much enraged at the outrage which had been perpetrated on Father Ephraim. Not only did the captain strongly approve of Father Zenon's plan but he promised to give it his support and to back him in its execution. The father, by means of the spies whom he had placed in the country, ascertained that the Governor of S. Thomé went every Saturday, early in the morning to say his prayers in a chapel half a league from the town, situated on a small hill dedicated to the Holy Virgin. He caused three iron gratings to be placed on the window of a small room in the convent, with two good locks on the door and as many padlocks, and having taken all these precautions he went to the captain of the fort, an Irishman of great personal bravery, who kept promise he had made him to aid in the ambuscade which was laid for the Governor of S. Thomé. He himself headed thirty of his soldiers, and accompanying Father Zenon they all went out of the fort towards midnight, and concealed themselves till daylight in a part of the mountain upon which this chapel of the Holy Virgin was situated, where they could not be seen. The Governor of St. Thomé, according to his custom, did not fail to go to the chapel shortly after sunrise, and when he got out of his pallankeen and ascended the hill, which was rough, on foot, he was immediately seized by the Irish captain and his soldiers, who emerged from the ambuscade with Father Zenon, carried him off to Madras to the convent of the Capuchins, and imprisoned him in the chamber which had been prepared for him. The Governor, much surprised at finding himself carried off in this manner, protested strongly to Father Zenon, and threatened him with the resentment of the King of Portugal when he heard of this outrage against a Governor of one of his towns. This was his daily discourse during the time he was kept in the cell, and Father Zenon simply replied that he believed he was much more gently treated at Madras than Father Ephraim was in the Inquisition at Goa, whither he, the Governor, had sent him; that he had only to cause the Father to be brought back, and they would replace him at the foot of the hill where he had been seized with as much right as the others had to carry off Father Ephraim. However, for five or six days the St. Thomé road was crowded with people who came to beseech the English President to exercise his authority and release the Governor. But the President only replied that he was not in his hands, and that after their action towards Father Ephraim he could not in common justice compel Father Zenon to release a person who was one of the authors of the injury done to his companion. The President contented himself with asking the Father to have the goodness to permit his prisoner to dine at his table, promising to surrender him whenever he wished; this request he obtained easily, but was unable afterwards to keep his promise.

The drummer of the garrison, who was a Frenchman, and

a merchant of Marseilles named Roboli, who was then in the fort, two days after the Governor of St. Thomé had entered it, offered him their services to aid him to escape, provided that they were well rewarded ; this he promised them, and also that they should have a free passage on the first vessel sailing from Goa to Portugal. The agreement being made, on the following day the drummer beat the reveille at an earlier hour than usual, and with great vigour, and at the same time the merchant Roboli and the Governor, tieing sheets together, let themselves down by the corner of the bastion, which was not high. The drummer at the same time left his drum and followed them quickly, so that St. Thomé being only a good half league from Madras, they were all three inside it before anything was known of their departure. The whole population of St. Thomé made great rejoicings at the return of the Governor, and immediately dispatched a boat to Goa to convey the news. The drummer and the merchant Roboli set sail forthwith and when they reached Goa bearing the letters of the Governor of S. Thomé in their favour every convent and wealthy house made them presents, and even the Viceroy himself, Dom Philippe de Mascarenhas, treated them kindly, and invited them to embark on his vessel intending to take them to Portugal with him ; but all three, the Viceroy and the two Frenchmen, died at sea.

In the meantine the imprisonment of Father Ephraim made a great sensation in Europe. M. de Château des Bois, his brother, complained of it to the Portuguese Ambassador, who not feeling too sure of his position, wrote promptly about it to the King his master ; so that, by the first vessels which left for Goa, an order was sent that Father Ephraim should be released. The Pope also wrote saying that if he were not set free he would excommunicate all the clergy of Goa. But all these letters were of no avail, and Father Ephraim had only the King of Golkonda, who loved him and who had done all he could to induce him to remain at Bhāgnagar, to thank for his liberty. The King had learnt from him some mathematics, like his son-in-law the Arab Prince, who had offered to build a house and church for the Father at his own expense. This he had afterwards done for two Augustin clerics who had come from Goa. The King was then at war with the Raja of the Province of Carnatica, and his army was close to

S. Thome ; as soon therefore as he heard of the evil trick which the Portuguese had played on Father Ephraim he sent an order to Mir Jumla, the General of his troops, to lay siege to St. Thomé and to kill and burn all if he could not obtain a definite promise from the Governor of the place that in two months Father Ephraim would be set at liberty. A copy of the King's order was sent to the Governor, and the town was so alarmed that nothing was to be seen but boat after boat setting forth for Goa in order to urge the Viceroy to take measures for Father Ephraim's speedy release. He was accordingly set free, and messengers came to tell him on the part of the Inquisitor, that he might leave. But although the door was open to him he refused to quit the prison till all the clerics in Goa came in procession to bring him forth. This they promptly did, and after he came out he went to pass fifteen days in the Convent of the Capuchins, who are a kind of Recollects. I have heard Father Ephraim many times say what distressed him most during his imprisonment was to witness the ignorance of the Inquisitor and his council when they examined him, and he believed that not one of them had ever read the Holy Scriptures.[10]

Abbé Carré in the account of his travels describes the case of the saintly Bishop M. d'Hyeropollis, who had been sent to India by the Holy College of foreign missions with the authority of the Pope but without the permission of the king of Portugal. As a result, he incurred the hatred of the Portuguese who tried to humiliate him and made repeated attempts to kidnap him in order to bring him before the Inquisition of Goa. The relevant passage from Abbé Carré's book is given below :

" By travelling all the next day, 23rd, I reached the town of Bicholim in the evening. I stayed with the Bishop, M. d'Hyeropollis, who lives here as a rule. He has a fine church and a seminary, which he was having much trouble in keeping up, owing to the persecutions, not only of the Moors and enemies of our Holy Faith, but also of the Portuguese at Goa, who disliked him so much that there was no indignity or insult that they have not inflicted on him, without consideration of his position. This saintly prelate has suffered all this injury with angelic patience

[10] *Tavernier's Travels in India* (Translated by V. Ball), Vol. I, London 1925, pp. 176-184.

and humility. In the evening after prayers, this good bishop took me aside for a private conversation. He told me all the insults continually received from these Portuguese, who had conceived such a hatred against him that they had tried several times to kidnap him in order to bring him before the Inquisition at Goa. They proposed to send him to Portugal by the first ship for punishment, because (said these Portuguese) he had come from Rome, and been sent by the Holy College of Foreign Missions with the authority of the Pope, but without the permission of the king of Portugal whom they alone recognized as the supreme spiritual and temporal head in India.[11]

Bishop M. C'Hyeropollis referred to by Abbé Carré, as shown by Sir Charles Fawcett in the footnote to the above passage, is the same person as Bishop Matheus Castro who was born in a Brahmin family at Divar (Goa) in 1607. He died in Rome in 1679. The writer of "*A Pearl to India*" states that Archbishop Christovão de Sá had refused to ordain him on the ground that he was born in a Brahmin family :

"On one occasion a well qualified Brahmin named Mathew de Castro was presented to him for ordination by the Provincial of the Carmelites. Christovão de Sá replied that he refused on principle to ordain Brahmins and nothing could shake him from this decision."[12]

The following biographical note appears in *Biographia Goana*, a work printed in Bombay but never published :

"Bishop Mathews de Castro was not only Vicar Apostolic but also Inquisitor General, whose jurisdiction extended over all the missions entrusted to his care."[13]

Another interesting case is that of Father D. Nobili, an Italian Jesuit, who adopted the garb of a Hindu *Sanyasi*, styled himself as a "Romak Brahmin" and succeeded in attracting hundreds of Hindus of Madura and surrounding areas into the Christian fold. Archbishop de Sá desired to drag him before the Inquisition and punish him for having lapsed into idolatry. His plans, however, were defeated as a result of a papal brief which

[11] *The Travels of the Abbé Carré in India, op. cit.*, Vol. I, 1947, pp. 203-4.
[12] Vicent Cronin, *A Pearl to India*, London 1959, p. 205.
[13] *Biographia Goana*, Bombay, p. 0.

required that his case should be investigated by a round table conference which would include fellow archbishops and other theologians. The writer of *A Pearl to India* observes :

" What he wanted was to sit on his primatial throne, flanked by his two Inquisitors and pass sentence on a wretched priest who lapsed into idolatry. The brief was intolerable and derogatory to the Primatial dignity. Archbishop de Sá would not accept it. He ordered his Inqusitors to write at once to the Grand Inquisitor of Portugal insisting that Nobili be judged by the Inquisition and by the Inquisition only."[14]

The Manual of Regulations of the Holy Office contains detailed instructions for the selection of Inquisitors and rules of conduct for their guidance. All officers of the Inquisition had to be natives of Portugal, Old Christians of pure blood, without the least suspicion of the taint of the race of Moors, Jews or persons newly converted to Christianity. Qualifications, and previous experience necessary for appointment as Inquisitors are also carefully specified. In particular, it is laid down that such persons must be at least 30 years of age, must have worked as Deputies and shown evidence of prudence, learning and virtue in that capacity. The Inquisitors are enjoined to live with great honesty and modesty so as to deserve the respect of all, and to use their great authority only for the purposes for which it was conferred on them. They were also required to be very discriminating in the choice of persons with whom they would associate and to visit only persons known for their sobriety and good habits. It was specifically laid down that they should not write letters or send messages in the name of the judicial committee of the Holy Office as experience had shown that this endangered the authority of the Inquisition.[15] It is obvious that the object of these instructions was to insulate the Inquisitors from unhealthy pressures and influences which might raise suspicion of their integrity and impartiality and to protect them from temptations to abuse their power for worldly ends. There is evidence to show, however, that the power was frequently abused and the personal lives of the Inquisitors were marked by ostentation and luxury and at times moral depravity. It will be remembered that

[14] Vicent Cronin, *op. cit.*, p. 208.
[15] *Regimento do Santo Officio de Inquisiçam*, Livro I, Titulo 3.

Tavernier states that when the Inquisition seized anyone, his person was searched, the furniture and other effects found in his house were inventoried to be returned to him should he be found innocent, but as regards gold and silver and jewels, they were not recorded and were never seen again "being taken to the Inquisitor for the expense of the trial."[16] We have also quoted in Chapter III Pyrard's account of the Inquisition of Goa, in the course of which he states that persons were seldom arrested unless they were rich. Dellon, in chapter XXIII of his account, describes as follows the opportunities available to the Inquisitors for amassing wealth :

"In addition to the honour, and unbounded authority and appointments, annexed to the posts of all the Inquisitors, they derive very considerable emolument in two ways. One arises from the sale of the effects of the prisoners, in which, it any rare or valuable article should be comprised, the Inquisitors have but to send a servant to bid for it (and few would dare to offer a greater price), whereby things are often obtained by them, for the half of their real worth. The other means of profit is still more important : when the produce of a confiscation is remitted to the Royal Treasury, the Inquisitors have the power of sending warrants at their pleasure, and for any amount, to answer the charges and secret occasions of the Holy Office, which are instantly satisfied, without any one daring to inquire the particulars of these privy expenses. By these means, almost the whole of the seizures return into their hands."[17]

There is evidence to show that some Inquisitors also resorted to other expedients to extort money. It will be remembered for instance, that in chapter VIII we mentioned how an agent of the Inquisitor Frei Manoel da Assumpção received 6000 *Xerafins* from the wives of certain Hindus who had been arrested by the Inquisitor, with a promise to secure the release of their husbands.

Shocking evidence that the Inquisition of Goa had sunk to depths of moral depravity which, but for the unimpeachable source from which the information comes, one would have considered almost incredible, is published by Dr. Antonio Noronha, a former Chief Justice of the High Court of Goa, in his monograph

[16] *Tavernier's Travels in India, op. cit.*, p. 184
[17] *Vide* Part II, p. 87.

" The Hindus and the Portuguese Republic." This is an extract from an oration given by the Archbishop of Evora at the Cathedral Church of Lisbon in 1897, on the occasion of the tricentenary of the death of Padre Antonio Vieira, to whom we referred earlier in this chapter. The Archbishop remarked :

" The Inquisition was an infamous tribunal at all places. But the infamy never reached greater depths, nor was more vile, more black, and more completely determined by mundane interests than at the tribunal of Goa, by irony called the Holy Office. Here the Inquisitors went to the length of imprisoning in its jails women who resisted their advances, and after having satisfied their bestial instincts there, ordering that they be burnt as heretics."[18]

One of the important functions entrusted to the Inquisition was the censorship of books. In the Manual of Regulations of the Inquisition, among the categories against whom the Inquisition was required to institute proceedings is mentioned that of persons who possess and read prohibited books.[19] We have mentioned earlier a case in which a woman denounced her own husband to the Inquisition for having possessed books on Protestantism.[20] Special officers of the Inquisition appointed for dealing with its function of censorship were known as *Qualificadores*. Their main duty was to examine books before they were printed locally, as well as printed books brought from outside, to see that they contained nothing against Catholic faith or good customs. They maintained catalogues of banned books. They also visited bookshops a number of times every year and, if they found therein any books which were banned or which contained anything against the Catholic religion or customs, asked the booksellers to separate them from other books and not to dispose of them and reported the matter to the Inquisitors immediately to enable them to take necessary action. On the death of a person who owned a library, they visited his residence and examined the library.[21]

As stated above, before a book could be printed a licence to

[18] *A India Portuguesa*, Vol. II, Nova Goa 1923, p. 263.
[19] *Regimento do Santo Officio da Inquisiçam*, f. 12.
[20] *Vide* Chapter III, pp. 28-9
[21] *Regimento do Santo Officio da Inquisiçam*, Livro I, Titulo X, ff. 50-52.

print had to be obtained from the Inquisitors. Such licences are printed at the beginning of all books published in Goa in the seventeenth century in Marathi or in the local dialect.

All books written in Sanskrit and Marathi, whatever their subject matter, were seized by the Inquisition and burnt on the suspicion that they might deal with idolatry. It is probable that valuable non-religious literature dealing with art, literature, sciences, etc., was destroyed indiscriminately, as a consequence. These activities had been initiated in Goa even before the establishment of the Inquisition. For instance, there is a letter dated November 28, 1548, in which D. Fr. João de Albuquerque proudly reports his achievements in that direction.[22] This attitude of suspicion and hostility to literature extended also to European literature as will be seen from the following resolution passed by the 5th *Concilio Provincial* held in 1606 :

" This Sacred Council directs, under pain of excommunication *latae sententiae*, all the captains of the fleet, soldiers and Christians of any rank or condition residing in this state, if they come into possession of any book brought from Dutch or English ships, or those of any other foreign nation, navigating in these parts, and in whatever language the book may have been written, not to read it or give it others. They are enjoined to hand it over to the Ordinary or the Board of the Holy Inquisition, or to its Commissaries, or to the Dean, and in their absence to the Vicar or Rector of the Church of the place where the book came into their possession. The same censure is to be applied to the Commissaries and the Vicars, should they read the books even though the titles may appear pious and devout, for the very reason that, as is the way of heretics, under such titles a lot of false and pernicious doctrines is contained against the truth and the purity of the Holy Catholic Faith. They should, therefore, with all care and diligence hand such books over to the Board of the Holy Office for executing the order concerning forbidden books. Let this Decree be published in all the established churches of this Province and in places where the ministers of His Majesty inspect the personnel at the time the fleet is about to sail."[23]

[22] Frederico Diniz d'Ayala, *Goa : Antiga e Moderna*, Nova Goa 1927, pp. 73-4.

[23] A. K. Priolkar, *The Printing Press in India*, Bombay 1958, pp. 168-9.

Boxes containing Prohibited Books were carried in procession during *Auto da Fé* and burnt.[24]

Some of the Inquisitors were not content with the destruction of indigenous literature but wished also to exterminate the indigenous languages and to replace them with Portuguese. Cunha Rivara in his " *Historical Essay on Konkani Language* " writes :

" The Inquisition cannot be absolved from a large share in the persecution of the vernacular ; and what is more, a larger part in the ruin of the Portuguese Empire in Asia.

" But we confine ourselves to what concerns the language. The whole system of the Inquisition aimed not only at the extirpation of superstitious and idolatrous beliefs, but also of innocent usages and customs retaining even a trace of the Asiatic society, which existed previous to the conquest by the Portuguese. Consequently the language was involved in this general proscription.

" One Inquisitor with eighteen years of service in the Inquisition of Goa, proposed to His Majesty, in the year 1731, the following : ' The first and the principal cause of such a lamentable ruin (loss of souls) is the disregard of the law of His Majesty, D. Sebastião of glorious memory, and the Goan Councils, prohibiting the natives to converse in their own vernacular and making obligatory the use of the Portuguese language ; this disregard in observing the law, gave rise to so many and so great evils, to the extent of effecting irreparable harm to souls, as well as to the royal revenues. Since I have been though unworthy, the Inquisitor of this State, ruin has set in the villages of Nadorá (sic), Revorá, Pirná, Assonorá and Aldoná in the Province of Bardez ; in the villages of Cuncolim, Assolná, Dicarpalli, Consuá, and Aquem in Salsete ; and in the Island of Goa, in Bambolim, Curcá, and Siridão, and presently in the village of Bastorá, in Bardez. In these places some members of village communities, as aiso women and children have been arrested and others accused of malpractices ; for since they cannot speak any other language but their own vernacular, they are secretly visited by *Botos*, servants and High Priests of Pagodas who teach them the tenets of their

[24] *Regimento do Santo Officio da Inquisiçam*, f. 142.

sect and further persuade them to offer alms to the Pagodas and to supply other necessary requisites for the ornament of the same temples, reminding them of the good fortune their ancestors had enjoyed from such observances and the ruin they were subjected to, for having failed to observe these customs ; under such persuasion they are moved to offer gifts and sacrifices and perform other diabolical ceremonies, forgetting the law of Jesus Christ which they had professed in the sacrament of Holy Baptism. This would not have happened had they known only the Portuguese language ; since they being ignorant of the native tongue the *Botos*, *Grous* and their attendants would not have been able to have any communication with them, for the simple reason that the latter could only converse in the vernacular of the place. Thus an end would have been put to the great loss among native Christians whose faith has not been well grounded, and who easily yield to the teaching of the Hindu priests.'

"We do not know what to admire in such a proposal of the Inquisitor, his malice or foolishness. Undoubtedly it is the height of malice to affirm that Goan Councils had prohibited the natives to talk in their mother tongue, and had obliged them to speak the Portuguese language alone. It is foolishness to make people believe that through the vernacular alone could the *Botos* and other Hindu priests explain the tenets of their belief and sect with a view to convincing the native Christians.

"It will be clear from the reading of VIII and IX that council, far from forbidding the use of the vernacular, had rather recommended its use for the teaching of Christian doctrine."[25]

A printing press was established in Goa in 1556 and a large number of books were printed there until 1674. It is significant that none of these contain any reference to the activities of the Inquisition. The only reference I could find was an indirect one in a passage contained in an old *Purana*, popularly ascribed to Francisco Vaz de Guimarães, which was published for the first time in 1845 but composed much earlier. In this passage it is stated that many Christian converts do not conform to the teachings of their religion but secretly worship Hindu Gods in their

[25] Priolkar, *op. cit.*, pp. 207-9.

homes and, as a consequence, are taken to Goa year after year, obviously as prisoners of the Inquisition :

Murâda Christão âssunxim,
pâtiça nahim deta sudecharâxim,
anim pungitân henduâmchê deu,
âpulê gharim.
Hi vartâ nohê zuthi,
haixê carnito zana' tumim,
varsachê varsâ gonuiâ zâtâna,
gê henduamchê deu mânitâna.[26]

Detailed information which would provide an accurate idea of the activities of the Inquisition of Goa, such as, data relating to the number of cases tried, proportions of cases in which different types of sentences were imposed, the number of persons who died in its prisons before trials or during trials as a result of torture or otherwise, or were burnt at the stake, is unfortunately not available. In the *Biblioteca Nacional* of Lisbon there is a manuscript work called *Reportorio General de Inquisição de Goa* (General Calendar of the Inquisition of Goa) written by João Delgado Figueira, who worked as Promotor, Deputy and later as Inquisitor in the Inquisition of Goa. This deals with the activities of the Inquisition during the period 1561 to 1623 and states that during this period of 63 years 3,800 cases were tried by the Holy Office. Baião writes that during the period 1561 to 1774, 16,172 cases were tried by the Inquisition.[27] A list of the Acts of Faith celebrated by the Goa Inquisition, compiled from the *Reportorio* and other sources by Elkan Nathan Adler, corresponding member of the Royal Academy of History of Spain, is reproduced hereunder:

1562, Sept. 20 ; Nov. 15. 1563, June 27 ; Dec. 5. 1564, Oct. 27. 1565, Aug. 19 ; Dec. 23. 1566. Feb. 10 ; Dec. 22. 1567, June 15. 1568, Jan. 18 ; Jan. 28. 1569, July 17 1571, April 12. 1572, Oct. 12 ; 1574 May 18. 1575, Sept. 4. 1576, Oct. 28. 1577, Sept. 1. 1578, Aug. 17. 1579, Sept. 6. 1580, Dec. 4. 1581, Nov. 2. 1582, Dec. 14. 1585, Nov. 10. 1587, Sept. 13. 1590, Dec. 8. 1596, Dec. 8. 1600. 1601, Jan. 30. 1605. 1606, Nov. 19. 1607, Dec. 9.

[26] *Declaração Novamente Feita da muito dolorosa Morte e Paixão do Nosso Senhor Jesus Christo, Cantha* V, 57-8, Bombay 1845.
[27] Baião, *op. cit.*, vol. I, p. 293.

1610 Oct. 17. 1612 June 3. 1618 Nov. 18. 1623 Dec. 10. 1624. 1628 Feb. 7. 1635 Aug. 26. 1640 March 14. 1650 April 4. 1651 Dec. 3. 1653 Dec. 14. 1654 Mar. 27. 1655, Dec. 19. 1656, April 9; May 11, 12; Oct. 16. 1657, Mar. 16; Oct. 21. 1658, Oct. 6; Oct. 16. 1660, March 14. 1662, March 29. 1664 May 13. " Meza " i.e. auto in private. 1673 Dec. 1676 Jan. 12. 1685, Dec. 9. 1685 " Mezas " 1686, Jan. 10, " Meza ", July 21, 1687, Jan. 19. 1688, March 28. 1689 March 29; Dec. 11. 1690, Oct. 8. 1693 Nov. 1. 1697 April 21; Nov. 3. 1698 Dec. 14. 1700 March 27; March 28. 1701 Feb. 20, Sept. 4. 1703 Nov. 18. 1705 May 24. 1708 June 17. (1711 Nov. 22.) 1715 Oct. 27. 1716 June 7; Dec. 13. 1717 Sept. 5. 1718 June 19; Oct. 2. 1719 Sept. 15. 1722 Nov. 11. 1723 Nov. 14. 1725 Mar. 4; Nov. 11. 1726 Nov. 17. 1727 Nov. 23. 1730 Nov. 26. 1732 Jan. 13; Dec. 14. 1733 Jan. 3; June 21; July 21; Dec. 13. 1734 Sept. 5; 1736 Jan. 15; Aug. 16; Dec. 30. 1741 Dec. 17. 1742 Dec. 23. 1744 Jan. 19. 1745 Dec. 5. 1747 Dec. 10. 1749 March 25. 1750 Dec. 6. 1752 Jan. 9. 1753 May 27. 1754 Aug. 18. 1755 Dec. 14. 1756 Aug. 18. 1757 May 15. 1758 Nov. 12. 1761 Feb. 1. 1763 May 13. 1764 May 13. 1765 March 17. 1765 10 " Mezas ". 1766 Sept. 21. 1768 May 29. 1769 May 7. 1771 Febr. 3. 1773. Feb. 7.[28]

Process No. 15·028 in the records of the Inquisition of Lisbon is a list of the prisoners who participated in the Act of Faith celebrated on January 12, 1676, of whom Dellon was one. Baião, in the first volume of his book on the Inquisition of Goa gives the following synopsis of this list :

Men : Deceased who were absolved 2; Persons absolved 2; Infidel persons 13; Persons who would not abjure 6; For sodomy 1; First abjuration *de levi* 9; Second abjuration 10; Persons who abjured *de vehemente* 4; First abjuration in form 10; second abjuration in form 10; Third abjuraton in form 6; Deceased received 3.

Women : Deceased who were absolved 2; persons absolved 2; Infidel persons 6; Persons who abjured *de levi* 5; Persons who

[28] Elkan Nathan Adler, *Auto de Fé and Jews*, Oxford University Press, Oxford 1908.

abjured *de vehemente* 6; First abjuration in form 8; Second abjuration in form 6; Deceased received 8; Relaxed in person 2; Relaxed in effigy 4.[29]

Some other lists of this type of the prisoners of the Inquisition of Goa are found in the records of the Inquisition of Lisbon.

The Inquisition of Goa was abolished for the first time during the regime of D. José I in 1774 when the national policies were being guided by the liberal minister Marquez de Pombal. The suggestion that the Inquisition of Goa be abolished emanated from the Inquisitor General Cardinal Cunha. He pointed out that the Inquisition was established at a time when Portugal had vast colonial possessions and carried on a prosperous trade in the East. These had since then been lost almost wholly and in recognition of this change the viceroy had been replaced by a *Capitão Geral* and a *Chanceler Ouvidor* and the High Court by three *Juizes de Fora.* In the Portuguese colony of Brazil, even in cities where High Courts existed, only Commissaries of the Inquisition were appointed. After consulting the *Conselho Geral,* he had therefore, come to the view that in the present circumstances it would be illogical to continue to have a Tribunal for the limited area of Goa, inhabited mainly by Hindus and infidels outside the pale of the Church. The suggestion was approved by the king on April 6, 1773.[30] On February 8, 1774 the Inquisitor General ordered the Inquisition of Goa to release all prisoners, whether already sentenced or under trial, to place all the incomplete processes in boxes and send them to the *Conselho Geral* by the first available ship, to hand over cash to the Board of Royal Revenues and houses and movable property to the governor, and to hand over the secret archives to the Commissary. Marquez de Pombal on February 10, 1774 sent the relevant order of the Inquisitor General to the Governor of Goa and ordered that it should be acted upon promptly and effectively, firmly ignoring any attempts of the Inquistors to postpone or delay its execution.[31]

Soon thereafter the death of D. José I in 1778 and the succession of Maria I, drove Pombal from power and there was a complete change in the political climate of Portugal. As a result we find

[29] Baião, *op. cit.*, Vol. I, p. 435.
[30] *Ibid.*, p. 372.
[31] *Ibid.*, p. 374.

the same Inquisitor General Cunha, who had himself proposed the abolition of the Inquisition in 1773, clamouring for its reinstatement on the ground that Christian religion in India was in peril. He pointed out that incontestable evidence had shown that soon after the extinction of Inquisition, Hindu rites were being openly practised, Hindu temples erected and there was an imminent danger that the native converts would revert to their old practices and conversion of others would be rendered extremely difficult, if not impossible. Opinions of some of the old officials of the Inquisition of Goa were obtained. In his report dated February 28, 1778, José Antonio Ribeiro da Mota, who had been an Inquisitor in 1774, pleaded for its re-establishment on the following grounds :

(*i*) The people of Goa do not speak Portuguese and, as a consequence never acquire an adequate conception of Christianity and Portuguese culture nor rational love for Portuguese government and religion. Hence the effect of the very efficient schools of Christian doctrine in Goa as also of the other corrective and educative activities of the Inquisition was very shortlived. It is therefore necessary that the Inquisition should be functioning continuously and permanently.

(*ii*) Since the extinction of Inquisition the Hindus who had been restrained in the practice of their religion through fear of and great respect for the Inquisition have been practising their religion openly and bad Christians who were in hiding have come out into the open. Soon after the abolition of the Inquisition, he himself saw innumerable Hindus not only from the Portuguese territories but also from the neighbouring areas, gathered in Goa to worship at a temple which is traditionally believed to exist inside a famous tank, very deep and constructed under a waterfall in a cocoanut garden near the Church of Trinity; and the whole city resounded with their chants and music.

(*iii*) A Commissary of the Holy Tribunal, without the respect and the punitive machinery of the Holy Tribunal, would be inadequate for the task. He could at best find time to take down denunciations and forward them to Portugal and it would be inconvenient to send the accused to Portugal for being corrected or indoctrinated by the Inquisition of Lisbon.[32]

[32] *Ibid.*, pp. 387-390.

Manuel Marques de Azevedo, another old officer of the Inquisition of Goa, also favoured the re-establishment of the Inquisition. In his reply he refers to "the vague voice of complaint of the rigor of the Inquisition" raised by "an impenitent heretic" in a publication in the French language which had been accepted as true by the public and even by some good Catholics in Portugal.[33] This is an obvious reference to Dellon's account of the Inquisition of Goa, and indicates how it contributed to the ultimate abolition of the Inquisition by drawing public attention to the injustice and cruelty of its procedures.

In April 1778 the Inquisition of Goa was revived but its procedures were in future to conform to a new Manual of Rules and Regulations which was to replace the old Manual prepared by the Inquisitor General D. Francisco de Castro. In a letter dated April 4, 1778 the Inquisitor General directs the Inquisitors to carry their work with moderation as prescribed in the new Manual "seeking the conversion of the Infidels and sinners with more sweetness and suavity than rigour." The Inquisitors were also instructed to submit all sentences of relaxation of the accused to the secular power to the *Conselho Geral* for being confirmed and moderated, even though the accused or their Procurators did not appeal against these sentences. It may be mentioned that a policy of moderation had been laid down for the Inquisition of Portugal in 1774, the year in which the Inquisition of Goa was first abolished. "In 1774 a new *Regimento* was issued by the Inquisitor-General, Cardinal da Cunha, in the preface of which the Jesuits are accused of having perverted the forms of procedure, causing all the evils with which it had afflicted the land. The new code removed many of these abuses of the old and king José in the decree approving it, repeated the accusation of the Jesuits, holding them responsible for the ferocious and sanguinary corruptions, incompatible with the principles of natural reason and religion, which had rendered the Inquisition a horror to all Europe and had created within the monarchy an independent and autocratic body of ecclesiastics."[34]

The revived Tribunal continued to exist in a moribund condition for over thirty years. Available documentary evidence

[33] *Ibid.*, p. 391.
[34] Lea, *op. cit.*, vol. III, pp. 310-11.

indicates that most of the accused during these years were sentenced to spiritual penances. On May 2, 1801, the governor reported that although the moderation of the present tribunal had caused people to forget the terrors which in the past had led to the emigration of innumerable traders from Goa, during his tenure of office in India of 19 years, he had not come across a single occasion on which Inquisition had to deal with a dangerous apostate heretic and usually it dealt with only persons of most abject condition. He therefore suggested that the tribunal be abolished and replaced by a Commissary appointed by the Inquisitor General. Ground was thus prepared for the final abolition of the Inquisition of Goa.

In a commercial treaty with Great Britain dated February 19, 1810, the Portuguese government accepted the principle of permitting in Goa and its dependencies free tolerance of any and all religions. As a consequence Conde de Linhares on November 2, 1811 informed the British Minister Plenipotentiary that orders for the abolition of the Holy Tribunal would be issued during the next monsoon. On June 16, 1812, the Prince Regent informed the viceroy, Conde de Sarzedas, that he had decided to abolish the Inquisition of Goa for all time and that the principle of tolerance of all cults should be recognised.[35] The royal orders were promptly complied with.

I propose to conclude this Chapter with a brief discussion of the historical role of the Inquisition.

Portuguese historians are generally agreed that the Inquisition contributed in a large measure to the decline of the Portuguese power in India. Cunha Rivara writes :

" The Inquisition cannot be absolved from a large share in the persecution of the vernacular ; and what is more, a larger part in the ruin of the Portuguese Empire in India."[36]

Portuguese statesmen had foreseen that this would be the inevitable consequence of the activities of the Inquisition, and warned the king from time to time. As a remarkable instance of this, I would like to mention a letter addressed to the king on

[35] Baião. *op. cit.*, Vol. I, p. 415.
[36] Priolkar, *op. cit.*, p. 207.

December 19, 1729 by viceroy João Saldanha da Gama. The opening paragraph of this letter runs as follows :

" All the ruin of this State consists visibly in the lack of commerce,which lack arises from two reasons ; first, the horror with which the merchants, who are only Hindus or Muslims, view the proceedings of the Holy Office, not only on account of the diabolic passion with which they feel their rites have been vilified ; but also on account of what they suffer in its prisons where they elect to die by not changing their custom of not eating or drinking in front of the Christians nor any viands prepared by hands of persons not belonging to their caste; and as the castes are many, it is not possible to provide separate prisons for different castes. The other reason is the violence of imprisonment, of which I gave an account to Your Majesty."

The viceroy proceeds to add that these merchants appreciate the justice and equity of the Portuguese laws and are aware of the violence from which they frequently suffer in the territories of both the Asiatic and other European rulers. Yet, owing to the fear of the Inquisition they prefer to migrate to the neighbouring territories and man the factories and commerce of the English and the French. They continue to long to return to the Portuguese territories and would agree to do so on condition that they are not punished by the Holy Office, if they perform their rites behind closed doors, without offence to the public and without the attendance of Christians ; and also that the Holy Office does not admit as witnesses against them persons of their castes who denounce them out of malice and spite. The viceroy proceeds :

" These are the conditions under which all the merchants offer to return to the dominions and forts of Your Majesty with their ships and their families. I do not know the law by which the Inquisition can take cognisance of the offences of persons who never were Catholics and I see that on account of the excessive number of persons of this quality who have been imprisoned, the entire province of the north is depopulated, the admirable factories of Thana lost, which at present are beginning to be established at Bombay..."[37]

[37] Cunha Rivara, *Ensaio Historico*, *op. cit.*, pp. 346-8 , (Doc. 50).

Another significant document bearing on the same point is a letter addressed to the king by the same viceroy on January 18, 1727, in connection with a proposal that the Portuguese should buy back the island of Bombay from the English. In an enclosure to this letter, the viceroy estimates that the island yields a revenue of about 1,60,000 *Xerafins* but proceeds to add :

" I must add a warning that the major part of the revenues depend on the commerce and traffic which at present exists in the said island in conjunction with the liberty of conscience which is observed there."

Cunha Rivara, editor of *Archivo Portuguez Oriental* in which this document is published, brings out its significance in the following note :

" This document, which is of considerable interest to the history of Bombay, also shows that the government of Portugal at this time considered it possible to buy the island from the English ; and above all it is remarkable for the good sense with which the viceroy indicates to the Court of Lisbon the harm which has been caused in India as a result of the persecution of the infidels by the Holy Office, and the advantages which have accrued to the English in Bombay as a result of the liberty of conscience."[38]

In Chapter VIII we have seen how the Indians who had embraced Christianity lacked the capacity even to undertake government jobs which the Portuguese were anxious to give them, and did not possess the necessary knowledge and ability to carry on commerce. Most of them had become Christians to secure the privileges and material advantages which conversion brought and it was natural that they should prefer a life of comfort and ease to one of enterprise and hard work. These converts could not therefore take the place of the Hindus and Muslims who had been driven away by the terror of the Inquisition.

In the first volume of his work on the Inquisition of Goa, Baião reproduces in full an anonymous manuscript, apparently written soon after the reinstatement of the Inquisition in 1778, copies of which are available in the *Biblioteca de Ajuda* and the *Biblioteca Nacional* of Lisbon. The writer, in the light of an

[38] Cunha Rivara, *op. cit.*, Fasc. VI, suppl. ii, pp. 287-292.

analysis of the historical role of the Inquisition of Goa, concludes that interests of religion, church as well as of state demand its total abolition. It will be interesting to review briefly some of the arguments advanced by this anonymous writer.

The writer points out how at one time the Portuguese dominated the commerce of the East and were the masters of an extensive empire. This empire soon dwindled to Goa, Daman and Diu in India and Macau in China and, in his opinion, the cause of this misfortune was indisputably the Inquisition. He states that D. João III had agreed to the establishment of the Inquisition in Goa on condition that it should concern itself only with the Christian population and that the others should be permitted perfect liberty of conscience. He proceeds :

"The condition subject to which king D. João III admitted the Inquisition in Goa was ignored soon after his death ; the cult of other religions was no longer tolerated ; the attendance of merchants diminished appreciably and commerce began gradually to extinguish ; even the natives of the land started to emigrate ; the Portuguese who had settled in India sought means of subsistence in foreign dominions ; there were no people for defence but Manuel Severim de Faria and other writers state that more than 30,000 Portuguese served in the armies of the enemies and in the dominions of the neighbouring princes. The peoples of Ceylon were treated with great barbarity. The tombs of the emperors of China in the island of Calainpni were pillaged. The temples on the Coast of Mohatos were razed and those who came to weep over the ruins of their temples were hanged. The customs of the Portuguese degenerated into a mixture of avarice, cruelty and devotion. The kings of Portugal could no longer touch the product of the tributes, which more than 150 princes of the East used to pay them ; these tributes, receipts of the customs and taxes were not available for the maintenance of the fortresses and necessary armament of the navy. The defenders of the Portuguese establishments were born of Avarice and did not possess the daring of their fathers. Within a short time, the Portuguese under the pretext of religion, came to be the scourge and horror of the peoples."

The writer points out that in the Portuguese dominions the Inquisition and the secular government, two equally powerful bodies, worked independently for ends which were frequently opposed to each other and could not collaborate for the good of the state. He gives some instances to illustrate how the political aims of the government were at variance with those of the Inquisitors and points out that such instances could easily be multiplied.

Referring to the effect of the Inquisition on commerce he writes :

" The Portuguese held the navigation of India for the purpose of trade. The Inquisition and commerce are incompatible.

"Commerce necessitates that people of different nations should come together more often and that they should be permited to practice their cults publicly, since religion is the bond which holds men together.

" The Inquisition divides, puts men to flight and terrorises them, since it is based on intolerance. Had it been established in London and Amsterdam these cities would have been deserted and miserable today. When Philip II wished to introduce it in the provinces of Flanders, the interruption of the commerce was one of the main causes of the revolution.

"France and Germany happily were saved from the scourge. They had horrible wars of religion. These ended but the Inquisition once established remained for all time in Portugal and in India."

The writer points out that the establishment of the Inquisition of Goa was followed by that of the convents of various religious orders which are always its satellites and that one traveller noticed 60 convents in which more than 20,000 friars were fed, not counting the Jesuits. The commerce of Goa was ultimately drawn into these convents and brought religion into disgrace. The clergy received an unlimited number of ships without awaiting permission of the king and enriched themselves. The writer expresses the view that while abolishing the Inquisition steps should also be taken to curb the growth and activities of these convents also.[39]

[39] Baião. *op. cit.*, Vol. I, p. 398.

Another consequence of major historical significance which resulted from the methods and activities of the Inquisition was the profound misunderstanding of the nature of Christianity which they implanted in the Indian mind. The intolerance, ruthlessness, cruelty and terror which characterised its activities were far removed from the spirit of the Christian Gospels with its emphasis on compassion and love and it was only natural that its victims should have drawn the inference that the Christian God in whose name these activities were carried on was a primitive deity of vengeance and wrath.

Ill. No. 1. **Standard of the Goa Inquisition, bearing the image of St. Dominic, founder of the Inquisition.**

Part II

ACCOUNTS GIVEN BY DELLON AND BUCHANAN OF THE INQUISITION AT GOA

DELLON'S
ACCOUNT OF THE INQUISITION
AT
GOA

Reprinted from the English translation printed by Joseph Simmons, Queen Street, Hull, in 1812 for I. Wilson, Lowgate. The original French copy from which the translation was made, was printed at Paris in 1684. The translator omitted chapters 3, 4, 5, 6, 7, 8, 42 and 43 as he thought their inclusion "would tend only to increase the size and expense of the book, if he retained the account of the different places visited by M. Dellon."

ADVERTISEMENT

By the Author

IT is but too common to find books whose pompous titles promise a great deal, but which, deceiving the reader's expectation, contain anything but what they profess. A different method has been adopted in the present work; and those who will take the trouble to peruse it will confess, that the title inadequately describes the contents.

I have confined myself to giving a faithful relation of what I have observed in the Inquisition, without interrupting it by many remarks; leaving my readers at liberty to make them for themselves. Those who have some slight knowledge of the Holy Office, will have no hesitation to believe all that I relate, and that I have not exaggerated anything; and, however extraordinary the proceedings and formalities of the Inquisition may appear, the reader may be assured that I have stated nothing but what is strictly true.

I do not pretend to censure the Inquisition itself; I am even willing to admit that the institution may be good; and it is certain that in those places where it originated, so much severity has not been exercised as in Spain and Portugal, and in the countries dependent on those crowns where it has been planted; but like all human establishments, which, though pure in design, are subject to relaxation and abuse, it is not surprising that these have also found their way into the tribunals of the Holy Office.

It is then the abuse only, of which I complain; yet the inquisitors who affect such profound secrecy as to everything respecting their tribunals, may be displeased at the liberty of exposing matters the concealment of which so materially concerns them; but, besides that the disclosure may, if they choose, be advantageous to themselves, I have considered it my duty no longer to withhold from the public a communication which must be of the highest utility to it; in fact, it is important that those who, from curiosity or avocations, reside in places where the Holy Office exercises its jurisdiction, should be informed what they ought to avoid or to do, in order to elude its power, and to prevent the experience of a misfortune like that which is the subject of this narrative.

CHAPTER I

The motives of giving this account to the public.

EVERY one knows in general what is meant by the Inquisition; that it is established in certain places, as Italy, Spain, Portugal, and the greatest part of the countries which are dependent upon them; and that the judges execute a system of jurisprudence, unknown to the tribunals, with extreme rigour over the people under their power. It is also understood that the exercise of this severity is not equal nor general; as the Inquisition in Spain is more severe than that in Italy, and less so than that in Portugal and its colonies. The maxims of this unprecedented jurisprudence, their examination, and many of their results, may be found in several publications; but I know of no one who has dared to speak of what passes under the secrecy of the tribunal. Its officers are too deeply interested in maintaining its jurisdiction, to withdraw the veil; and as to those who, having had transactions with them, are acquainted with their practices, and may have reason to be dissatisfied with them, the dread of the horrid tortures inflicted on those convicted of breaking the oath of secrecy imposed before their liberty is restored, renders the mysteries of the Inquisition so impenetrable, that it is almost impossible ever to learn the truth, without being so unfortunate as to be conducted into its prisons, and thus acquiring experimental knowledge; or from the information of one who has happily not sunk under that misfortune, and who, when enclosed in the frightful solitudes of the Holy Office, must have carefully noted all that occurred during his detention, and after his liberation can relate in safety what he has suffered and observed.

These various reasons operate to prevent many persons from being acquainted with the transactions of this formidable tribunal. And as, next to the duty we owe to God, we have none more incumbent than that of serving our neighbour, and more especially the public, I conceive myself bound to present it with a recital of my sufferings, and observations in the prisons of the Inquisition; to which I shall subjoin what I have been told by persons worthy of credit, whom I have known intimately, both during the period of my incarceration and since my release.

I have long hesitated as to the publication of this account; for eight years have elapsed since my return to France, and upwards of four since the account was written. I was afraid to offend the Holy Office and to break my oath; and my apprehension was increased by some pious but timid people, who entertained similar sentiments. Others equally religious, but whom I thought more enlightened, afterwards convinced me, that it was important to the public in many respects to be thoroughly instructed as to this tribunal, and that the relation might even be serviceable to the gentlemen of the Holy Office, if they knew how to profit by it, and still more so to those who have the power to regulate its proceedings, and restrain its jurisdiction: and that with regard to an oath, so unjustifiably extorted as that exacted by the Inquisition, under the dread of being burnt, general utility was a sufficient dispensation to the conscience of the party taking it, and consequently imposed a sort of obligation upon him to communicate what he knew.

Such are the motives which have induced me to withhold, and at length to publish, this account; and if the retention has deprived the world of a particle of useful information, it will at least excuse me from the charge of precipitation, and prove that the recital is not influenced by the ill-usage I have sustained.

It remains only to observe, that what I have to say of the Inquisition of Goa, ought to be understood of those of Portugal and Spain; for, though the latter is less cruel than the two others, inasmuch as the public executions, called Acts of Faith, are less frequent in that country; and though ignorance is more prevalent in the Indies than in Portugal; yet it may be inferred from a narrative which appeared in the Gazette of France of the 22nd of August 1680, that the same spirit, the same rules, and the same rigour direct all the executions of the Inquisition in each of those countries; since there are circumstances there stated even more horrible than those of the Act of Faith in which I bore a part.

CHAPTER II

Ostensible causes of my imprisonment.

I was staying at Damaun, a town in the East Indies, in possession of the Portuguese, to rest from the fatigues I had endured in various voyages, and to recruit myself for the more ample gratification of my passion for travelling, but where I had hoped to find repose, I encountered the commencement of trouble infinitely greater than those which I had previously borne.

An unfounded jealousy imbibed against me by the governor of Damaun was the true cause of the prosecutions I have suffered from the ministers of the Inquisition. It may easily be supposed that this was not alleged in the accusation brought against me; but, to serve the revenge of the governor, other pretexts were used, and the means at length contrived to banish me from the Indies, in which I might else have passed the remainder of my life.

It must be allowed that though the avowed grounds might be unsatisfactory to persons instructed in the faith and the truth, they were quite sufficient with a people actuated by such prejudices and principles as the Portuguese; in which light they appeared to be so plausible, that it was not until the conclusion of the affair that I discovered the real motives of my arrest.

The first opportunity which I gave to my enemies to resort to the Inquisition for my ruin, was a conversation with an Indian priest, a Theologian of the order of St. Dominic:—But, before I proceed, I ought to say, that though my conduct might not be entirely conformable to the sanctity of the religion in which I was baptized, I have ever been attached to the faith of my ancestors, that is, to the Catholic, Apostolic and Roman Church; and that God hath endowed me with more respect for its doctrines, than the generality of Christians seem to feel towards them. I have always delighted in hearing and reading, and never read anything with more enthusiasm than the Holy Scriptures, as well the Old as the New Testament, which I usually carried about my person. I had taken pains to acquire a knowledge of scholastic theology, because in extensive travels all descriptions of men, of every religion and sect, are to be met with ; and I disputed freely with Heretics and Schismatics. I possessed several books upon the subject, and had received much information, both from discourse and study, during the leisure afforded by my voyages, and my residence in various parts of India. I therefore conceived that I was able to enter the lists with even professed Theologians, and innocently fell into the snare with this priest. I lodged with the Dominicans, at their pressing invitation, and we lived together in great kindness and familiarity. I had even rendered them services on several occasions, to prove my gratitude for the honour they had done me, and the friendship that they testified. We frequently entered into conversation, and that which I had with the priest I have named, was upon the effects of baptism. We agreed upon the three kinds which the Catholic Church acknowledges ; and it was merely for the sake of argument, and not from doubt, that I proposed to deny the efficacy of that which is called *Flaminis* ; and to support my opinion, I adduced the passage, "*Except a man be born of water and of the spirit, &c.*" (John III. 5). I had scarcely ceased speaking when the good father withdrew without making any reply, as if he had been called away by some urgent business, and, as it appears, went to denounce me to the Commissary of the Holy Office. I was often afterwards in his company, and as he shewed no coolness towards me, I was far from thinking him unfriendly.

I have frequently been where little cabinets, on which are painted the figures of the Holy Virgin, or some other saint, have been carried round. The Portuguese are accustomed to salute the image, and those who are devoted to the fraternity place their alms in the box. Every person is at liberty to give or not ; but the kiss cannot be dispensed with, without offending the assistants. I was then only twenty-four years of age, and had not all the prudence which a person ought to have who lives amongst strangers, to whose customs he should conform as much as possible ; and as I had not witnessed these ceremonies before, I sometimes refused to receive and kiss the cabinet,—whence it was concluded, (surely too rashly) that I despised the image, and was consequently heretical.

I once happened to be at the house of a Portuguese gentleman, whose son was to be bled for some indisposition ; and I observed that the youth had an ivory image of the Holy Virgin in his bed, which he reverenced much, and often kissed and addressed himself to it. This mode of worshipping image is usual amongst the Portuguese, and gave me some disturbance ; because, being misinterpreted by the Heretics, they are thereby more than by any other reason prevented from returning to the Church. I told the youth that if he did not take care, his blood would spill upon the image ; and, on his replying that he could not part with it, I intimated that it would embarrass the operation. He then reproached me by saying, that the French were Heretics, and did not worship images. To which I answered, that we ought to honour them ; and that if we might be allowed to use the word " *Worship* ", it could be with reference to those of our Saviour alone, whilst the adoration related to the person only represented by them ; and I quoted the Council of Trent, session 25.

About the same time, it chanced that one of my neighbours came to me, and seeing a crucifix at the head of my bed, said, " If you should happen to bring any female home with you sir, do not forget to cover this image !" " How !" said I, " do you think it is possible to hide ourselves from God ; and, you like dissolute women after locking up their rosaries and relics, believe you may abandon yourself without delinquency to all sorts of excess ? Pray, sir, entertain more elevated sentiments of the deity, and do not fancy that a slender veil can conceal our sins from the eyes of God, who clearly penetrates every secret of our hearts. Is this crucifix more than a piece of ivory ?"

Here we ended ; and my neighbour, on retiring, acquitted himself of his supposed duty, by denouncing me to the Commissary of the Inquisition ; for it is proper to state, that every person resident in places subject to the Holy Office is obliged, under pain of the greater excommunication, reserved to the Grand Inquisitor, to denounce, within thirty days, whatever he has heard or witnessed on matters within the cognizance of the tribunal; and because many do not fear the penalty, or doubt whether they have incurred it ; in order to oblige the people to implicit obedience to this command, the inquisitors have declared, that those who fail in making this denunciation within the time prescribed, shall be reputed guilty, and punished as if they had themselves committed the crime they have not revealed. The consequence of which is, that friends betray their friends, fathers their children, and children, through zeal without discretion, forget the duty which God and nature impress upon them towards those from whom they derive existence.

The obstinacy with which I objected to wear a rosary contributed to confirm the belief of my heresy, no less than my refusal to salute the images. But what tended more than anything to my imprisonment and condemnation was, that being in a company where moral justice was treated of, I said, "that it deserved rather the term of injustice; since man, judging from appearances which are often deceptious, was liable to make inequitable decisions; and that God, only knowing things as they are, he alone could be called truly just." Some one present observed "that, generally speaking, what I had said was true; but a distinction was to be made;—for if true justice was not to be found in France, they had the advantage of a tribunal whose decrees were not less just, nor less infallible than those of Jesus Christ." Well knowing that he alluded to the Inquisition, I asked, if he thought the inquisitors less human, or less subject to their passions than other judges? "Do not answer me in that manner," replied the defender of the Holy Office; "if the inquisitors composing the tribunal are infallible, it is because the Holy Ghost perpetually dictates their decisions." I could not long endure a discourse which appeared to me to be so irrational; and to prove to him by example that the inquisitors were anything but what he represented them to be, I related to him the adventures of Father Ephraim de Nevers, a Capuchin, and Apostolic Missionary in the Indies, who, as M. de la Boulaye le Gou informs us in his Travels, had been arrested by the Inquisition from pure malice about seventeen years before, and had been confined and ill-treated for a length of time; and I concluded by telling him, that I did not doubt that this priest was more virtuous and more enlightened than those who had caused him to be immured in a prison, without permission even to repeat his breviary. I concluded by saying, that I thought it was fortunate for France that this severe Tribunal had not been introduced there, and most happy for myself that I was not subject to its jurisdiction. This conversation was exactly reported to the Father Commissary; and, added to what I had broached before, ultimately occasioned the process against me.

(Titles of the Chapters omitted in the translation).

CHAPTER III

A concise description of the Cape de Verde, the Cape of Good Hope, and the Isle of Bourbon.

CHAPTER IV

Description of the Isle of Dauphing or St. Lawrence.

CHAPTER V

Departure from the Isle of Dauphing for the Indies. Description of Mosambique, the Isle of Socotora and the Red Sea.

CHAPTER VI

Containing an account of what is remarkable at Surat.

CHAPTER VII

Concerning the different kingdoms of Malabar, between Ceylon and Cape Camorin and Goa.

CHAPTER VIII

An abridged description of the city of Goa, Chaoul, Basseen, Damaun, and other small towns.

CHAPTER IX

Visit to the Commissary of the Inquisition, to prefer my own accusation, and request his advice.

NOTWITHSTANDING the inviolable secrecy which the Inquisition exacts upon oath, from all who approach its tribunal, some rumour reached me of the depositions made against me; and the dread of falling into the hands of the Holy Office, impelled me to go to the Commissary, from whom I expected counsel and protection, because I had been introduced to him by persons of respectability, and he had always pretended friendship to me from the time of my arrival at Damaun.

I related to him ingenuously, and step by step, what had occurred; and then requested he would instruct me how I should behave myself in future: assuring him that I had no bad intention, that I was ready to correct myself, and to retract whatever I might have advanced which he deemed to be improper.

The good father confessed that my proceedings had offended many, that he was convinced that my intention had not been bad, and that there was not even in what I had said anything positively criminal; but he advised me, nevertheless, to accommodate myself a little to the habits of the people, and to speak less freely of such subjects; and particularly respecting images, which I had repeatedly declared, and had attempted to prove by reference to the scriptures and the fathers, ought not to be worshipped; that the people, it was true, were led away by some slight errors, which passed for genuine religion, but that it did not become me to undertake to correct and reform them.

I thanked the Commissary for his good advice, and left him with much satisfaction; because I knew that, being my own accuser, before I was convicted, I could not, by the laws of the Inquisition, be further charged. I was also extremely delighted with the justice and integrity of this good father, who not thinking me culpable, had freely given me directions how to conduct myself with such caution for the future, as not to give occasion for the slightest shadow of suspicion.

CHAPTER X

Containing the real causes of my detention, and the manner of my arrest.

ALTHOUGH what I have stated in the preceding Chapters was more than sufficient for my destruction, according to the maxims of the Inquisition, and the customs of the country; matters would not have proceeded either so far, or so hastily, if the governor of Damaun, Manuel Furtado de Mendoza, had not been instigated by the jealousy to which I have alluded. His dissimulation was such, that he appeared to be one of my best friends, though secretly pressing the Commissary of the Holy Office to write to the Inquisition at Goa, to communicate to them the expressions I had used; being determined not to suffer the opportunity to escape, which I had inadvertently afforded him, of making sure of me, and driving me from Damaun for ever. The cause of the governor's jealousy was, the frequent but innocent visits which I had paid to a lady whom he admired, (and by whom he was truly beloved, which I then knew not,) and, as he judged from appearances only, he imagined I was more favourably received than himself.

A black priest, Secretary to the Holy Office, who lived opposite the lady's house, was as much enamoured as the governor; and had repeatedly solicited her to gratify his infamous passion. even when at confession, as the lady herself informed me.

On noticing my attentions, he became as jealous, as the governor; and although he had hitherto been on friendly terms with me, and I had even done him some important services, he eagerly joined with Don Manuel Furtado in oppressing me.

The rivals, thus united, urged the Commissary so unremittingly, that upon the information, which, at their entreaty, he sent to Goa, he received an order from the inquisitors for my arrest; which was executed in the evening of the 24th of August, 1673 on my return from the house of a lady of great respectability, called Signora Donna Francisca Pereira, the wife of one of the principal gentlemen of the town, Manuel Peixote da Gama. This lady, who was about sixty years of age, considered herself indebted to me for the lives of her eldest daughter, and her grand-daughter ; and indeed I was so fortunate as to be of service. The daughter fell sick when the mother was away from home, and the unskilfulness of a Pundit, or Indian physician, had reduced her to the last extremity, when I was called in. I treated the disorder as I thought proper, and she recovered. On the mother's return, (overjoyed at the restoration of her beloved daughter,) her grand-child, who was, if possible, more endeared to her, became indisposed, and was in greater danger than her aunt had been ; but, as before, I was not sent for the little invalid at first, but delayed until her case was desperate. I found her in a high fever, and although on the point of delirium, the Indian physician, instead of letting her blood, had covered her head with pepper, which I immediately caused to be removed. My applications were successful, and in a few days she was perfectly convalescent. From that time the lady, impressed with gratitude, overwhelmed me with presents, and wishing that I should reside near her, had allotted me a house opposite to her own. It was on the very day on which she presented me with this house and as I was quitting the mansion of this generous lady, in order to return to my residence, when the Criminal Judge of the town accosted me, and commanded me to follow him to the prison; whither I was conducted, without deigning to acquaint me by what authority, until after I entered it.

Great as was my surprise when this officer arrested me, yet, as I felt conscious of no crime, and believed that at the most I had been apprehended for some slight matter, I imagined (with sufficient reason) that Manuel Furtado, who had always professed much regard for me, would not suffer me to remain all night in prison ; but when my conductor told me that it was by order of Inquisition, my astonishment was so extreme that I was for some time motionless. On recollecting myself a little, I requested to speak to the Commissary, but to complete my distress, they told me he had set off that day for Goa. So that no comfort was left me but the hope which every one encouraged, that I should be soon discharged ; because the Holy Office was not only just in its decisions, but it was infinitely more disposed to mercy, and especially towards those who confessed their faults with a good grace, without long solicitation.

All these fine speeches did not prevent me feeling my present misfortune very sensibly, and the company of my friends, who failed not to visit me, so far from consoling, afflicted me the more, by the comparisons I drew between their condition and my own.

As I had no enemies but concealed ones, they easily intermixed with my best friends. The governor and the black priest, who wished for nothing so much as my being taken away, well knew how to dissemble their jealousy and malice ; the former, by sending some officers of his household to assure me that he participated in my distress, and to offer me anything that was in his power ; and the other by coming to the gate to shed a few false tears, which joy rather than condolence caused to flow.

CHAPTER XI

Description of the prison of Damaun. I write to the Inquisitors without success. The extreme misery of the prisoners.

THE prison of Damaun is adjacent to, but below the level of river, and is consequently damp and unhealthy. A few years since it was inundated, by a hole which had been made in the wall by some prisoners for the purpose of escaping.

The walls are very thick. The prison consists of two large halls on the ground floor, and one above ; the men being confined in the lower, and the women in the higher story. The largest of the lower halls is about forty feet in length, by fifteen feet in breadth, and the lesser one is about two-thirds of those dimensions. About forty persons were confined in these rooms, without any other place for answering the ordinary demands of nature ; and where the collected water formed a pool in the centre of each apartment. The women had no other convenience on their floor ; but with this advantage, that the water ran off from their hall and filtered through the boards into ours, which thus became the reservoir of both. The only receptacle for our other excrements, was a large tub, emptied but once a week, and engendering an immense quantity of worms, which crawled over the floor, even upon our beds.

Whilst I continued in this prison, the pains which I took to have it cleansed rendered it rather less disgusting; but though I often obliged them to throw on even fifty buckets of water in a day, the stench was intolerable.

So soon as I was immured in this melancholy abode, and seriously contemplated my mischance, I readily discovered its occasion, and resolved to omit nothing which was likely to bring it to a termination.

My friends perpetually inculcated, that the best and surest mode of regaining my liberty was to make a voluntary confession of what I might even conjecture only to be the ground of accusation against me. Willing, therefore, to avail myself of their counsel, I wrote to the Grand Inquisitor at Goa; I told him candidly everything of which I supposed I might be accused, and beseeched him to believe that if I had erred, it was rather from levity and imprudence, than from any ill intention. My letter was faithfully delivered; but, contrary to my wishes, and the hope of my friends, I received no answer, and was allowed to languish in this noisome and dark dungeon, along with several blacks, who, as well as myself, had been arrested by order of the Holy Office.

The considerate benevolence of the generous Donna Francisca, which was undiminished during the whole period of my imprisonment at Damaun, made it rather more supportable. That noble lady was not content with sending me mere necessaries only, but I daily received from her sufficient to maintain four persons, both plentifully and luxuriously. She herself took the trouble to prepare my victuals, and the slave who brought them was regularly accompanied by one of her grandsons, to witness the delivery, lest any of her domestics, or the gaoler, might be suborned to poison me; and, as she could not personally visit me, she caused her husband, her children, or her sons-in-law, to come to me every day.

The other prisoners were not so fortunate. As there is no appointed subsistence for them, the magistrates refer the charge to the charity of those who may be disposed to bestow it; and there being but two persons in the town who distributed food to them regularly twice a week, (the greater part having nothing during the remainder,) they were reduced to so pitiful a condition, as to contribute, in no small degree, to increase my own.

I gave them all I could spare from my allowance; but some of these poor wretches, who were not confined in the same apartment, were so pressed by hunger as to be compelled to devour their own excrements. Upon this occasion I learnt, that some years before, about fifty Malabar pirates, having been taken and thrown into this prison, the horrible famine which they suffered induced forty of them to strangle themselves with the linen of their turbans.

The distress I witnessed induced me to write to the governor and the principal people in the town, who at length had the kindness to send some relief to the wretched victims of the Holy Office.

CHAPTER XII

The return of the Father Commissary. My removal to Goa.

THE Father Commissary, as I have already stated, saw nothing criminal in the confession I had voluntarily made to him; and though it had been otherwise, I ought, according to the laws of the Inquisition, to have remained at large; but as that was not the intention of the governor or the black priest, the good father, superseding the laws in their favour, had accused me as a dogmatizing heretic. He might have sent me to the Inquisition at Goa immediately upon my imprisonment, and had he so done I should have been liberated three months afterwards, at the Act of Faith in December; but it not according with the views of my rivals that I should be free so soon, the Commissary, so far from transporting me to Goa, went thither himself, to avoid my remonstrances and petitions, and did not return until after the celebration of the Act of Faith, that is, towards the latter end of December. Whether he might not employ the four months of his absence in representing me to the Inquisitor as a very bad and dangerous man, whom it was necessary to remove out of the Indies, I am ignorant; but I have reason to suspect he did so, from the affected severity of my sentence, which was considered to be extraordinary, even in Portugal.

The Commissary returned on the 20th of December with the flotilla, which, at that season, usually escorts merchant ships from Goa to Cambay.

The Father, who had an order to cause all the prisoners of the Inquisition to embark in the galliots, gave me notice to be ready to depart when the fleet returned from Cambay.

M. I'Abbé Carré passing through Damaun, on his return from St. Thomas's, where M. de la Haye then was, with much difficulty obtained permission to see me; and had the goodness to come to me on Christmas eve, and also the next day, when he departed for Surat.

I wrote again to the Commissary, and entreated him, through different persons, that he would permit me to speak to him; but neither my letters, nor the solicitations of those who interested themselves for me, could prevail upon him; so justly apprehensive was he of being reproached for his insincerity.

About this time, a Portuguese, called Manuel Vas, with whom I was intimately acquainted, being accused of having a wife in Portugal, was arrested by an order of the Holy Office for having married a second at Damaun, and was lodged in the same prison with me.

My benevolent protectress being informed that I was to be transferred to Goa, was not neglectful to furnish me with provisions sufficient for a much longer voyage than that I was about to take. Part of fleet returning from Cambay on the last day of December, the Commissary sent chains and fetters for the prisoners who were to depart with it. The blacks were chained together two and two, but some of them were so debilitated by hunger, that their feet, which they had not power to use, were unloosed on their embarking. The Portuguese and myself were honoured with separate irons; and the Commissary had the politeness to intimate that I might have the choice of those destined for his countryman and myself. To profit by his civility, I chose the most commodious, though the heaviest; and was conveyed with my feet in fetters in a Palanquin to the banks of the river, where I met several of my friends, whom I was allowed to embrace on exchanging our adieus. The Governor, who was there also, omitted nothing that might persuade me that he was concerned at my misfortune, and expressed a thousand hypocritical wishes for my speedy release and happy return. The sight of my friends, and their tears, augmented my affliction; but no circumstance gave me greater pain than being refused the privilege of taking leave of my benefactress, whom I was ardently desirous to thank for all her kindness. At last, after many sorrowful compliments, I was forced into a boat, and put on board one of the galliots of the little fleet, which waited only for the orders of the general.

CHAPTER XIII

Departure from Damaun. Arrival at Basseen, and abode there. Arrival at Goa.

ALTHOUGH several of the galliots and vessels had not yet arrived from Diu and Cambay, the General, Louis de Mello, made the signal for those which were at Damaun, to sail on the 1st day of the year 1674, for Basseen, to wait until the remainder of the fleet should join. As the wind was fair, and we had only twenty leagues to traverse, we reached Basseen the day following; and, immediately after the anchors were dropt, the prisoners were landed, and conducted to the prison for security, whilst the fleet continued in the port. I was taken there with the rest; and a friend of mine, who had recently settled at Basseen, having unsuccessfully attempted to obtain permission to visit me, expressed in a letter, which he had considerable trouble to get conveyed to me, how much he commiserated my fate.

The prison of Basseen is more spacious and less filthy than that of Damaun. We found there many companions in misery, whom the Commissary of the Inquisition at that town had detained for some time, in expectation of an opportunity to send them to Goa.

They were all chained as we were. We re-embarked on the seventh, and all the fleet being assembled, and provided with necessaries we weighed anchor and sailed the next day.

Nothing remarkable occurred during the rest of the voyage; we were always within sight of land, and with a favourable breeze arrived on the fourteenth on the bar of Goa.

Our captains having previously apprized the Inquisitor, we were landed the next day, and led by his order to the Inquisition; but this not being an audience day, one of the officers conducted us to the prison of the Ordinary, that is, of the Archbishop of Goa, called by the Portuguese "*Aljouvar*." I was one of the first who entered it, and afterwards saw all our unfortunate company, which had been dispersed during the voyage, come in by degrees.

This prison was more foul, dark, and horrible than any one I had seen, and I doubt whether there can be one more nauseous and appalling. It is a sort of cavern, where the day is but just distinguishable through an extremely narrow aperture, where the subtlest sun-beam can scarcely penetrate, and where a clear light is never beheld.

The stench was excessive; for there was no other place for the necessities of the prisoners than a well sunk in the floor, in the midst of the cavern, which it required some resolution to approach; from which cause part of the ordure remained upon the brink, and the greatest part of the prisoners did not even go so far, but made their evacuations all around. When night approached, I durst not lie down for fear of the swarms of vermin, and the filth which every where abounded, but I was constrained to recline against the wall. Yet, shocking as is the *Aljouvar*, I would have preferred it to the neat and light cells of the Holy Inquisition; because here I had the blessings of society and conversation, but in the prisons of the Holy Office I was informed those enjoyments were debarred.

CHAPTER XIV

The manner in which I was conducted to the Inquisition, and the observances used there towards prisoners on their entrance.

I HAD begun to flatter myself that I should be permitted to remain in the *Aljouvar*, until my business was settled, as I was not removed during that day and the ensuing night; but all my hopes vanished, when an officer came about eight o'clock in the morning of the 16th of January, with an order to take us to the *Santa Casa*, which was immediately executed. On account of my fetters, it was with great difficulty that I reached the place to which I was conducted, yet with these sad appendages we were obliged to walk from the *Aljouvar* to the Inquisition; and, having been assisted in ascending the steps, I entered, along with my companions, into the great hall, where some Smiths attended to knock off our irons. I was the first person summoned to the audience.

After crossing the hall, I was ushered into an antichamber, and thence into the apartment where my judge was seated. This place, which is called by the Portuguese, "*Mesa do Santo Officio*," which signifies "the Board of the Holy Office," was adorned with tapestry, composed of taffety, in stripes of blue and citron colour. At one extremity, was a large crucifix in relief, reaching almost to the ceiling. In the centre of the room was a platform, upon which stood a table, about fifteen feet in length, and four broad, with several armed chairs placed around it. At one end of this table, and on the same side as the crucifix, the Secretary sat on a folding stool. I was placed opposite to him. Near me, on the right, in an armed chair, was the Grand Inquisitor of the Indies, Francisco Delgado de Matos, a secular priest, about forty years of age. He was alone, because the second of the two Inquisitors, usually resident at Goa, and who is always a religious of the Dominican order, had recently gone to Portugal, and his successor had not been appointed.

Immediately upon entering the audience chamber, I cast myself at the feet of my Judge, with the design of affecting his feelings by my suppliant attitude; but he would not suffer it, and commanded me to rise. Having asked my name and profession, he interrogated me if I knew the occasion of my arrest, exhorting me to confess it freely, as the only means of obtaining a prompt discharge. After satisfying him as to the two first inquiries, I told him that I believed I did know the cause of my detention, and that if he would have the goodness to hear me, I was ready instantly to become my own accuser. I added tears to my entreaties, and again prostrated myself before him; but my Judge, without the slightest emotion, said, that there was no haste; that he had other matters more important than mine to attend to, and that he would let me know when he should have leisure for it; and taking up a little silver bell, which was laid before him, rang for the *Alcaide*, or gaoler of the Holy Office, who came in and led me into a long gallery, not far distant, into which the Secretary almost directly followed us. My trunk was brought in and opened in my presence. I was thoroughly searched, and everything about me was taken away, even to some buttons, and a ring which I wore on my finger, without leaving me anything but my rosary, my handkerchief, and some pieces of gold which I had sewn into one of my garters, and which they neglected to examine. An exact inventory was immediately taken of the rest of my property, but which has since proved to have been wholly useless, as nothing of value was ever restored to me, although the Secretary then declared that everything should be given back upon my release; and the Inquisitor himself often afterwards reiterated the same promise.

The inventory being finished, the *Alcaide* took me by the hand, and led me, bare-headed to a little cell, about ten feet square, in which I was locked up alone, and saw no one until my supper was brought in the evening. As I had eaten nothing either that day or the preceding, I gladly took what was given to me, which enabled me to take some rest during the night. When my breakfast was brought the next morning, I requested to be allowed some books, and my combs; but I found that books were not permitted to any person, not even the Breviary to priests; and that I should have no use for combs, as they cut off my hair without delay, which is the practice with all prisoners of whatever rank or sex, so soon as they enter the prisons of the Holy Office, or the next day after at the latest.

I shall here break off the recital of what relates to myself, for the purpose of briefly describing the house itself, and the regulations and formalities observed in it.

CHAPTER XV

Description of the Inquisition at Goa.

THE palace of the Inquisition, called by the Portuguese *Santa Casa*, or the Holy House, is situated on one side of the great square, opposite the cathedral dedicated to Saint Catherine. It is extensive and magnificent; in the front are three entrances, of which, the centre is the largest, and opens upon the grand staircase ascending to the hall which I have mentioned. The two other portals severally lead to the apartments of the Inquisitors, which are sufficiently commodious for considerable establishments. Within, are various apartments for the officers of the house; and passing through the interior, there is a vast edifice divided into distinct masses or squares of buildings, of two stories each, separated by small courts. In each story is a gallery, resembling a dormitory, containing seven or eight small chambers, ten feet square; the whole number of which, is about two hundred. In one of these dormitories, the cells are dark, being without windows, and smaller and lower than the rest; as I had occasion to know from the circumstances of having been taken to see them, on complaining that I was too rigorously treated, in order to satisfy me that I might fare worse. The rest of the cells are square, vaulted, whitewashed, clean, and lighted by a small grated and open window, placed at a height above the reach of the tallest man. All the walls are five feet thick. Every chamber is secured by two doors, one opening inwards, and the other without; the inner door is made in two divisions, is strong, well-fitted, and opened by the lower half in the manner of a grate; in the upper part is a little window, through which, the prisoners receive their food, linen, and such other necessary articles as can be so conveyed. There is a door to this opening, guarded by strong bolts.

The outer door is neither so thick nor so strong as the other, but it is entire and without any aperture. It is usually left open from six o'clock in the morning until eleven, in order to ventilate the chamber through the crevices of the inner door.

CHAPTER XVI

Treatment of the prisoners.

TO each person whom misfortune brings into these Holy Prisons, are given an earthen pot filled with water to wash in ; another of a better kind, also filled with water to drink ; with a *Pucaro,* or vessel made of a sort of sigillaceous earth, common in the Indies, and which keeps the water fresh, even if retained in it for some time ; a brush to sweep the chamber ; a mat to spread on the platform for sleeping ; a large close-stool pan with a pot cover, which is changed every fourth day, and serves also for receiving the filth collected by the broom.

The prisoners are tolerably well kept. They have three meals daily. Breakfast is brought at six, dinner at ten, and supper at four in the afternoon.

The breakfast for Blacks, is generally *cange,* or water thickened with rice ; and their other meals always consist of rice and fish.

The Whites are treated more delicately. In the morning, a soft roll, weighing about three ounces, with fried fish and fruits ; or on Sundays, and sometimes on Thursdays, a sausage. On the latter days, also, they have meat to dinner with a roll, as in the morning ; a dish of rice and some ragout, with abundance of sauce to mix with the rice, which is prepared with water and salt only. On other days, they have nothing but fish to dinner. The suppers chiefly consist of bread, fried fish, a dish of rice, and a ragout of fish or eggs, the sauce of which may be eaten with the rice ; but not any flesh, not even on Easter-day. I imagine that this regimen is used as much for the sake of economy, (fish being very cheap in the Indies,) as to mortify those who have incurred the pain of the greater excommunication ; and at the same time, it preserves them from the cruel disorder which the Indians call *Mordechi*, proceeding from indigestion, and which is frequent and fatal in these climates, especially in a place where exercise cannot be taken.

The sick receive every necessary attention with the greatest care. Physicians and surgeons visit them when required, and if the disease becomes dangerous, confessors are introduced ; but the Viaticum and Extreme Unction are never administered in this house, nor is either Sermon or Mass ever heard there.

Those who die in prison, are interred within the house without any ceremony ; and if, according to the maxims of the Tribunal, they are deemed to have incurred capital punishment, their bodies are taken up, and their remains preserved to be burnt at the Next Act of Faith.

As it is always hot in the Indies, and no books are allowed to any person in the Inquisition, the prisoners never behold fire or any other light than that of day. In each cell there are two platforms for the purpose of reposing upon, as it sometimes happens that two persons are confined together. In addition to the mat which is given to every prisoner, Europeans have a checked counterpane, which serves for a mattress ; there being no need of a covering, except to avoid the persecution of the Mosquitos which are in such numbers as to occasion one of the greatest inconveniences endured in this melancholy abode.

CHAPTER XVII

Of the different officers of the Inquisition.

THERE are two Inquisitors at Goa. The chief, called the Grand Inquisitor, is always a secular priest ; and the second, a religious of the order of St. Dominic. The Holy Office has also officers denominated Deputies of the Holy Office, who are very numerous, and of all orders of religious. They assist at the final decision of the cases of criminals, and in preparing the accusations against them ; but do not attend the Tribunal, unless summoned by the Inquisitors. There are others called *Qualificadores* of the Holy Office, to whom is committed the charge of examining the propositions in such works as are suspected to contain anything contrary to the purity of the Holy Faith ; but who do not assist at the judgements, and come to the Tribunal only to make their reports.

There are besides, a Proctor and Solicitor ; and Advocates for such prisoners as wish to have them ; but whose assistance is better adapted to extract their private opinions, and to deceive rather than to defend them ; and even if their fidelity was unsuspicious, their protection would be useless to the Accused, to whom they are not permitted to speak, except in the presence of their Judges, or of persons who are sent to make a report of the conference.

The Inquisition has other officers called Familiars of the Holy Office, who are, properly speaking, the Tipstaffs of the Tribunal. Persons of all ranks, even Dukes and Princes, are proud of being admitted to this noble function. They are employed to arrest those who are accused and it is customary to depute a Familiar of equal rank with the party to be apprehended. These officers have no wages, and they deem themselves sufficiently rewarded by the honour conferred upon them in serving so holy a Tribunal. They wear the honourable distinction of a gold medal, engraved with the arms of the Holy Office. When one of them is ordered to make an arrest, he goes alone ; and having declared to the party that he is summoned by the Inquisitors, the latter is obliged to follow him without reply ; for , on the slightest resistance, every body would assist the execution of the warrants of the Holy Office.

There are also attached to the institution, several Secretaries, "*Marentios* ", or Tipstaffs, properly called Inspectors ; an *Alcaide*, or Gaoler, and Guards, to watch the prisoners, and carry them their food and other necessaries.

CHAPTER XVIII

The deportment of the Officers of the Inquisition towards the prisoners.

As all the prisoners are separated, and it rarely happens that two are confined in the same cell, four persons are more than sufficient to guard two hundred. A perpetual and rigid silence is preserved in the Inquisition, and those who venture to utter their complaints, to weep, or even to pray to God too loudly, are liable to be beaten by the Guards; who, on hearing the slightest noise, hasten to the spot from whence it proceeds, to require silence; and if a repetition of the order be not obeyed, they open the doors, and strike without mercy. This serves, not only to correct the party who receives the chastisement, but also to intimidate the rest; who, from the profound stillness which reigns around, all hear his cries and the sound of the blows. The *Alcaide* and the Guards are always in the galleries, and sleep there during the night.

The Inquisitor, attended by a Secretary and Interpreter, visits every prisoner about once in two months, to inquire if anything is wanted, if the victuals are brought at the appointed times, and if there are any complaints to be preferred against the officers; and as soon as answers are returned to these three questions, the door is instantly closed. In effect, these visits are made for no other purpose than to display that justice and goodness, of which there is so much parade in this Tribunal; but they produce neither comfort nor advantage to the prisoners who may be disposed to complain, nor are they ever treated with more humanity in consequence.

Such of the prisoners as are wealthy have no better allowance than those who are poor, the latter being provided for by the confiscations levied from the former; for the Holy Office seldom fails to seize all the property, real and personal, of those who are so unfortunate as to fall into its hands.

CHAPTER XIX

Formalities observed in the Inquisition.

WHEN a person is arrested by the Inquisition, he is first asked his name, and profession or quality, and is then required to render an accurate statement of all his effects. To induce him to do this the more readily, he is assured, in the name of Jesus Christ, that if he is innocent, all that he shall so declare will be faithfully returned to him; but otherwise, even though he should be acquitted, such articles as may be discovered to belong to him, and not included in the list, will be confiscated. From the universal prepossession entertained of the sanctity and integrity of this Tribunal, it frequently happens, that a person, whose conscience reproaches him with no crime, and gives him no reason to doubt that his innocence will be acknowledged, and his liberty consequently restored, without hesitation exposes his most private and important concerns.

It is not, however, without some plausibility, that the public mind is prejudiced in favour of this Tribunal; which, considered externally only, dispenses justice with more lenity and charity, than any other known jurisdiction. Those who voluntarily become their own accusers, and testify their repentance before they are apprehended, are allowed to be at large without fear of imprisonment. It is true, that those who do not accuse themselves until after their arrest, are deemed guilty, and are condemned as such; but no one is sentenced to any temporal punishment extending to death, who is not clearly convicted. Two or three witnesses only, as in lay jurisdictions, are here considered too few for conviction; and, though two witnesses are sufficient to obtain an order for a person's apprehension, seven at least are necessary for his condemnation. However palpable his guilt, or enormous the offence, the Holy Office is satisfied with the ecclesiastical penalty of excommunication, and the confiscation of property; and should the criminal be amenable to the civil courts, if he confesses his crime, he is, for the first time, exempt from all temporal and corporal punishment. The Holy Office intercedes for him, suspends the secular arm, and obtains his pardon, if to be procured by interest or entreaty.

It is true, that should he repeat his offence, the Inquisition cannot again save him ; but it abandons him with reluctance, and only delivers him to the civil judge, upon his promising that if the relapsed criminal should receive sentence of death, it shall be executed without effusion of blood. Here is tenderness !

But after saying all that can be alleged in favour of the Holy Office, some particulars must be added, which will explain the nature and extent of this apparent lenity and kindness. The witnesses are never confronted ; all descriptions of people are received as witnesses, even such as are interested in the death and condemnation of the accused ; he is not suffered to make any remark upon the evidence of persons the most notoriously underserving of credit, and the most defective in their testimony. The number of the witnesses is often reduced to five ; in which are comprehended supposed accomplices, whose depositions are extracted by torture, and who, to save their own lives, avow what they have not done ; and the accused himself, who confessing on the rack of crime of which he is guiltless, is also reputed as a witness. The number of seven is often substantially reduced to none, from being composed of convicts, who are really innocent of the offences imputed to them, but whom the Inquisition renders effectually criminal, by compelling them, either from dread of the stake, or by torture, to accuse the guiltless in order to save themselves. To make this mystery intelligible it should be noticed, that amongst the crimes cognizable in the Inquisition, there are some which may be committed by one person alone, as blasphemy, impiety, &c. There are others which cannot be committed without one accomplice at the least, as sodomy ; and others again, which require several, as assisting at the Jewish Sabbath ; participating in those superstitious assemblies which the converted Idolaters so reluctantly relinquish, and which are denominated Magic and Witchcraft, because they are held in order to discover secret matters, and penetrate into futurity by means which cannot naturally lead to such results.

It is in regard to such crimes as cannot be perpetrated without one or more accomplices that the proceedings of the Holy Office are the most extraordinary.

The Jews having been expelled from Spain by Ferdinand, king of Arragon, and Isabella of Castille, his queen, sought refuge in Portugal where they were allowed to settle on the condition of embracing Christianity, at least in outward profession. As the Jewish name is everywhere odious, the Christian families are distinguished from the converted Jews, whose decendants, however remote, are termed, even to this day, *New Christians* ; and as, in course of time, some of them have formed matrimonial connections with the old Christians, their issue are daily reproached with being in part new, which the Portuguese express by saying, "*Tem parte de Cristam novo* ; " so that, though their grandfathers and great grandfathers may have been Christians, these unfortunates are unable to procure admission into the number of "*Cristam velhos*" or Old Christians. The families which are thus directly or partially descended from Jews, being well known in Portugal, and the objects of hatred and malevolence to some, are obliged to associate together, for the interchange of mutual services, which they cannot receive from others ; and this very union increases the contempt and aversion which are entertained towards them, and is the general occasion of their troubles.

CHAPTER XX

The injustice committed in the Inquisition towards those accused of Judaism.

TO elucidate this matter, I will suppose that a *New Christian* indeed, but who is nevertheless most sincerely and truly a Christian, though descended from one of those unfortunate families, should be arrested by order of the Inquisition, and accused not by seven witnesses only, but by fifty. Such a man, convinced of his own innocence, which he trusts will be indubitably acknowledged, will have no hesitation in presenting an exact inventory of all his property, relying upon its being faithfully restored to him. Yet the door of his prison will be scarcely closed, before every thing that he has, is sold by auction ; for assuredly, restitution will never be made.

After some months have elapsed, he is sent for to the Audience, where he is asked if he knows the cause of his imprisonment. To this, of course, he answers in the negative. He is then exhorted to consider seriously, and confess, as his only chance of freedom; and is then remanded to his confinement. Some time afterwards; he is again brought in, and many times interrogated to the same purport, without producing any other answer than before. But when the period of the *Auto da Fé* approaches, the Proctor waits upon him, and declares, that he is charged by a great number of witnesses, of having *Judaised*; which means having conformed to the ceremonies of the Mosaic law; such as not eating pork, hare, fish without scales, &c. of having attended to solemnization of the sabbath, having eaten the Pascal Lamb, &c. He is then conjured "by the bowels of the mercy of our Lord Jesus Christ," (for such are the terms affected to be used in this Holy House,) voluntarily to confess his crimes, as the sole means to save his life; and the Holy Office desires, if possible, to prevent his losing it. The innocent man persists in denying what he is urged to confess; he is, in consequence, condemned as "*convicto negativo*," (convicted, but confessing not,) to be delivered over to the secular power, to be punished according to law, that is, to be burnt.

Notwithstanding this, he is continually exhorted to accuse himself, and provided he does so before the eve of the Act, he may escape death. But if he persists in asserting his innocence in despite of all exhortation and solicitation, and even the torture to which he is subjected, to compel him to be his own accuser; the order for his death is delivered to him on the Friday immediately preceding the Sunday of the celebration. The decree is signified in the presence of a Tipstaff of the Lay Courts, who casts a cord round the hands of the pretended culprit, to testify that he has taken possession of him, on his abandonment by ecclesiastical justice. A confessor is then introduced, who remains with him day and night and perseveres in pressing him most urgently to confess the charges against him, in order to save his life. Should he continue in his denial until Sunday, he is cruelly executed; and should he accuse himself, he is rendered infamous and wretched for his whole life. If the advice of his confessor and the fear of punishment induce him to acknowledge crimes which he has not committed, he must demand to be conducted to the audience, which is instantly granted. Being brought before his Judges, he is first required to confess his guilt, and then to entreat for mercy, as well for his crimes as his obstinate denial of them ; and, as they assume the supposition, that his avowal is sincere, he is obliged to detail all his faults and all his errors ; and the testimony which has been deposed against him being communicated to him, in order to comply with the requisition to the utmost, he repeats all that he hears.

He, perhaps, then concludes, that he shall be discharged ; but he has other things to perform, which are infinitely less easy than what he has hitherto done ; for the Inquisitors, by degrees, begin to urge him in this way—" If thou hast observed the law of Moses, and assembled on the Sabbath day as thou sayest, and thy accusers have seen thee there, as appears to have been the case, to convince us of the sincerity of thy repentance, tell us who are thine accusers, and those who have been with thee at these assemblies."

It is not easy to assign the motive, why the gentlemen of the Holy Office oblige these pretended Jews to conjecture who are the witnesses against them, unless it is, that the witnesses of the Sabbath are considered as accomplices ; but how is the poor wretch that is innocent, to divine who they are ? and, though he were guilty what is the use of naming them to the Holy Office, which knows them already, because it has received their depositions, upon which, alone, he is treated as such ? In all other cases, the names of the witnesses are concealed from the criminal, to screen them from his reproaches ; but here he is made to guess them. Admitting that they are accomplices, the Inquisition knows them no better by their being named. If they have been forced to avow their offence in the prisons of the Inquisition, they either remain there still, or have been in them ; and the Holy Office can have no interest in making the accused name them, which cannot render him more innocent, nor them less culpable. The offender and the witness are equally in the power of the Inquisition ;—what then is the object of these Judges ? If it is only to compel him to impeach all his accomplices, by his attempts to name all his witnesses, that might be of service if he were really guilty ; but, if he is not, this imposition is of no other use than to harass the innocent :—and so it is, for the poor *New Christian* being obliged to mention people whom he does not know, to the Inquisitor who does, (for otherwise, the avowal of a crime of which he is not guilty, would avail him nothing) reasons much in this manner :—" Those who have accused me, must necessarily be my relations, my friends, and my neighbours ; and in fine, some of the New Christians with whom I have associated, for the Ancient Christians are never apprehended or suspected of Judaism ; and probably, these very persons are placed in the same situation with myself ; I will, therefore, accuse them in return :" and as it is impossible that he should exactly guess those who have deposed against him, in order to make up the number of his six or seven accusers, he names a great many innocent persons who have never thought of him—against whom, however, he himself becomes a witness by this declaration ; upon which, they are arrested, and kept in the prisons of the Holy Office, until, in course of time, seven witnesses (like the one I have described,) are mustered against them, and ensure their condemnation.

CHAPTER XXI

The practices of the Inquisition.

IT may be inferred from what has been said in the preceding Chapter, that the miserable victims of the Inquisition reciprocally impeach each other ; and that, consequently, a man may be perfectly innocent, although there are fifty witnesses against him ; and yet, innocent as he is, if he should not accuse himself, or guess freely, he is delivered up to the executioner as fully convicted ; which would happen less frequently if the accuser, witnesses, and accused were confronted.

The practice observed towards persons suspected of Judaism and what has been said in respect to them, is to be understood of persons charged with Sorcery, from having attended the superstitious assemblies I have mentioned ; and here the difficulty of naming the witnesses is increased, because they have not, like the New Christians, to look for their accusers and accomplices in a certain class ; but must find them indiscriminately and fortuitously amongst their acquaintances, friends, kindred, enemies, and persons connected with no sect whatever ; which is the more embarrassing to the innocent in these casual and extorted accusations, as he must denounce a greater number, to recognize in such a crowd of innocent persons, the witnesses respecting whom he is interrogated.

The effects of those who are executed and of those who confess, are alike confiscated, because they are equally reputed guilty. The Inquisitors do not so much desire the death as the property of their victims ; and as, according to the laws of the Tribunal, apostates, and such as persevere in denying their accusations, are alone delivered to the secular arm, the Judges do everything in their power (not omitting torture, which they have the goodness to inflict to the extreme, in order to save their lives) to induce them to confess. But the true reason, which makes them so anxious that a man should be his own accuser, is, that having declared himself to be guilty, the world has no right to doubt that his property is justly forfeited. The remission of the penalty of death to these pretended criminals, confounds weak minds, by an ostentation of mercy and apparent justice; and tends not a little to maintain the opinion of the sanctity and lenity of this Tribunal, which could not long exist without this artifice.

It may be proper to observe here, that those who have thus escaped death by their extorted confessions, are strictly enjoined, when they leave the prisons of the Holy Office, to declare that they have been treated with great tenderness and clemency, in as much as their lives, which they justly merited to lose, have been spared. Should any one, who has acknowledged that he is guilty, attempt to vindicate himself on his release, he would be immediately denounced and arrested, and burnt at the next Act of Faith, without hope of pardon.

CHAPTER XXII

Other acts of injustice, commonly committed by the Inquisition.

THE Judges of the Holy Office might readily ascertain the truth or falsehood of the charge of Judaism, would they take the trouble to investigate the matter without prejudice ; and to consider, that of an hundred persons condemned to be burnt as Jews, there are scarcely four who profess that faith at their death; the rest exclaiming and protesting to their last gasp, that they are Christians, and have been so during their whole lives; that they worship our Saviour as their only true God; and that on his mercy, and the merits of his adorable sacrifice, alone, they repose their hope; but the cries and declarations of these unfortunates, (if one may so call those who suffer for not avowing a falsehood,) fail to touch these gentlemen, who imagine, that this authentic confession of their faith, which so many make at the very moment of death, deserves not the smallest consideration; and who believe, that a certain number of witnesses, whom the fear of being burnt only obliges them to accuse the innocent, are sufficient to screen them from the the vengeance of God. But if so many Christians, deemed to be Jews, are unjustly delivered to the executioner in all Inquisitions; neither less great, nor less frequent injustice is committed in the Indies, towards those accused of Magic or Sorcery, and condemned to be burnt for those crimes.

To place this in a proper light, it should be premised, that the Heathens, whose religion abounds with superstitious rites,—(as, for instance, to divine the issue of an undertaking or disease—whether one is beloved by a certain person —the thief who has stolen what is lost—and other things of the like nature)—cannot so readily nor so entirely forget these things, but they often recur to them after they are baptized. This will be thought the less extraordinary if we recollect, that in France, where the Christian religion has been established for so many ages, persons are yet to be found who believe in, and practise many of, these impertinent ceremonies, which even time has not caused to be forgotten; that the Heathens, so recently converted, have passed the greatest part of their existence in Paganism; and that those who live in the states of the King of Portugal, are subjects or slaves, who change their religion in the expectation of better treatment from their Lords or Masters. Yet these faults, which in rude and ignorant people appear rather to deserve stripes than the stake, are expiated by that cruel punishment, by all those who are convicted thereof according to the maxims of this Tribunal,—for the second time, if they have confessed the first,—or for the first, if they persist in denying. The Inquisition also punishes, not only Christians who fall, or are accused of falling, within the cases under its cognizance ; but Mahometans, Heathens, or other Strangers of whatever persuasion, who commit any of the prohibited offences, or who publicly exercise their religion in the countries subject to the King of Portugal ; for though that Prince tolerates liberty of conscience, the Holy Office interprets the permission, that strangers may live in their own Faith, but are liable to be punished as criminals if they practise its ceremonies. And, as in the territories of the Portuguese in India, there are more Mahometans and Heathens than Christians ; and the Inquisition, which punishes apostate Christians with death, never sentences to that penalty those who have not been baptized, though they should relapse a hundred times into the same errors, but generally commutes it for banishments, corporal correction, or the galleys ; the dread of being liable to be sentenced to the flames, hinders many from embracing Christianity ; and the Holy Office, instead of being useful in these parts, for the propagation of the Faith, deters people from the church, by rendering it an object of horror to them. From the continual chain of accusations, which is the necessary consequence of what has been stated, and the ease by which any person can denounce his enemies with impunity, the prisons of the Inquisition are never long empty ; and though the Acts of Faith are celebrated, at the latest, every two or three years, it frequently happens, that at each, there are two hundred prisoners, and often more.

CHAPTER XXIII

Some particulars relating to the Officers of the Inquisition.

THERE are four Inquisitions in the Portuguese dominions, viz :—In Portugal, those of Lisbon, Coimbra, and Evora ; and in the East Indies, that of Goa. These are all sovereign Tribunals, without appeal in all matters within the extent of their respective jurisdictions. The Inquisition of Goa comprehends all the countries possessed by the crown of Portugal, to the Cape of Good Hope. Besides these four Tribunals, there is a Grand Council of the Inquisition, in which, the Inquisitor General presides. This Tribunal is the chief, and whatever is done in the others, is reported there. In addition to the honour, and unbounded authority and appointments, annexed to the posts of all the Inquisitors, they derive very considerable emolument in two ways. One arises from the sale of the effects of the prisoners, in which, if any rare or valuable article should be comprised, the Inquisitors have but to send a servant to bid for it, (and few would dare to offer a greater price,) whereby things are often obtained by them, for the half of their real worth. The other means of profit is still more important: when the produce of a confiscation is remitted to the Royal Treasury, the Inquisitors have the power of sending warrants at their pleasure, and for any amount, to answer the charges and secret occasions of the Holy Office, which are instantly satisfied, without any one daring to inquire the particulars of these privy expenses. By these means, almost the whole of the seizures return into their hands.

All the Inquisitors are nominated by the King, and confirmed by the Pope, from whom they receive their bulls. At Goa, the Grand Inquisitor alone, has, or claims the privilege of a carriage, and receives more respect than the Archbishop or the Viceroy. His authority extends over all descriptions of persons, as well Lay, as Ecclesiastic; except the Archbishop, his Grand Vicar, (who is generally a bishop,) the Viceroy, and the Governors in case of the Viceroy's decease; but he can cause any of these to be arrested, after previously informing the court of Portugal, and receiving secret orders from the Soverign Council of the Inquisition of Lisbon, called "*Conselho Supremo.*" This Tribunal assembles every fifteen days, unless some extraordinary occasion should require it to be convened oftener; but the inferior councils regularly meet twice a day, from eight to eleven in the morning, and from two to four in the afternoon—and sometimes later, especially previous to the Acts of Faith, when the sitting is often prolonged until ten in the evening.

On the final decision of the cases, besides the *Deputados* who attend officially, the Archbishops or Bishops of those places where the Inquisition is established, have a right to be present, and preside upon all the judgments pronounced. But it is time to return to what concerns myself.

CHAPTER XXIV

In what manner I was conducted to the first Audience, and the result.

IMMEDIATELY after I was shut up in the prisons of the Holy Office, I was informed, that when I wanted anything I had only to knock gently at the door, and the guards would attend, or to ask for it when my meals were served; and that if I wished for an audience, I was to address the *Alcaide*, who, as well as the guards, never speaks to the prisoners without a witness. I was also taught to believe that my liberation would be the consequence of confession, which caused me to importune those officers to take me before my Judges; but, after all my tears and entreaties, this favour was not granted until the 31st day of January, 1674. On that day the *Alcaide* entered with a guard, about two in the afternoon. I dressed myself as he directed, and left my cell uncovered and barefoot. The *Alcaide* walked before, and the guard followed me, in which order we proceeded to the door of the audience room; where the *Alcaide* advancing a little forwards, made a profound obeisance, and withdrew to give me room to enter alone. I found there, as on the former occasion,the Inquisitor and Secretary. I threw myself on my knees, but was commanded to rise, and be seated. I placed myself on a bench at the end of the table beside my Judge. Near me, upon the table, was a Missal, upon which, previous to my further proceeding, I was directed to lay my hand, and swear to declare the truth and preserve secrecy. These oaths are exacted from every one who is brought to this Tribunal, either as a witness, or as amenable to its jurisdiction.

I was then asked if I knew the cause of my imprisonment, and had determined to confess it; and having signified that I wished to do so, I minutely repeated all that I have already stated, touching Baptism and the worship of Images; without mentioning what I had advanced respecting the Inquisition, which at that moment I did not recollect. The Judge enquired if I had not something else to say; and, finding that I had related all that I could remember, instead of releasing me as I had expected, he terminated this fine audience in nearly the following terms :—" That I had very properly resolved to become my own accuser, and that he conjured me in the name of our Lord Jesus Christ, fully to confess all that I knew ; that I might experience the goodness and mercy extended by this Tribunal, towards those who appear to be truly sorry for their offences, by making a sincere and voluntary acknowledgment."

My confession and his exhortation being concluded and taken down in writing, they were read aloud, and signed by me ; after which the Inquisitor rang the bell for the *Alcaide*, to re-conduct me to my chamber.

CHAPTER XXV

My second and third Audiences.

ON the fifteenth of February, I was again taken before my Judge, without any solicitation on my part ; which induced me to conclude that I was to be discharged. So soon as I entered the room, I was interrogated anew, if I had anything further to say, and exhorted to conceal nothing, but to candidly confess all my sins. I answered, that after the closest consideration, I could not recollect anything I had not previously represented. My own name, those of my father, mother, brothers, grandfathers, great grandfathers, godfathers, and grandmothers were required ; and whether I was " *Cristam de oito dias* " (an eight-days' Christian),—for in Portugal, children are baptized on the eighth day after the birth, and the mothers do not leave the house to go to church, until the fortieth day after their accouchement, if ever so propitious.

My Judge seemed surprised when I told him, that in France it was not the custom to defer baptism until the eighth day ; but that infants were baptized there as early as possible. From the observance of these formal ceremonies, it would seem, that notwithstanding the detestation shown by the Portuguese towards the Jews, they themselves possess not genuine Christian principles. But this is not all the mischief :—It may often happen, that the children die without being regenerated by the sacrament of baptism, and thus be eternally excluded from heaven. For the sake of the ceremonial purification (which ought to be considered as having been abrogated by the publication of the gospel,) the Portuguese women do not scruple to break the ordinances of the church, which command all Christians to assist at the holy sacrifice of the Mass on Sundays and Feasts, if not prevented by lawful impediments.

I was next asked what was the name of the Clergyman by whom I was baptized, and in what diocese and town; and finally, if I had been confirmed, and by what Bishop. Having satisfied these enquiries, I was ordered to kneel down, to make the sign of the Cross, to repeat the Lord's Prayer, the *Ave Maria*, the Creed, the Commandments of God and the Church, and the *Salve Regina*; when the Audience concluded as before, with a conjuration, "*by the bowels of the mercy of our Lord Jesus Christ,*" to make immediate confession. This being committed to writing, read in my presence, and subscribed with my signature, I was sent away.

From the beginning of my confinement, I had been greatly distressed, and had wept incessantly; but on returning from this second Audience, I entirely abandoned myself to grief; being convinced, that what was required from me was impossible, as my memory did not furnish what I was solicited to avow. I attempted to put an end to my existence by fasting. I received, indeed, the food which was brought to me, because I could not refuse it without being liable to be beaten by the Guards, who carefully notice, when the dishes are returned, whether sufficient nourishment has been taken; but my despair enabled me to deceive all their caution. I passed several days without tasting anything; and to prevent its being discovered, I threw part of what was given me into the close-stool. This extreme fasting deprived me of rest; and my sole employment was to weep. But during these days of anguish, I reflected on the errors of my past life, and acknowledged the justice of God which had hurled me into this abyss of misery. I even believed that it was intended as the means of my recall and conversion; and being somewhat revived by these thoughts, I heartily implored the aid of the Blessed Virgin, who is the consolation of the wretched, and the asylum and refuge of the sinner; and whose protection I have so often enjoyed, as well in the prison as in many other events of life, that I cannot now repress this public testimony of my experience.

At length, having made a more particular, or rather more happy recollection of what I had said or done during my residence at Damaun, I remembered the opinions I had asserted respecting the Inquisition and its integrity. I immediately demanded audience, which however I did not obtain until the sixteenth of March.

When summoned, I had no doubt that my business would be dismissed the same day, and that after the confession I was prepared to make, I should be discharged; but at the very moment that I fancied I was on the accomplishment of all my wishes, I suddenly found these delightful hopes destroyed; for having detailed everything I had said about the Inquisition, I was cooly informed that that was not what was expected; and having nothing more to communicate, I was instantly remanded, without even taking my confession in writing.

CHAPTER XXVI

Despair impels me to suicide.

I WAS now arrived at the most insupportable period of my captivity; for rigorous as it had hitherto been, I had at least the satisfaction of having borne it with some degree of patience, and had sought to derive advantage from my misfortunes. Religion teaches us, that the greatest calamities are real blessings to those who make a proper use of them; I must therefore ever deem that portion of my life alone infelicitous, wherein I committed sins so enormous, as not to be justified or extenuated by the cruelty of those who exacted impossibilities from me, under pain of being burnt; for no extremity can excuse despair, which is the greatest and last of evils.

I had determined to omit the mention of my despondency, and of the attempts which I made to destroy myself. But it has been suggested to me that the circumstance was material, because the inexcusable rigour of the Inquisition may probably drive many into the same state ; and because it is of importance to know, not only the extent of these evils considered in themselves, but also the shocking consequences which are but too frequent. If rational and well-educated persons, who know their duties and keep in the light of the Faith, yield under these extremities, what may not be apprehended from so many ignorant people, without instruction, principally recent converts from Paganism, whose doctrines have taught them during almost all their lives to regard despair as heroism ? I acknowledge that the unpropitious issue of my last Audience, the success of which I had so fully anticipated, was an annihilating stroke ; and, regarding liberty as a blessing I could never hope for, I abandoned myself so entirely to grief and despair, that I was almost distracted. I had not forgotten that self-destruction is prohibited, and had not any intention to rush into eternal ruin ; but I had no wish to live, and so much desire to die, that my reason was disturbed. I imagined that I had discovered a middle course between the desperate resolution of a sudden death, and that natural termination of life for which I could not bear the thoughts of waiting ; and I hoped for the divine forgiveness, if I could attain it slowly and by the ministration of another. I therefore feigned indisposition from a feverish attack. A *Pundit*, or Pagan Physician, was introduced, who did not even take the trouble to count my pulse, and asserted that I was actually in a fever.

He ordered me to be bled five times, on five successive days ; and as my design in using this remedy was far otherwise than his, (which was to restore me to health, whilst mine was to finish a miserable existence,) the instant I was left alone, I untied the bandages, and suffered the blood to flow, until it filled a pot which was capable of containing eighteen ounces. I repeated these excessive evacuations after every bleeding, and taking at the same time scarcely any nourishment, I was (as may be supposed) reduced to the most extreme debility.

The *Alcaide*, observing the great change in my appearance, was surprised, as well as the Pundit, at my distressing condition, from which they conceived such slender hopes of my recovery, that they were obliged to report it to the Inquisitor—who directed them to propose that I should confess myself; and, as I did not think that I could live, I began to repent of what I had done, and not wishing to lose both soul and body at once, I consented that a Confessor should be sent for. A religious of the order of St. Francis attended accordingly, and having fully confided to him my whole case, I received much consolation, and was induced by his excellent counsel to do everything in my power towards the restoration of my health.

I permitted him to communicate what had occurred to the Inquisitor confidentially; and from that day, (which was Good Friday,) they carefully supplied me with everything necessary for the speedy reparation of the strength I had lost with my blood; and to enliven the melancholy which preyed upon me, a black prisoner accused of magic, was confined along with me, and remained in my cell for five months.

During this period I was more rational, and suffered less from ennui; but so soon as I was thought to be convalescent, my companion was removed; and the privation of this comfort soon occasioned me to relapse into the same state in which I was before.

CHAPTER XXVII

Despair drives me to fresh excesses.

THE removal of my companion made me more furious than ever. I beat my breast and face, and, not satisfied with that, I sought for means, which before I wanted sufficient resolution to use, to kill myself. I was sensible that this could not be effected by a second pretence of indisposition; which, if I had attempted in case it should have been necessary to bleed me, proper care would have been taken to prevent such effusion of blood as I had before encouraged. Inspired by despair, it occurred to me that notwithstanding the scrupulous search which I had undergone on my first imprisonment, I had secreted some pieces of gold by sewing them into a ribband, fastened round my leg below the knee like a garter. I broke one of these coins; and by friction against an earthen vessel, contrived to sharpen and point a piece in the form of a lancet with which I determined to cut the arteries of my arm. With this view, I took every requisite precaution, and inserted it as far as I could; but, with all my pains, I could not obtain my object, and instead of the arteries, opened only the veins above them. Being rendered quite desperate, I pierced both arms, until I fainted from weakness, and fell on the floor in my blood, which flowed into every part of the room; and assuredly, if the special providence of God had not caused my door to be opened, for the purpose of bringing me something at an unusual time, I should have miserably lost my life and soul.

The astonishment of my guards when they saw me, may be imagined. They called the *Alcaide*, and entering together they bound up my wounds, and succeeded in bringing me to myself. The circumstances being reported to the Inquisitor, he ordered me to be brought before him; I was carried by four men and laid down upon the floor, my extreme weakness preventing me from standing or sitting.

The Inquisitor bitterly reproached me, and commanded the attendants to take me away, and handcuff me in order to hinder me from tearing away the bandages, which were tied round my arms. This was instantly obeyed, and not only were my hands chained, but a collar of iron was put on my neck and fastened to the manacles with a padlock, in such a manner that I could not even move my arms. This measure increased my irritation. I threw myself upon the ground, dashed my head against the pavement and the walls; and, had I been left in this situation, I should have certainly liberated my arms and destroyed myself; but, being watched, my actions soon evinced that all severity was unavailable, and that milder treatment would be more advisable.

My irons were taken off; the most deceitful promises were made; my chamber was changed; and another companion was given to me, who was made responsible for my safety. This was also a black prisoner, but much less civilized than the one I had before. It pleased God, who had preserved me from so great a crime, to dissipate the despair into which I had fallen, and thereby to bless me more than those who have committed suicide in the prisons of the Holy Office, where the door of all human comfort is closed upon its wretched inmates for ever. My new companion continued with me about two months. When I became rather more composed he was removed, though the languor I felt was so extreme, that it was with difficulty I could rise to receive my meals from the door at two paces distant. After a year had thus passed, from mere dint of suffering I became as it were habituated to it, and God finally gave me patience to endure, without making any further attempt upon my life.

CHAPTER XXVIII

My fourth Audience, in which the Proctor pronounces sentence of death against me.

I HAD been eighteen months in the Inquisition, when my Judges being informed that I was able to appear, caused me to be conducted to an Audience for the fourth time. They asked me if I had resolved to declare what was required; and on replying that I could not remember anything which I had not said before, the Proctor of the Holy Office presented himself with the informations laid against me.

On my former examinations I had accused myself; they were satisfied with hearing me without entering into any explanation, and I was remanded to my cell as soon as I had finished what I had to say; but on this occasion I was formally impeached, and a time allotted for my defence. My own confessions were included in the depositions. The facts themselves were true, as I had voluntarily admitted, and in that respect I had therefore no defence; but I wished to convince my Judges that the facts were not so heinous as they appeared. I represented to them, that with regard to my opinions upon Baptism, I had not had any intention to controvert the doctrines of the church, but that the passage "*Except a man be born of water and of the spirit, he cannot enter into the kingdom of God,*" having struck me as very particular, I had requested an explanation. The Grand Inquisitor appeared to me to be surprised by the passage, which every one knows by heart, and I was astonished at his surprise. He enquired where it was to be found. I said in the gospel of St. John, chap. iii. verse 5. He called for a New Testament, turned to the passage and read it, but did not explain it to me, He seemed, however, glad to pass it over, by telling me. that it was sufficiently expounded by tradition ; as not only those who have died for the sake of our Lord Jesus Christ without having been formally baptized, but also those who have been cut off in the intention of being baptized and in sorrow for their sins, are in effect considered as being baptized.

Upon the subject of Image-worship, I said that I had not asserted anything that was not authorized by the Holy Council of Trent, and quoted the passage from the 25th Session, treating of the Invocation of Saints and of Holy Images. " The Images of Christ, of the Virgin Mother of God, and of the other Saints, are to be kept ; and that respect is due to them, and worship to be imparted, so as that by the images before which we prostrate ourselves, we should adore Christ and honour the Saints whose resemblance they bear."

My Judge seemed to be more astonished by this reference than he was by the preceding ; and, having found it, closed the book without giving me any explanation.

Such ignorance in persons who are appointed to decide upon matters of Faith, is incomprehensible ; and I own that I should reluctantly trust myself as to the fact, although I witnessed and perfectly recollect it, if I had not learnt from the publications of Mr. Tavernier, that, reserved as Father Ephraim de Nevers was upon everything relating to the Inquisition, under which he suffered so much, he did intimate that nothing had been so intolerable to him as the ignorance of its ministers.

The Proctor, on reading the informations, stated, that besides what I had admitted, I was accused and fully convicted of having spoken contemptuously of the Inquisition and its Officers, and even with disrespect of the Sovereign Pontiff and against his authority ; and concluded, that the contumacy I had hitherto displayed, by neglecting so many delays and benignant warnings which had been given to me, was a convincing proof that I had entertained the most pernicious intentions, and that my design was to teach and inculcate heretical opinions; that I had consequently incurred the penalty of the greater Excommunication ; that my property was confiscated to the crown, and myself delivered over to the secular power, to be punished for my crimes according to law, that is, to be burnt.

I leave it to my readers to imagine the effect of these cruel denunciations of the Proctor of the Holy Office upon my mind ; yet I can truly aver, that, terrible as they were, the death to which I was sentenced, appeared to me to be less dreadful, than the prolongation of my slavery. The agony of spirit and contraction of heart which I felt, did not prevent me from replying to the fresh charges which had been brought against me, that as to my intentions they had never been bad, that I had ever been a true Catholic, and that all those with whom I had associated in the Indies, could testify it, and especially Father Ambrose and Father Yves, both French Capuchins who had frequently confessed me ; (—I have since learnt, that the latter was actually at Goa at the very time that I referred to him as an evidence in my favour ;)—that I had even travelled sixteen leagues to keep the feast of Easter ; that, had I been heretically inclined, I could easily have established myself in those parts of the Indies, where perfect liberty of conduct and speech were tolerated, and not have chosen the states of the King of Portugal for my abode ; that I was so far from declaiming against the Faith, that I had often disputed with heretics in its defence ; that, indeed, I remembered that I had expressed myself too freely respecting the Tribunal before which I stood, and the personages who belonged to it, but was surprised to find, that what had been so slightly treated when I acknowledged it a year and a half before, was now attributed to me as a grievous crime ; that as to what related to the Pope, I did not recollect that I had ever mentioned him in the manner stated in my accusation, but if they would detail the particulars, I would speak honestly and truly to the charge.

The Inquisitor then addressing me said, that I should have time for considering the article which regarded the Holy Pontiff ; but that he was astonished at my impudence in asserting that I had confessed the charge touching the Inquisition, as he was confident I had never opened my mouth upon the subject; and that if I had made any such declaration within the period I had represented, I should not have been so long detained.

I so well remembered what I had said, and the answer I had received; I was moreover so indignant at finding myself trifled with,—that had I not been compelled to retire as soon as I had signed my examination, I could not have refrained from insulting my Judge; and if I had had strength and liberty in proportion to the courage which my anger inspired, I possibly should not have been content with opprobrious language only.

CHAPTER XXIX

I am frequently taken to the Audience. Various remarks upon occurrences in the Inquisition.

I WAS summoned to three or four Audiences in less than a month afterwards, and was urged to confess what I was accused of respecting the Pope. It was even intimated, that the Proctor had found an additional proof against me, but which in fact differed in no respect from what had been before alledged. What manifestly shews that this was nothing but a falsehood invented for the purpose of extracting my sentiments, is, that any specification of what it was pretended I had advanced was refused; and it being ultimately perceived, that nothing could be drawn from me, the point was no longer pressed, and this article was not inserted in the publication of the process against me at the Act of Faith. In these latter Audiences, however, it was attempted to make me admit that my design in the facts I had avowed, was to support Heresy; but this I never would assent to, for nothing could be more removed from truth.

During the months of November and December, I every morning heard the cries of those to whom the torture was administered, and which was inflicted so severely, that I have seen many persons of both sexes who have been crippled by it, and, amongst others, the first companion allotted to me in my prison.

No distinctions of rank, age, or sex are attended to in this Tribunal. Every individual is treated with equal severity; and when the interest of the Inquisition requires it, all are alike tortured in almost perfect nudity.

It occurred to me, that before I entered the prisons of the Holy Office, I had heard it mentioned, that the *Auto da Fé* was usually celebrated on the first Sunday in Advent, because, in the service for that day, is read a portion of the gospel which describes the day of Judgement; and the Inquisitors affect that this ceremony is its lively and natural prototype. I was also confident that there were several prisoners; the dead silence which reigns in this mansion having afforded me opportunity to ascertain, with tolerable exactness, how many doors were opened at the hours of repast. In addition to this, I was almost certain that an Archbishop had arrived in the month of October, (the see having been vacant nearly thirty years,) from the extraordinary ringing of the bells of the cathedral for nine days successively; to which period, it is neither the custom of the churches in general, nor of that of Goa in particular, to extend the solemnization of any remarkable feast; and I knew that this Prelate had been expected before my imprisonment.

From all these reasons I inferred that I should be released in the beginning of December; but when I saw the first and the second Sundays in Advent pass, I began to fear that my liberation or punishment was postponed for another year.

CHAPTER XXX

By what means I discovered that the Auto da Fé was to be performed. on the ensuing day; and the description of the dresses given to the prisoners for their appearance at that ceremony.

HAVING persuaded myself that the *Auto da Fé* was always celebrated in the beginning of December, and not observing any preparations for the awful ceremony, I reconciled myself to another year of suffering; but when I the least expected it, I was on the eve of quitting the cruel captivity in which I had languished for two years. I remarked, that on Saturday the eleventh of January, 1676, as I gave my linen as usual to be washed, the Officers declined taking it till the next day. On reflecting upon this unusual circumstance, and not being able satisfactorily to account for it, I concluded that the celebration of the *Auto da Fé* might take place on the morrow; and my opinion was the more confirmed, or rather converted into certainty, when, immediately after vespers had chimed at the cathedral, the bell rang for matins, which had never happened before during my imprisonment, except on the eve of the Feast of the Holy Sacrament, which is celebrated in the Indies on the Thursday following the Sunday after Easter, on account of the incessant rains which fall there at the period when it is solemnized in Europe. It may be supposed that joy would have begun to resume its place in my heart, when I believe that I was on the point of leaving the tomb in which I had been buried alive for two years; but the terror which was occasioned by the dreadful denunciations of the Proctor, and the uncertainty of my fate, augmented my anxiety and grief to such a degree, that I passed the remainder of the day and part of the night under feelings which would have excited compassion from any but those into whose hands I had fallen.

When supper was brought to me, I refused it; and because, contrary to custom, I was not entreated to receive it, when the door was shut I gave way entirely to the melancholy which possessed me; but, after many sighs and tears, overpowered by vexation and deathly images, I dropped asleep about eleven o'clock.

I had not slept long before I was awoke by a noise occasioned by the guards in drawing back the bolts of my cell. I was surprised by the approach of persons bearing lights, to which I was unaccustomed, and the hour contributed to increase my alarm.

The *Alcaide* gave me a garment, which he ordered me to put on, and to be ready to follow him when he should call for me; and then retired, leaving me a lighted lamp. I had neither power to rise nor to reply; and when left alone, I was seized with so general and violent a trepidation, that, for more than a quarter of an hour, I could not summon resolution even to look upon the dress which had been brought. At last I arose, and prostrating myself before a cross which I had scrawled upon the wall, I recommended myself to God and resigned my lot into his hands: I then put on the dress, which consisted of a jacket with sleeves down to the wrists, and trousers hanging over the heels; both being of black stuff with white stripes.

CHAPTER XXXI

The preparations for the Act of Faith, and the various marks of distinction given to the prisoners, according to their degrees of criminality.

I HAD not long to wait after I had dressed myself. The gentlemen whose first visit was made a little before midnight, returned about two in the morning, and conducted me into a long gallery, where a great number of my companions in misery were already assembled, and arranged against the wall. I took my place in the rank, and many others arrived after me. Although there were nearly two hundred men in the gallery, every one preserved profound silence; as in this great number, there were scarcely any to be distinguished amongst the others; and as all were habited in black, these persons might have been mistaken for so many statues placed upon the wall, if the motion of their eyes, the use of which alone was allowed them, had not shown that they were alive.

The place in which we were, was lighted by a few lamps, whose gloomy rays displaying so many black, sad, and devoted objects, seemed an appropriate prelude to death.

The women, who were apparelled in the same stuff as the men, were in an adjoining gallery, where we could not see them; but I observed that in a Dormitory at a little distance from that in which we stood, there were also several prisoners, and some persons clothed in black dresses, who occasionally walked about the apartment. I did not then know what this meant, but a few hours after I learnt that the persons in that apartment were condemned to be burnt, and that those who walked were their Confessors.

Being unacquainted with the forms of the Holy Office, although I had before so anxiously wished to die, I imagined that I was amongst the number of the condemned ; but was somewhat encouraged by the observation, that there was nothing in my habiliments different from the rest, and that it was improbable that so many persons as were dressed like myself would be put to death.

When we were all arranged against the wall of the gallery, a yellow wax-light was given to each ; and some bundles of robes made like Dalmatics or large Scapularies were brought in. These were made of yellow stuff, with crosses of St. Andrew painted in red both in front and behind. It is thus that those are distinguished who have committed, or are adjudged to have committed, offences against the Christian Faith, whether Jews, Mahometans, Sorcerers, or Heretic Apostates. These vestments are called *Sambenito.*

Such as are considered as convicted, and persist in denying the charges against them, and those who have relapsed, wear another kind of Scapulary called *Samarra*, the ground of which is of a grey colour. A portrait of the wearer is depicted on both sides, placed on burning firebrands, with ascending flames, and surrounded by demons. Their names and crimes are inscribed beneath the picture. Those who have confessed after sentence has been pronounced and before leaving the prison, have the flames on their *Samarras* reversed, which is called *Fogo revolto*. The *Sambenitos* were distributed to twenty Blacks accused of Magic, to one Portuguese who was charged with the same crime, and was moreover a *New Christian*, and, as half measures would not satisfy the revenge of my persecutors, who were resolved to degrade me as much as possible, I was compelled to wear a garb similar to those of the Sorcerers and Heretics, although I had uniformly professed the Catholic, Apostolic, and Roman Faith, as my Judges might have been easily informed by many persons, both foreigners and my own countrymen, to whom I had been known in various parts of India. My apprehension now redoubled ; conceiving that if, amongst so great a number of prisoners, twenty-two only received these disgraceful *Sambenitos*, they must be those to whom no mercy was intended.

When this distribution was made, I noticed five pasteboard caps, tapering to a point like a sugar loaf, and entirely covered with devils and flames of fire, with the word "*Feiticero.*" (Sorcerer) written round the fillet. These caps are called, *Carochas*, and are placed upon the heads of the most guilty of those accused of Magic; and as they happened to be near me. I expected to be presented with one. This, however, was not the case. From that moment, I had no doubt that these wretches would indeed be burnt; and as they were as ignorant as myself of the forms of the Holy Office, they assured me afterwards, that they themselves had also thought their destruction inevitable.

Every one being thus accoutred according to the character of his offence, we were allowed to sit down upon the floor, in expectation of fresh orders.

At four in the morning, some domestics followed the guards in order to distribute bread and figs to such as chose to partake of them; but, though I had taken no supper the preceding night, I was not disposed to eat, and should not have taken anything, if one of the guards had not come up to me and said, "Take your bread, and if you cannot eat it now, put it in your pocket, for you will be hungry before you come back." These words afforded me infinite satisfaction, and dissipated all my terror by the hope which they inspired of my return; and I took his advice.

At length the day dawned about five o'clock; and the various emotions of shame, grief, and terror with which all were agitated, might be traced in our countenances; for, though each was joyful at the prospect of deliverance from a captivity so severe and insupportable, the sentiment was much alloyed by the uncertainty of his fate.

CHAPTER XXXII

The order of procession to the Act of Faith.

THE great bell of the cathedral tolled a little before sunrise as a signal to the multitude to assemble for the august solemnity of the *Auto da Fé*, which is the triumph of the Holy Office; and we were then commanded to go forth one by one. In passing from the gallery to the great hall, I remarked that the Inquisitor was seated at the door and a Secretary standing near him; that the hall was filled by the inhabitants of Goa, whose names were entered in a list which he held; and that as each prisoner came out of the gallery, he called for one of the gentlemen in the hall, who immediately advanced to the prisoner to accompany him, and act as his godfather at the Act of Faith.

These godfathers have the charge of the persons they attend, and are obliged to answer for, and represent them until the Feast is concluded; and Messrs. the Inquisitors affect to consider them as much honoured by the appointment. My godfather was the General of the Portuguese ships in the Indies. I went out with him, and when I got into the street, I saw that the procession was headed by the community of the Dominicans, who have this privilege because St. Dominic, their patron, was also the founder of the Inquisition. They were preceded by the banner of the Holy Office, in which the image of the founder was represented in very rich embroidery, with a sword in one hand and an olive branch in the other, with the inscription, "*Justitia and Misericordia.*"

These Religious were followed by the prisoners singly, each holding a taper, and having his godfather by his side. The least guilty marched first, and, as I was not reckoned as one of the most innocent, more than a hundred went before me. Like the rest, my head and feet were bare, and I was greatly annoyed during the procession, which continued upwards of an hour, by the small flints, with which the streets of Goa are covered; causing the blood to stream from my feet.

We were led through the principal streets, and everywhere regarded by an immense crowd, which came from all parts of India, and lined all the roads by which we passed; notice having been given from the pulpit in the most distant parishes, long before the Act of Faith was to be celebrated.

At length, overwhelmed with shame and confusion, and fatigued by the walk, we arrived at the church of St. Francis, which had been previously fitted up for the celebration of the

Auto da Fé. The high altar was hung with black, and six silver candle sticks with tapers of white wax were burning upon it. Two seats resembling thrones were erected, one on each side of the altar; that on the right being destined for the Inquisitor and his Council, and the other for the Viceroy and his Court. At some distance, opposite the high altar, and nearer to the entrance, was another altar, with ten missals laid open upon it; and from thence to the door, a passage about three feet in width was railed in; and on each side, benches were placed for the culprits and their godfathers, who sat down in the order in which they entered the church; so that the first were nearest the altar. So soon as I was seated, I attended to the procedure observed as to those who followed me; I remarked that those to whom the horrible *Carochas* had been given, marched the last of our party, and immediately after them a large crucifix was carried, with the face towards those who preceded it, and was followed by two persons and the statues of four others, as large as life, accurately executed, and which were placed upon long poles, accompanied by the same number of chests filled with the bones of those represented by the statues, and each carried by a man. The front of the crucifix being turned upon those who walked before, signified that mercy had been extended to them, by their deliverance from the death they had justly merited; and, on the contrary, that those behind had no favour to hope for. Such is the mystery which pervades every thing in the Holy Office.

The manner in which these wretches were clothed, was equally calculated to excite horror and pity. Not only the living persons, but the statues also, had each a *Samarra* of grey stuff, painted all over with devils, flames, and burning fire-brands; upon which, the portrait of the wearer was naturally represented on both sides, with his sentence under-written in large characters, briefly stating his name and country, and the nature of the crime for which he was condemned. With this strange garment, they also wore those frightful *Carochas*, covered, like the robe, with demons and fire.

The little chests which enclosed the bones of the deceased, the proceedings against whom had been conducted either before or after their deaths, or prior to, or pending their imprisonment, for the purpose of giving colour to the confiscation of their property, were also painted black, and covered with flames and devils.

It is here necessary to mention, that the jurisdiction of the Inquisition is not limited to the living, or to those who have died in prison ; but processes are often instituted against persons who have been dead many years before their accusation. When any important charge is preferred against a person deceased, his body is taken out of his tomb, and, on conviction, consumed at the Act of Faith ; his estates are seized, and those who may have taken possession compelled to refund. I state nothing but what I have witnessed ; for one of the statues produced on this occasion represented a man who had died a long time before ; against whom a process had been instituted, his remains disinterred, his effects confiscated, and his bones (or perhaps those of some other person who had been buried in the same place) burnt.

CHAPTER XXXIII

Containing an account of the transactions at the place where the Auto da Fé was celebrated.

THESE wretches having entered in the funeral equipage I have described, and being seated in the places appointed for them near the door of the church, the Inquisitor, attended by his Officers, came in, and placed himself upon the throne, prepared for him on the right of the altar ; whilst the Viceroy and his Court took possession of that on the left. The crucifix was laid upon the altar, between the six candles, and every one being stationed at his post, the church was filled by the crowd. The Provincial of the Augustins ascended the pulpit, and preached for half an hour ; and, notwithstanding the embarrassment and mental uneasiness which I felt, I could not help noticing the comparison which he drew between the Inquisition and Noah's Ark ; in which, however, he marked this distinction, that the creatures which entered the Ark, left it on the cessation of the deluge with their original nature and properties ; whereas the Inquisition had this singular characteristic, that those who came within its walls, cruel as wolves and fierce as lions, went forth gentle as lambs.

L. No. 6. *Samarra*, with a portrait the wearer placed on burning fire-ands and surrounded by demons, and *rocha*, conical cap. Dress worn by ose who were condemned to be burnt ve. (See pt. II, pp. 52-53).

ILL. No. 7. *Sambenito*, with the Cross of St. Andrew Dress worn by those who had avoided death by self-accusation. (See pt. II, p. 52).

Ill. No. 8. Procession to the *Auto de Fé.*

At the head of the procession is the banner of the Holy Office. Then follow the Dominic friars. Next follow the prisoners, the least guilty marching first. Each prisoner holds a taper and has his Godfather by his side. Then follow effigies of the dead prisoners carried on poles, each accompanied by a chest containing the bones of the deceased. (See pt. II, pp. 53-56).

Ill. No. 9. Celebration of the *Auto de Fé* in the church of St. Francis (Goa). (See pt. II, pp. 56-57).

Ill. No. 10. *Campo Sancto Lazaro* in Goa, where condemned prisoners were burnt. (See pt. II, p. 60).

On the conclusion of the sermon, two Readers alternately appeared in the pulpit to declare aloud the accusations, and announce the punishments to which the criminals were sentenced.

As the publication of the proceedings against each party commenced, he was conducted by the *Alcaide* into the middle of the Aisle, where he continued standing with a lighted taper in his hand, until his sentence was delivered; and, as it is presumed that all the criminals have incurred the penalty of the greater Excommunication, when this was done, he was led up to the altar where the missals were placed; upon one of which, after kneeling down, he was directed to lay his hands, in which posture he remained, until there were as many persons as books. The Reader then discontinued the proceedings, and in an audible manner pronounced a confession of Faith, which the criminals were previously bidden to repeat after him, with heart and voice, and at the end of which, each returned to his station, and the reading was resumed.

I was summoned in my turn, and found that the charge against me involved three points; one of which was, the having maintained the inefficacy of the Baptism Flaminis; another, having asserted that Images ought not to be worshipped, and having blasphemed against the representation of a crucifix in ivory, by saying that it was a piece of ivory; and the last, that I had spoken contemptuously of the Inquisition and its Ministers—but above all, the bad intention from which I had uttered these things. For these offences I was declared Excommunicate, and, by way of atonement, my goods were forfeited to the King, and myself banished from the Indies, and condemned to serve in the galleys of Portugal for five years; and moreover to perform such other penances, as might be expressly enjoined by the Inquisitors.

Of all these punishments, that which appeared to me the heaviest, was the indispensable necessity of quitting India, in which I had intended to travel for some time; but this disappointment was in some measure compensated by the prospect of being soon delivered from the hands of the Holy Office.

My confession of Faith being finished, I returned to my place, and then availed myself of the hint which had been given me by the guard, to keep my bread; for the ceremony having lasted the whole day, every one present ate something in the church.

CHAPTER XXXIV

The prisoners are absolved, and those sentenced to the stake delivered over to the secular power. The ceremonies observed on this occasion.

WHEN the causes of those, to whom mercy was extended by the boon of their lives, were concluded, the Inquisitor left his seat, to assume the Alb and Stole; and attended by about twenty Priests, each bearing a wand, came into the centre of the church; where, after several prayers had been read, we were severally released from Excommunication, (which it was stated we had incurred) by a stroke from the Priests on our clothes.

I cannot resist mentioning a circumstance, which will shew the excessive superstitition of the Portuguese in matters relating to the Inquisition. During the procession, and whilst we remained in the church, the person who was my godfather, (though I frequently addressed him,) would not speak to me, and even refused me a pinch of snuff which I requested; so apprehensive was he, that in so doing, he should participate in the censure under which he conceived me to lie; but the moment I received absolution, he embraced me, presented his snuff-box, and told me that thenceforth he should regard me as a brother, since the church had absolved me.

This ceremony being concluded, and the Inquisitor re-seated, the wretched victims to be sacrificed by the Holy Inquisition were ordered to advance separately. There were a man and a woman, and the images of four men deceased, with the chests in which their bones were deposited. The man and woman were black native Christians accused of magic, and condemned as Apostates; but, in truth, as little Sorcerers as those by whom they were condemned.

Two of the four statues also, represented persons convicted of magic; and the others, two new Christians, who were said to have Judaised. One of these had died in the prisons of the Holy Office ; the other expired in his own house, and his body had been long since interred in his parish church ; but having been accused of Judaism after his decease, as he had left considerable wealth, his tomb was opened, and his remains disinterred to be burnt at the *Auto da Fé* ; whence it may be inferred, that the Holy Inquisition affects, in imitation of our Saviour, to exercise its power on the quick and the dead.

The proceedings against these unfortunates were then read, all of which concluded in these terms; " that the mercy of the Holy Office being prevented by their relapse or contumacy, and being indispensably obliged to punish them according to the rigour of the law, it gave them up to the secular power and civil justice, which it nevertheless entreated to regard with mercy and clemency these miserable creatures, and if they were liable to capital punishment, that it should be inflicted without effusion of blood."

At the conclusion of these words, a Tipstaff of the Lay Court approached, and seized his victims, each previously receiving a slight blow on the breast from the *Alcaide* of the Holy Office, to testify that they were abandoned.

How benevolent is the Inquisition, thus to intercede for the guilty ! What extreme condescension in the magistrates, to be satisfied, from complaisance to the Inquisition, with burning the culprits to the very marrow of their bones, rather than shed their blood !

Thus terminated the Act of Faith ; and whilst these wretches were conveyed to the banks of the river, where the Viceroy and his Court were assembled, and where the faggots on which they were to be immolated had been piled the preceding day, we were re-conducted to the Inquisition by our godfathers, without any order of procession.

Although I have never been present at an execution of persons abandoned in this manner by the Holy Office, yet having had authentic accounts from persons who have witnessed many such occasions, I will relate, in a few words, the formalities which are observed.

So soon as the condemned arrive at the place where the Lay Judges are assembled, they are asked in what religion they wish to die ; without referring in any manner to the proceedings against them, which are presumed to have been perfectly correct, and the prisoners justly condemned, the infallibility of the Inquisition being never questioned. Upon this question being answered, the executioner lays hold of them, and binds them to the stake, where they are previously strangled if they die Christians, and burnt alive if they persist in Judaism or Heresy, which so seldom happens that scarcely one instance has been known in four Acts of Faith, though few have passed without a great number having been burnt.

The day after the execution, the pictures of those who have been put to death are carried through the Dominican churches. The heads alone are represented, laid on burning fire brands. Their names are inscribed beneath, with those of their father and country, the description of the crime for which they are condemned, and the year, month, and day of their execution. If the party has fallen twice into the same offence, these words are added to the foot of the portrait, "*Morreo queimado, por Hereje relapso*" (he was burnt as a relapsed Heretic.)—If, having been accused but once, he persists in error, it is altered to—"*por Hereje contumos* ;" but as this case rarely happens, there are not many pictures with this inscription. Again, if having been accused but once by a sufficient number of witnesses, he perseveres in asserting his innocency, and even professes himself a Christian to the last, it is stated "*Morreo queimado, por Hereje convitto negativo,*" (that is, he was burnt for a convicted Heretic, but without confession ;) and of these, there are a great many. It is certain that of a hundred *negatives*, ninety-nine at the least are not only innocent of the crime which they deny, but, besides their innocence, have the further merit of preferring death to the falsehood of acknowledging themselves guilty of a crime of which they are incapable ; for it is not possible that a man assured of his life if he confesses, should persist in denying, and choose to be burnt rather than avow, a fact, the confession of which would save his life.

These frightful figures are placed in the nave and above the grand entrance of the church, as so many illustrious trophies consecrated to the glory of the Holy Office ; and when this part is full, they are arranged in the aisles near the door. Those who have been in the great church of the Dominicans, at Lisbon, may have observed several hundreds of these affecting representations.

CHAPTER XXXV

My final departure from the Inquisition. We are conducted to a private house to receive instruction for some days.

I WAS so fatigued and so exhausted at my return from the Act of Faith, that I felt not less eagerness to re-enter my cell in order to rest myself, than I had some days before expressed to leave it. My godfather accompanied me into the hall, and the *Alcaide* having conducted me into the gallery, I hastened to shut myself up, whilst he attended the rest. I threw myself upon my bed, in expectation of supper, which was nothing but bread and some figs. the bustle of the day having impeded the business of the kitchen. I slept better than I had done for many nights preceeding, but so soon as it was light, I waited impatiently what was to be done with me. The *Alcaide* came about six o'clock for the dress I had worn during the procession, which I cheerfully relinquished, and, at the same time, wished to give him the *Sambenito*, but he would not receive it, as I was to wear it every Sunday and Holiday until the entire accomplishment of my sentence. Breakfast was brought about seven o'clock, and soon after I was directed to collect my clothes together, and to be ready to go when I should be called for.

I obeyed this last order with the utmost promptitude. About nine, a guard opened my door ; I took up my bundle upon my back, as I was directed, and followed him to the great hall, where the greater part of the prisoners were already assembled.

After remaining there some time, about twenty of my companions, who had been sentenced the day before to be whipped, and were now brought for the purpose of receiving the infliction from the hands of the hangman through all the streets of the town, entered ; and being thus collected, the Inquisitor appeared, before whom we knelt to receive his benediction, kissing the ground at his feet. The Blacks, who had few clothes, were then ordered to take up those of the Whites. Such of the prisoners as were not Christians were instantly sent to the places prescribed by their sentences ; some into exile, and others to the galleys, or the powder manufactory, called " *Casa da Pulvera* ; " and such as were Christians, as well Blacks as Whites, were conducted to a house expressly hired for them in the city for some time, for the purpose of receiving instructions. The halls and passages of the house were appropriated for the lodging of the Blacks ; and we that were Whites, were placed in a separate chamber, in which we were locked up during the night, having the range of the house in the day time, with liberty to converse with those who came to see us. Every day there were two catechisings ; one for the Blacks, and another for the Whites ; and Mass was regularly performed, at which we all assisted, as also at Matins and Vespers.

During my abode in this place, I was visited by a Dominican monk, one of the friends I had known at Damaun, where he had been a Prior. This excellent priest, oppressed with age and infirmities, no sooner knew that I was liberated, than he hired a palanquin to come to see me. He lamented my disaster, embracing me tenderly, and assuring me that he had had many fears for me ; that he had often enquired after my health and the state of my affairs, from the Father, Agent for the prisoners, who was his friend, and of the same order as himself, but notwithstanding he had been long without obtaining a satisfactory answer ; and that, at last, after much entreaty, all that he could learn was that I was alive.

I derived much consolation from the visits of this Religous, and my being obliged to leave the Indies was equally distressing to us both. He had the goodness to come to me repeatedly ; urged me to return to India when I was at liberty ; and sent me several things for the voyage, which my condition and necessities precluded the hope of procuring.

CHAPTER XXXVI

I am reconducted to the Inquisition, to hear the Penances imposed upon me.

AFTER remaining in this house until the 23rd of January, we were then conveyed to the hall of the Inquisition, and thence separately summoned to the Board of the Holy Office, to receive from the Inquisitor a paper containing the penances to which he was pleased to sentence us. I went in my turn, and was directed to kneel down, after laying my hands upon the Gospels, and in that posture to promise to preserve the most inviolable secrecy concerning all that had passed and had come to my knowledge during my detention. My Judge then gave me a writing signed by his hand, expressing what I was to perform; and as this document is not long, I conceive that it is best to transcribe it, as accurately translated from the Portuguese.

List of Penances to be observed by—

1st. In the three ensuing years he shall confess and communicate;—during the first year, once a month;—and the two following, at the feasts of Easter, Whitsuntide, Christmas. and the Assumption of our Lady.

2nd. He shall, if practicable, hear Mass and a Sermon every Sunday and Holiday.

3rd. During the first three years he shall repeat, five times every day, the Lord's Prayer and *Ave Maria*, in honour of the five wounds of our Saviour.

4th. He shall not form any friendship nor particular intimacy with Heretics or persons holding suspicious doctrines, which may prejudice his salvation.

5th and lastly, He shall be inflexibly reserved as to every thing which he has seen, said, or heard, or the treatment which has been observed towards him, as well at the Board as in the other places of the Holy Office.

FRANCISCO DELGADO e MATOS.

Who can say on perusing these penitentiary canons, that the Inquisition is too rigorous? On receiving this paper, I kissed the ground, and retired into the hall, to wait until the rest had gone through the like formality. On departing, we were separated, and I know not what became of the remainder of the company; but about a dozen of us only were taken to the *Aljouvar*, the official prison in which I had been confined for one day on my arrival at Goa before my entrance into the Inquisition. Here I continued until the 25th, when an officer of the Holy Office came to carry me in iron on board of a vessel which was ready to sail for Portugal.

CHAPTER XXXVII

Remarks upon the preceding account.

I SHALL interrupt the recital of my adventures, by making some reflections on what I have already stated; and begin by an examination of the injustice I have sustained from the Inquisition.

The first instance, is the treachery of the Commissary of Damaun; who, after I had declared to him what I had said regarding the Holy Office, gave me such hypocritical counsel, and caused me to be arrested to gratify the resentment of the governor; although the practice of the Inquisition is, to leave those who have spontaneously accused themselves at large. I am aware of what this father has said in his vindication, that I had not made my accusation in form; but that was a defect of which he ought to have apprised me: I was young and a foreigner, and should have instantly complied with it—but this paltry pretext was necessary to satisfy the governor.

The next thing, of which I think, I have cause to complain, is with reference to the same Commissary, I mean his maliciously detaining me at Damaun until the month of January, instead of sending me to Goa immediately after my imprisonment. Had he done so, my business would have been investigated before the end of November, and I should have been released at the Act of Faith which was celebrated that year in the beginning of December; but not having been transferred till after the Act of Faith, it was owing to him that I remained in the prisons of the Holy Office two years longer than I ought; because few are discharged, except at the funeral ceremony, called the *Auto da Fé* which occurring but once in two or three years, it is an aggravation of the misfortune to be cast into the sacred cells immediately after they have been cleared, and to remain there until a sufficient number of prisoners is collected to perform the Act of Faith with greater eclat.

The refusal of the Inquisitor at my third audience, to take my confession of what I had advanced against the Inquisition; and the falsehood of the assertion which he dared to make long afterwards, that I had not declared the fact which was charged upon me as so heinous an offence, was one of the things which affiicted me the most during my confinement, and is not the least subject of my grievances.

I may also justly complain, that the Inquisitor wished to lay a new snare for me, when on confessing my opinions concerning the Holy Office, and the circumstance which had long before happened to Father Ephraim de Nevers, he asked me, "if I defended the errors of that priest;" but though I well knew that the innocence of the Father had been fully established, and that he had been arrested from invidious motives, I replied "that I did not pretend to defend any one, having enough to do to defend myself."

I think too, that I am justified in believing that I was sent into Portugal, for the express purpose of pleasing the Viceroy and the Governor of Damaun, who was his relation; as out of upwards of two hundred persons who left the Inquisition when I did, I was the only one compelled to leave the Indies for Europe.

The cruelty of the guards, by whom I was often maltreated both by words and deeds, in order to force me to receive food and medicine when I was indisposed, deserves, in my opinion, to be noticed; for though they have some pretence for obliging the prisoners to take nourishment and remedies, they surely ought to use the same means only which are resorted to for other invalids, to whom stripes and blows are never administered to make them drink broths and physic.

I cannot refrain from objecting to the title of *Holy* assumed by the Inquisition. It is indeed difficult to apprehend wherein its sanctity consists; and in what manner a Tribunal, which violates the sacred laws of Charity, and the ordinances of Jesus Christ and the Church, can be termed Holy. Our Lord commands Christians to reprove those who fall, charitably and privately; and it is not until after many warnings have been despised, and they have become incorrigible, that he wishes them to be denounced to the church, in order that this Holy Mother may, by her authority, make a final effort to bring back her rebellious children to their duty by the imposition of penances, and, if necessary, even by the thunders of Excommunication; without, however, depriving them of some spiritual aid, such as the word of God and good books, by means of which, they may be cured of their estrangement. But the Holy Inquisition, in a course of conduct wholly opposite, enjoins all those who acknowledge its authority, not only under pain of Excommunication, but also under corporal and most cruel penalties, to denounce at once and without notice, those whom they may have seen commit, or have heard to say anything contrary to its institutions; and to caution those who err either before or after their denunciation, would not be a less offence, nor would escape with a slighter punishment in this Tribunal, than to neglect making the declaration within the limited period.

Was there ever any conduct so unjust as to shut up Christian people for many years in a narrow prison without books, (since even the Breviary is not allowed to priests;) without any exhortation to encourage them to suffer patiently; without hearing Mass, either on Holidays or Sundays; without administering the Eucharist, even at Easter, which all Christians are compelled to receive under danger of committing a mortal sin; and without being strengthened by the holy viaticum and extreme unction, at the hour of death? Who can conceive a conduct so astonishing, and so contrary to Christian charity? In lay jurisdiction, if the criminals are ever so wicked and loaded with guilt, they assist at Mass, and have the privilege of reading pious works, calculated to inspire them with repentant thoughts ; those who have a right to the Breviary, are permitted to repeat it and perform their duty ; such priests and religious persons as will take the trouble, are allowed to visit them in their dungeons, to comfort or confess them ; they communicate not only at Easter, but also as often as they are disposed ; and, when sick, the last sacraments are not withheld from them. Wherefore, then, in the Holy Office, and Ecclesiastical Tribunal, (the sole principle of which should be to cultivate sentiments of benevolence and mercy,) are the Judges so obdurate and unfeeling, as not only to deprive of all human consolation, those whom misfortune has thrown into their power, but to study with the utmost anxiety, to withdraw from these poor wretches the very means which God has chosen for the participation of his grace ?

I appeal to the gentlemen of the Holy Office, for the truth of what I have stated ; and if it be true, my readers will determine what right the Inquisition has to be called Holy.

I shall only add, that though the Inquisition sometimes grants safe-conduct to such as are in a place of security, but wish to come to make their voluntary accusations ; it is, however, prudent not to rely upon them entirely. This Tribunal is not too scrupulous in breaking its words ; and when it pleases, it can find sufficient excuse for not observing it, as I shall prove by an instance.

I knew a Religious of the order of St. Dominic, called Father Hyacinth, at Surat ; who for many years had renounced his convent and his habit, living in a very dissolute and scandalous manner. A woman with whom he cohabited, and who had borne him several children, died. The loss affected him, and induced him to think of changing his course of life. He resolved to return to his convent at Basseen ; but because all the Portuguese, and particularly Priests and Religious, who have resided much amongst the Indians, are obliged on returning to the states under the dominion of the Portuguese, to present themselves to the Inquisition, and make an exact declaration of their mode of life, in order to avoid being arrested, this Religious, whose conscience, perhaps, reproached him with some matter relative to the Holy Office, wrote before he left Surat, to the Inquisitor at Goa for a safe-conduct, that he might go thither to prefer his own accusation, which was instantly granted.

He departed upon this feeble assurance, and went to Basseen, where he was not suffered to resume his religious habit, until he was previously absolved by the Inquisition ; for which purpose he went to Goa, and presented himself at the Board of the Holy Office, to which he was summoned various times, and after being strictly examined, received absolution, and was sent back to the Vicar General of his Order, who restored his habit, and reinstated him in the functions of Preacher and Confessor. He then supposed the business to be settled, and prepared to return to Basseen, where his convent was established ; but when on the point of embarking in a galliot, to the great surprise of his friends he was taken up and thrown into the prisons of the Holy Office ; whose ministers had granted him absolution with so much facility, that they might strike their blow with more effect. In fact, the poor Friar, deceived by this fictitious and dissembled pardon, had caused property of considerable value, which he had acquired during his residence at Surat, to be brought to him. All was confiscated by the Inquisition, which could not have been effected without the manoeuvre of pledging to this unfortunate Priest, a promise the performance of which was never intended ; and that the Inquisitors might not be charged with having violated their safe-conduct, they artfully circulated a report, that since his absolution they had discovered other crimes which he had not confessed.

This Priest, who was imprisoned a few days after I was, remained there when I left the prison, for he did not appear at the Act of Faith ; nor was his process read, which would not have been omitted had he died in the Inquisition ; so that he probably continued until the ensuing Act.

This circumstance was told me by a Religious of the same order, who visited me after my release ; and the example ought to convince travellers and residents in the countries where the Inquisition is established, to be not merely circumspect in their words and actions, but not even to trust the assurances and safe-conduct which the Inquisitors or their Commissaries may propose to give them, how trifling soever may be the apparent cause of suspicion.

CHAPTER XXXVIII

History of Joseph Pereira de Meneses.

AS examples afford the best instruction, I shall briefly relate what happened to one of the first men in Goa, Joseph de Pereira de Meneses. Being captain general of the fleets of the King of Portugal in the Indies, he was ordered by the governor to sail with a fleet to relieve Diu, which was besieged by the Arabs. He departed, and having reached Basseen, was detained there longer than he wished by contrary winds ; during which time the Arabs took Diu, sacked it, and returned loaden with booty before the succour arrived. The general, who came too late, gave his directions and went back to Goa, where, as soon as he landed, the Governor, Antonio de Mello de Castro, and the declared enemy of Joseph Pereira, caused him to be arrested, and charged him with having purposely stopped at Basseen to avoid fighting, and thus, by his cowardice and negligence, contributed to the destruction and pillage of Diu, for the relief of which he had been dispatched and as neither the governors, not even the Viceroy himself, can cause a person of rank to be arrested without an express order from the court of Portugal, Antonio de Mello being unable to put his enemy to death, sentenced him to a punishment still more cruel, viz. to be led through the streets of the city by the hangman, with a cord tied round his neck, a distaff in his hand, preceded by a herald proclaiming that this was done by the royal order, the criminal having been attainted and convicted to cowardice and treason.

This severe sentence was executed, notwithstanding the solicitations of the prisoner's friends ; and after being conducted in this disgraceful manner along the thoroughfares of Goa, no sooner had he re-entered his prison, than a Familiar of the Holy Office took him to the Inquisition.

This event surprised every one; it being well known that Joseph Pereira could not be accused of Judaism, as he was not a New Christian, and had always lived in a reputable manner. The approaching Act of Faith was impatiently awaited, for ascertaining the cause of his imprisonment and the issue of the affair; but though the celebration occurred at the conclusion of the year, he did not appear, nor was his cause notified, which increased the general astonishment.

It should be premised that Joseph de Pereira had some time before had a difference with a gentleman of his acquaintance, but to whom he had been reconciled. This false friend, who never lost sight of his revenge, bribed five of Pereira's domestics to accuse him at the Inquisition of sodomy, and cited them as witnesses to his having committed the fact with a page, upon which both were arrested. The page being possessed of less firmness than his master, who he knew was in the prisons of the Holy Office, as well as himself, and not doubting that he was charged with the same crime of which the Proctor had declared himself guilty, intimidated by the menaces of the Inquisitors, afraid of being burnt, (as he certainly would have been had he persisted in denial,) and seeing no other means of saving his life, confessed that he was guilty of an offence which he had not committed, and thus became the seventh witness against his master; the accuser, by the rules of the Inquisition, being accounted one. His confession preserved him, and at the next act of Faith he was dismissed with a sentence of banishment to Mosambique.

In the meantime Pereira continued to assert his innocence. He was condemned to the stake, and would have been burnt at the same Act of Faith in which his page appeared, if the repeated protestations which he made of his innocence, and the personal regard which his Judges had uniformly felt toward him, had not induced them to defer the execution of the sentence, in order to see if they could not extort his confession, or receive further information on the subject. He was therefore reserved for another Act of Faith, which was celebrated the ensuing year, in consequence of the prisons having been filled sooner than usual.

In the course of the year, the accuser and the witnesses were several times examined; and one of the Judges taking it into his head to interrogate them apart, whether the moon shone or not on the night when they said they had seen their master perpetrate the crime their asnwers varied. Upon which they were put to the torture, and retracted all that they had advanced against their master, whose innocence being thus acknowledged, those who had appeared against him were taken into custody. Pereira was, discharged at the first Act of Faith as acquitted, and the witnesses and the accuser were produced at the same Act with myself. The first were condemned to the galleys for five years, and the gentleman transported for nine years to the coast of Africa.

It may be presumed that if the witnesses had been confronted, the Inquisitors would not have fallen into this embarrassment, nor the accused into the risk of being immolated by the Holy Office to the anger and resentment of his enemy; who ought, as I think, along with his accomplices, to have been punished by the same mode of death, to which this innocent gentleman was devoted; and there is no doubt that this ill-timed clemency of the Inquisition but too frequently gives occasion to similar attempts.

CHAPTER XXXIX

Circumstances relating to other Persons who were discharged with me at the Act of Faith.

TWO young married gentlemen in the vicinity of Basseen, who were in the Portuguese navy, protected a soldier of that nation who had rendered them some service. These gentlemen being at Goa after a cruise, and desirous of passing the rainy season (which in India is called winter) at home, left this young soldier at Goa, where he pretended to have some business to transact, to follow them in a few days. Immediately upon their departure he married, left Goa within two days, and returned to Basseen a few days after his masters. Soon afterwards, an advantageous match being offered to him, he embraced it, and married a second time. To enable him to do so he prevailed upon these gentlemen to certify to the Curate that he was a bachelor; which they did in perfect ignorance of his marriage. In a short time after this he went to Goa to visit his first wife, and was followed thither by the brother of his second; who on hearing of his former marriage, denounced him to the Inquisition. He was arrested, and on ascertaining by whom his being an unmarried man had been attested, an order was sent to the Commissary of Basseen to seize them. These two gentlemen, more unfortunate than culpable, were conveyed to Goa in irons, and thrown into the prisons of the Holy Office, were they remained eighteen months. They appeared at the Act of Faith, and were condemned to an exile of three years on the coast of Africa. The bigamist was banished to the same place for seven years, on the expiration of which he was to return to his first wife. The pedigree of one of these gentlemen had the blemish of *Christam Novo*; and as persons so circumstanced are always suspected of being bad Christians, he was asked at the Audience if he was not a Jew, and conversant with the Mosaic Law. Astonished by these questions, apprehensive lest the misfortune of his birth should involve him in distress, and not being too well instructed in the Christian religion, he conceived that it would be the wisest course he could adopt, and the most calculated for his vindication, to speak disrespectfully concerning Moses, declaring that he cared nothing about him, and had no acquaintance with him, to the great amusement of the Judges.

Among those who were discharged at the Act of Faith, I observed one who had a gag in his mouth fastened to his ears, and was informed by the publication of his process, that it was for having spoken blasphemously in jest. In addition to the disgrace of appearing in this state, he was sentenced to transportation for five years.

CHAPTER XL

My departure from Goa. Arrival at the Brazils. Short Description of the country.

I WAS conveyed in irons on board a vessel on the road bound for Portugal, and committed to the custody of the boatswain, who undertook to deliver me to the Inquisition at Lisbon, and the captain having received his final dispatches, we weighed anchor the 27th of January, 1676, and on the same day my chains were taken off.

Our voyage to the Brazils was favourable. We arrived there in the month of May. On dropping anchor in the Bay of All Saints, my guard took me ashore to the Governor's palace, and thence to the public prison, where I was left in charge of the gaoler. I remained in the prison all the time the ship was in the port, but by the favour of some friends I had in the country, I was allowed to be at liberty in the day time, and shut up during the night only.

The prison of the Bay is more commodious than any I had seen, except those of the Holy Office. Above the ground floor, which is tolerably clean and well lighted, there are several apartments appropriated for persons charged with slighter offences, or who are rich or well connected. There is also a chapel in which the Holy Mass is celebrated on Fridays and Festivals; and there are many charitable persons in the town, who contribute to the necessities of the prisoners.

(The remainder of this chapter contains an account of the Brazils and St. Salvador; and mentions the author's departure for Lisbon on the return of the fleet from Portugal in the beginning of September.)

CHAPTER XLI

The most remarkable Events of the Voyage. Arrival at Lisbon.

AT the commencement of the voyage we had contrary winds, and with much difficulty doubled Cape St. Augustine; having been more than a fortnight in accomplishing what in tolerable weather is usually effected in three or four days.

Though our people did not fare so well as they had done on the voyage from Goa, having nothing but *Cassada* and salted or smoked provisions to eat, and water to drink; we had but few sick, and not more than three or four died. I have not any doubt that the constant use of sugar mixed with water and *Cassada*, and the profusion of dried fruits which we had taken on board before we left the Bay, contributed greatly, by increasing the natural vigour of the constitution, to exempt us from that cruel disease the scurvy; debility being, as I apprehended, the sole cause of the malady.

Our stores had been much injured on our voyage from Goa to Brazil, and in spite of all the care that was taken to prevent its progress, few were so fortunate as not to experience some slight attacks; the majority were in a deplorable condition upon landing, and nearly thirty died before we arrived. On the passage from the Brazils to Portugal we enjoyed perfect health, but the frequent storms we encountered, and from which we were often in danger of perishing, precluded the enjoyment of the blessing, and we had the distress of seeing two men drowned without the possibility of assisting them.

We passed the island of Fernando da Noronha, which is small, and called after the name of the discoverer. It is uninhabited, though formerly it was used as a watering-place; but since some English left several large mastiffs there, either purposely or accidentally, those animals have multiplied to such an excessive degree, and become so extraordinarily wild, that no one can land without danger of being worried.

We continued our course to the latitude of the Azores, where the Portuguese have been long established, and from whence a large proportion of the corn for the consumption of the mother country is imported. The principal island is called Terceira, in which the King, Don Alphonso lived in a sort of exile until his brother, Don Pedro, apprehensive lest the Spaniards should get possession of his person, took him to Lisbon, and thence to the castle of Cintra, where he was confined till his death.

We had originally intended to anchor at Terceira; but the wind being adverse, we sailed by the islands of St. Mary and St. Michael, which we durst not approach from the unrelenting violence of the tempest.

A circumstance happened to me during the voyage, which I think deserving notice. As I one day went to the altar to receive the adorable body of Christ, the person who administered a Cordelier of Observance, remarked that I cast down my eyes when he said, "*Domine! non sum dignus*;" and though I had no other design by so doing than that of humbling myself in the presence of my God, this worthy Father, who had preconceived an indifferent opinion of me, from having been in the Inquisition, misinterpreted this mark of devotion, and a few days afterwards severely reproached me on account of it, and told me that I was still heretically inclined, because I did not even deign to look upon the Sacred Host, when he presented it to me. I leave it to others to judge whether this was not a rash conclusion; but though I took great pains to defend myself, and explain my motive, he declared, after all, that he could not entertain a better opinion of me.

As I do not intend to speak of what does not relate to the Inquisition, I shall not enter into the minute details of the voyage. I shall say only, that after many fatigues in common with the rest, and some private vexations, we arrived at Lisbon on the 16th of December, being the eleventh month after sailing from Goa.

Chapter XLII and XLIII contain a short Description of the City of Lisbon.

CHAPTER XLIV

I am conveyed to a Prison called the Galley. Description of this place.

IMMEDIATELY after coming to anchor, the master under whose care I was, gave notice of my arrival to the Inquisition, to which I was taken the next day; and thence by order of the Inquisitors, (who did not condescend to see me) to the prison called the Galley;—(to which, as the Portuguese do not use Galleys in their Marine, those who are sentenced to them by the Holy Office or the Lay Courts are sent.) I was chained by the leg to a man who had avoided the stake by confessing the night before his intended execution.

All the convicts were fastened in pairs by the leg, with a chain about eight feet long. Each prisoner had a belt of iron about his waist, to which, it might be suspended, leaving about three feet in length between the two. The Galley slaves are sent daily to work in the shipyards, where they are employed in carrying wood to the carpenters, unloading vessels, collecting stones or sand for ballast, assisting in the making of rope, or in any other labour for the Royal Service, or the Officers who superintend them, though ever so mean and degrading.

Amongst those condemned to the Galleys, are not only persons committed from the Inquisition and the Civil Tribunals, but also fugitive or intractable slaves, sent by their masters for correction and amendment, Turks who have been captured from the Corsairs of Barbary ; and all these, whatsoever may be their rank or quality, are alike employed in the most disgusting drudgery, unless they have money to give to the Officers who treat with unprecedented cruelty those who cannot make them occasional presents. This Land-galley is erected on the bank of the river, and contains two large halls, one above the other ; both are full, and the slaves lie on platforms covered with mats. Each has his head and beard shaved every month. They wear frocks and caps of blue cloth ; and have also a surtout of thick grey serge, which serves for a cloak by day, and a covering at night. These are all the clothes which are given to them, with a couple of shirts of coarse cloth every six months. Each prisoner has half a pound of extremely hard, and very black biscuit, daily ; six pounds of salt meat every month, with a bushel of peas, lentils, or beans, with which they do as they please. Such as have other means of support, usually sell their allowances to purchase something better. There being no allowance of wine, those who drink it, buy it at their own charge. They are conducted every morning early to the shipyard, which is half a league distant, and where they work incessantly at whatever is given to them to do, until eleven o'clock. From that time until one, is allotted for rest or refreshment. When one o'clock strikes, they are summoned to resume their tasks until night, and are marched back to the Galley.

In this place there is a chapel, in which Mass is said on Sundays and Festivals. Many well-disposed Ecclesiastics who reside at

Lisbon, often come to catechise and exhort the prisoners. In addition to the Royal allowance, frequent alms are bestowed, physicians and surgeons attend the sick, and if any should be dangerously ill, all the sacraments are administered to them. Persons committing any offence are flogged in a cruel manner, being extended on the ground with their faces downwards. They are held by two men, whilst a third beats them severely on the posteriors with a thick knotted cord, which sometimes tears away the skin and large pieces of flesh. I have often witnessed cases, when, after these chastisements, it has been necessary to make deep incisions, which have degenerated into ulcers, and long rendered these wretches incapable of working.

When a slave has business in the town, he is allowed to go out, and even without his companion if he chooses, on paying for a guard, who attends him everywhere.

On these occasions he carries the whole chain alone, which from its length is crossed over his shoulders, so as to hang down behind or before, as he may find least inconvenient.

CHAPTER XLV

I apply to the Inquisition for my Release, which I ultimately obtain.

THE day after my arrival in the galley, I was shaved, clothed, and employed like the other slaves ; but painful as I found this mode of life, the privilege of seeing and conversing with any one, rendered it far less irksome, than the dreadful solitudes of the Inquisition.

According to the terms of my sentence I had five years to pass in this bitter servitude, and there was no prospect of the least remission being accorded to one who had presumed to speak against the Inquisition. Yet the desire which every wretch naturally encourages to bring his misery to a close, induced me to consider in what manner I might recover my liberty, though I hardly dared to hope that it was feasible.

I immediately enquired if there were any French in Lisbon who could give me assistance ; and being informed that Monsieur **** , principal physician to the Queen of Portugal, was highly esteemed by that princess and the whole court, I addressed myself to him, and entreated that he would take me under his protection. He complied with my request in the most obliging manner, not only by promising me his influence in every respect in which he could be of any service, but also by offering me his purse and his table ; at which he did me the honour of placing me, notwithstanding my chains, whenever I had permission to go to his house. The dress of a galley-slave, did not lessen me in his estimation, and he had the goodness even to come to my prison to console me, when his leisure gave him opportunity.

I then wrote to my relations in France, to acquaint them of the deplorable condition to which I had been so long reduced, and to entreat them to make such interest for me as they might think whould have weight with the Queen of Portugal, whose intercession I wished to procure in my behalf.

Mr. ****, who was naturally generous and beneficent, understanding by letters from Paris, that some persons whom he respected had the goodness to exert themselves for my being set at liberty, redoubled his efforts for its speedy accomplishment.

By his advice I presented an ample memorial to the Inquisitors, wherein I recounted the causes of my arrest, and prayed that they would cause the excessive rigour with which I had been treated in the Indies to be relaxed.

No answer was given to this, nor to three other petitions which followed within two months. The occasion of this silence was that the post of Inquisitor-General was vacant, and Monseigneur Don Verissimo d'Alencantra, Archbishop of Braga, (who has been since created Cardinal,) having been appointed, had not taken possession of his office.

This prelate, for whose arrival I was incessantly praying, because I knew that upon him all my hopes depended, at length made his entry into Lisbon in the Passion Week ; but as the

Tribunals are not open during that period I was obliged to wait until after Quasimodo (or the Sunday after Easter).

Upon the Inquisitor-General's commencing to exercise the function of his office, I preferred a new petition, which was read in the Supreme Council, but produced no other effect than that Don Verissimo said that he could not believe my representation, as it was utterly incredible that a man should have been condemned to the galleys for five years for such a trifling matter.

This answer gave me so much the more pleasure, as every one assured me that this Prelate was noble, learned, and generous. I therefore preferred a request that he would take the trouble to examine my case, and satisfy himself whether I had stated anything that was false. This proposal was resisted in the Council; no one being disposed to sanction a revisal of the proceedings, because all the Tribunals of the Inquisition being sovereign, without appeal from one to another, it would be an infringement on the authority of that of Goa if its sentence should be reversed. In fact, I should never have obtained my liberation if the Inquisitor-General had not been most powerfully interested for me.

At last, after long solicitation, he suffered himself to be prevailed upon by the applications of many persons of rank, and especially of his niece, the Countess de Figueirol, who had a particular regard for the queen's first physician. Having directed the proceedings against me to be read before him, and being thus convinced that I had said nothing but the truth, and impressed with a sense of the injustice and ignorance of the Judges who had condemned me on the mere ground of ill-intention, he ordered that I should be set at liberty, adding at the foot of my last petition, in his own hand, "*Seja solto como pede e se vá para França*:"—that is "Let him be discharged according to his request, and let him go to France."

CHAPTER XLVI

My departure from Lisbon, and return to France.

My petition being thus answered by the Inquisitor-General in the Supreme Council, which meets once a week or once a fortnight, was sent to the Board of the Holy Office, where audience is given twice a day; and so soon as those gentlemen sent a Familiar to inform me that my discharge was granted, I asked if there was a vessel bound to France, that I might apprise the Inquisition and be embarked without delay.

I received this intelligence on the first of June, with such sentiments of joy as none but those who have been captives can imagine, but considering the difficulty of finding a ship and negotiating for my passage whilst I remained without liberty of acting. I represented by another memorial to the Inquisitors, that it would be impossible for me to avail myself of the favour they had conceded whilst I continued in chains, and without the means of ascertaining in so large a city as Lisbon what vessels entered or sailed from the port, unless I could go myself, or had anyone who would take the trouble to make diligent inquiry.

The gentlemen of the Ordinary Council, who had misconceived and strictly interpreted the expressions of the Inquisitor-General when he decreed my freedom, viz. "*he shall be discharged according to his request, and go into France,*" explaining the addition, which was intended as a special favour, as an absolute obligation to embark immediately, answered my memorial, that what I asked was allowed on giving security that I should stay no longer in Lisbon than was necessary for me to meet with an opportunity to leave it. This answer was communicated the 28th of June. I immediately went to acquaint the first physician with it, entreating him to finish what he had had the goodness to begin.

Some important business prevented his going to the Inquisition that day, but he went on the 30th in the morning, and having given security for me in four hundred crowns that I should leave the country, a Familiar was sent in the afternoon of the same day, the last of June, 1677, to the galley, to take off my irons and conduct me to the Holy Office, where being summoned into the presence of the Inquisitors, one of them asking if I knew the queen's physician, told me he had become surety for me, and that from that instant I was at liberty to go where I pleased; and then making me a motion to withdraw, I replied only by a profound obeisance, and thus escaped from the tyrannic power of the Holy Office, under the pressure of which I had groaned for nearly four years, reckoning from the day of imprisonment, which was the 24th of August, 1673, until the last of June, 1677. The first thing I did after quitting this terrible house was to go to the nearest church, and render thanks to God and the Holy Virgin for my deliverance. I next went to Mr. ***, who wept for joy and embraced me. I then returned to the galley, to give a last farewell to the poor wretches who had been the companions of my misfortune, and to bring away the few things which belonged to me.

I got as early information as possible when a ship would sail for France, being more anxious to return thither, and be no longer within the jurisdiction of the Inquisitors, than they could possibly be for my departure. I soon found one, and embarked. After a few slight fatigues, I had the happiness to arrive in perfect health in my native land.

CHAPTER XLVII

The History of a Gentleman, which unfolds the Spirit of the Holy Office.

I SHALL conclude this account of the Inquisition by the relation of what happened, in my own knowledge, to two persons with whom I was acquainted in the Galley, at Lisbon. They were there before me, and remained when I went out, and I had many very particular conversations with them both on the subject of their own affairs and mine.

The first of these unfortunate gentlemen was Major of a regiment when he was arrested. His descent being "*Christam Novo,*" he was accused of Judaism by persons who apparently had had no other means of saving their own lives but by declaring themselves guilty of the same crime, and naming many innocent persons in order to discover (as required) the witnesses against them.

The poor officer on being seized was thrown into the prisons of the Holy Office, and often examined for the purpose of drawing from his own mouth the cause of his apprehension ; but not being able to say that which he did not know, after being detained upwards of two years, it was signified to him that he was accused and convicted in due form of being an apostate Jew. This he positively declared was false, protesting that he had never deviated from the Christian religion, and denied all the charges brought against him. Nothing was omitted to induce him to confess. Not only his life, but the restoration of his property was promised. It was then attempted to intimidate him by threats of cruel death; but nothing could shake his resolution, and he boldly told his Judges that he would rather die innocent than save his life by a meanness which would load him with eternal infamy. The Duke d'Aveira, who was then Inquisitor-General, and earnestly desirous of preserving this prisoner's life, one day visited him, and urgently exhorted him to take advantage of the opportunity thus afforded for avoiding punishment. The accused displayed a determined resolution not to injure his own reputation by acknowledging crimes he had not perpetrated. Irritated by his obstinacy, the Inquisitor-General was so far transported as to exclaim, "*Cuides que aveis de ganhar*?" evidently meaning, "What then do you mean to do? Do you think that we may be deceived?" And with these words retired, leaving the prisoner at liberty to adopt his own course. The very extraordinary meaning conveyed in this speech excites reflections very opposite either to the honour of the Judge or of the Holy Office; as it almost implies, "We will rather cause thee to be burnt as guilty, than allow it to be supposed that we have imprisoned thee without cause."

In course of time, the period of the *Auto da Fé* advanced. After about three years' confinement the Major heard his sentence of death pronounced, and a Confessor was allotted to prepare him for it. This gentleman, who had hitherto been so firm, was moved by the approach and preparation of punishment, and on the eve of the ceremony acknowledged everything, however false, that was required against himself. He appeared in the procession with a *Samarra* covered with flames reversed, called in Portuguese, *Fogo revolto*, to signify that by his confession, though late, he had escaped death, after being justly condemned by the sentence of the Inquisition. In addition to the forfeiture of his goods, he was sent to the galleys for five years. He had been there more than two years when I came, and it was in this place and from himself that I learnt what I have related.

CHAPTER XLVIII

Remarkable History of another Gentleman.

A PORTUGUESE gentleman of the highest rank, who was *Christam Novo,* and extremely wealthy, called Louis Pecoa de Sá, having been concerned in many criminal proceedings in the Lay Courts, had incurred the hatred of many persons, who, in revenge, denounced him to the Holy Office as secretly professing Judaism with his family. In consequence, on the same day, himself, his wife, his two sons, his daughter, and some other relations who lived in his house, were arrested and taken to the Prisons of the Inquisition at Coimbra.

Louis Pecoa was first interrogated for the particulars of his property, of which his real estate alone produced upwards of 80,000 *livres* per annum, and which, as well as his personal property, has been seized by the Holy Office. He was then urged to declare the cause of his imprisonment, which from ingorance he was unable to do. Every means in use at the Inquisition was then adopted to compel him to confess his crimes ; but nothing could affect Louis Pecoa. At the expiration of three years the accusations against him and the fatal conclusions of the Promoter were signified to him in case he persevered in his refusal ; but instead of accusing he attempted to justify himself, declaring that every title of the accusations against him was false, demanded to know the witnesses who had deposed to them, whom he undertook to convict of perjury, and concluded by intimating to his Judges the means by which, if they chose, his innocence might be ascertained ; but the Inquisitors, disregarding all that he had alleged in his defence, seeing him persist in his denial of the charge, condemned him to the flames ; and his sentence was formally announced to him fifteen days before it was to be executed. The Duke de Cadaval, who was intimately connected with Louis Pecoa, and the particular friend of the Duke d'Aveira, occasionally enquired how his affair proceeded ; and being informed by the Inquisitor-General, that not having confessed, and being fully convicted according to the rules of the Holy Office, he could not escape unless he accused himself before the time. This information gave him considerable uneasiness. He wished to have an interview with the unfortunate gentleman, to prevail upon him to save his life on any terms, but that was impracticable. At last, he thought of a most singular and unexampled expedient. This was to extract a promise from the Inquisitor-General, that if he could persuade Louis Pecoa to confess even after his going out to the Act of Faith, he should not be put to death, though directly contrary to the laws of the Holy Office. This he obtained, and the day of the celebration of the *Auto da Fé* being appointed, he caused some friends of his and Louis Pecoa's to leave Lisbon, and post themselves at the gate of the Inquisition. When the procession commenced, and their unhappy friend came forth, they advanced.

Being condemned, his pile was already prepared; he wore a *Carrocha* and *Samarra*, covered with flames and devils, his picture naturally represented before and behind, placed upon burning fire-brands; his sentence inscribed beneath, and his Confessor walking by his side. His friends no sooner beheld him than, bursting into tears, they threw themselves on his neck, beseeching him, for the sake of the Duke de Cadaval, and all that was dear to him, to save his life. They told him the promise they had obtained, that he should not be executed if he would yet confess, and remonstrated that the loss of all his estate ought not to influence him, as the Duke, by whom they had been sent, had charged them to assure him that he would bestow on him more than he had been deprived of. All these reasons, nor the tears and entreaties of his generous friends made no impression on Louis Pecoa, who declared aloud that he had always been a Christian, that such he would die, and that all the charges against him were so many falsehoods invented by his enemies, and tolerated by the Holy Office to profit by his spoils. The procession being arrived at the place appointed, a sermon was preached, the proceedings were read, absolution was given to those whose lives were spared, and in the evening the publication of the causes of those who were to be burnt commenced; the deputies of the Duke de Cadaval redoubled their entreaties, and at length prevailed upon their friend to demand an audience. He arose, and said as he went along, "Come then, we will go and commit falsehoods to gratify our friends." An audience was conceded, and he was reconducted to the prisons; but the Act of Faith being concluded when he was summoned to the Board to confess, it was with difficulty he could determine to do so, and was often on the point of having his sentence confirmed without hope of mercy. Nevertheless, he finally declared every thing they required, and signed his confession. After two years had elapsed, he was sent to Evora, where he appeared at an Act of Faith, wearing a *Samarra* with reversed flames; and having been five years in the prisons of the Holy Office, he was sentenced for other five to the galleys, whither he was sent the next day, and there I became acquainted with him, and obtained the knowledge of what I have detailed.

This unfortunate person, who was a very accomplished gentleman, and a good Christian learnt upon his release that his wife and his daughter had died in the prisons shortly after they were confined; and that his two sons, less firm than himself, had made a timely confession, and being discharged some time before, were sentenced to banishment for ten years into Algarve. For his own part, he waited for the period of his deliverance, and intended to leave Portugal as soon as he could, and go to pass the rest of his life in some country where there was no Inquisition.

DR. BUCHANAN'S ACCOUNT OF THE INQUISITION AT GOA IN 1808*

...While the Author (Dr. C. Buchanan) viewed these Christian corruptions in different places, and in different forms, he was always referred to the Inquisition at Goa, as the fountain-head. He had long cherished the hope, that he should be able to visit Goa, before he left India. His chief objects were the following :

1. To ascertain whether the Inquisition actually refused to recognise the Bible, among the Romish Churches in British India.

2. To inquire into the state and jurisdiction of the Inquisition, particularly as it affected British subjects.

3. To learn what was the system of education for the Priesthood ; and

4. To examine the ancient Church-libraries in Goa, which were said to contain all the books of the first printing.

He will select from his journal, in this place, chiefly what relates to the Inquisition. He had learnt from every quarter, that this tribunal, formerly so well known for its frequent burnings, was still in operation, though under some restriction as to the *publicity* of its proceedings ; and that its power extended to the extreme boundary of Hindostan. That, in the present civilized state of Christian nations in Europe, an Inquisition should exist at all under their authority, appeared strange ; but that a Papal tribunal of this character should exist under the implied toleration and countenance of the British Government ; that Christians, being subjects of the British Empire, and inhabiting the British territories, should be amenable to its power and jurisdiction, was a statement which seemed to be scarcely credible ; but if true, a fact which demanded the most public and solemn representation.

* Extract from Dr. Claudius Buchanan's *Christian Researches in India* (Fifth Edition) London, 1812, pp. 149-176.

Goa : Convent of the Augustinians, **Jan. 23, 1808.**

On my arrival at Goa, I was received into the house of Captain Schuyler, the British Resident. The British force here is commanded by Colonel Adams, of His Majesty's 78th Regiment, with whom I was formerly well acquainted in Bengal.* Next day I was introduced by these gentlemen to the Vice-Roy of Goa, the Count de Cabral. I intimated to His Excellency my wish to sail up the river to Old Goa,† (where the Inquisition is,) to which he politely acceded. Major Pereira, of the Portuguese establishment, who was present, and to whom I had letters of introduction from Bengal, offered to accompany me to the city, and to introduce me to the Archbishop of Goa, the Primate of the Orient.

I had communicated to Colonel Adams, and to the British Resident, my purpose of enquiring into the state of the Inquisition. These gentlemen informed me, that I should not be able to accomplish my design without difficulty; since every thing relating to the Inquisition was conducted in a very secret manner, the most respectable of the Lay Portuguese themselves being ignorant of its proceedings; and that, if the Priests were to discover my object, their excessive jealousy and alarm would prevent their communicating with me, or satisfying my inquiries on any subject.

On receiving this intelligence, I perceived that it would be necessary to proceed with caution. I was, in fact, about to visit a republic of Priests, whose dominion had existed for nearly three centuries; whose province it was to prosecute heretics, and parti-

* The forts in the harbour of Goa, were then occupied by British troops (two King's regiments, and two regiments of Native infantry) to prevent its falling into the hands of the French.

† There is Old and New Goa. The old city is about eight miles up the river. The Vice-Roy and the chief Portuguese inhabitants reside at New Goa, which is at the mouth of the river, within the forts of the harbour. The old city, where the Inquisition and the Churches are, is now almost entirely deserted by the secular Portuguese, and is inhabited by the Priests alone. The unhealthiness of the place, and the ascendancy of the Priests, are the causes assigned for abandoning the ancient city.

cularly the teachers of heresy; and from whose authority and sentence there was no appeal in India.*

It happened that Lieutenant Kempthorne, Commander of His Majesty's brig Diana, a distant connection of my own, was at this time in the harbour. On his learning that I meant to vist Old Goa, he offered to accompany me; as did Captain Stirling, of His Majesty's 84th regiment, which is now stationed at the forts.

We proceeded up the river in the British Resident's barge, accompanied by Major Pereira, who was well qualified, by a thirty years' residence, to give information concerning local circumstances. From him I learned that there were upwards of two hundred Churches and Chapels in the province of Goa, and upwards of two thousand Priests.

On our arrival at the city,† it was past twelve o'clock: all the Churches were shut, and we were told that they would not be opened again till two o'clock. I mentioned to Major Pereira, that I intended to stay at Old Goa some days; and that I should be obliged to him to find me a place to sleep in. He seemed surprised at this intimation, and observed that it would be difficult for me to obtain reception in any of the Churches or Convents, and that there were no private houses into which I could be admitted. I said I could sleep any where; I had two servants with me, and a travelling bed. When he perceived that I was serious in my purpose, he gave directions to a civil officer, to clear out a room in a building which had been long uninhabited, and which was

* I was informed that the Vice-Roy of Goa has no authority over the Inquisition, and that he himself is liable to its censure. Were the British Government, for instance, to prefer a complaint against the Inquisition to the Portuguese Government at Goa, it could obtain no redress. By the very constitution of the Inquisition, there is no power in India which can invade its jurisdiction, or even put a question to it on any subject.

† We entered the city by the palace gate, over which is the Statue of *Vasco de Gama*, who first opened India to the view of Europe. I had seen at *Calicut*, a few weeks before, the ruins of the Samorin's Palace, in which Vasco de Gama was first received. The Samorin was the first native Prince against whom the Europeans made war. The empire of the Samorin has passed away; and the empire of his conquerors has passed away; and now imperial Britain exercises dominion. May imperial Britain be prepared to give a good account of her stewardship, when it shall be said unto her, "Thou mayest be no longer steward!"

then used as a warehouse for goods. Matters at this time presented a very gloomy appearance ; and I had thoughts of returning with my companions from this inhospitable place. In the mean time we sat down in the room I have just mentioned, to take some refreshment, while Major Pereira went to call on some of his friends. During this interval, I communicated to Lieutenant Kempthorne the object of my visit. I had in my pocket Dellon's Account of the Inquisition at Goa*; and I mentioned some particulars. While we were conversing on the subject, the great bell began to toll ; the same which Dellon observes always tolls, before day-light, on the morning of the *Auto da Fé.* I did not myself ask any questions of the people concerning the Inquisition ; but Mr. Kempthorne made inquiries for me ; and he soon found out that the *Santa Casa*, or Holy Office, was close to the house where we were then sitting. The gentlemen went to the window to view the horrid mansion ; and I could see the Indignation of free and enlightened men arise in the countenance of the two British officers, while they contemplated a place where formerly their own countrymen were condemned to the flames, and into which they themselves might now suddenly be thrown, without the possibility of rescue.

At two o'clock we went out to view the Churches, which were now open for the afternoon service ; for there are regular daily masses ; and the bells began to assail the ear in every quarter.

The magnificence of the Churches of Goa, far exceeded any idea I had formed from the previous description. Goa is properly a city of Churches ; and the wealth of provinces seem to have been expended in their erection. The ancient specimens of architecture at this place far excel any thing that has been attempted in modern times in any other part of the East, both in grandeur and in taste. The Chapel of the Palace is built after the plan of St. Peter's at Rome, and is said to be an accurate model of that paragon of architecture. The Church of St. Dominic, the founder of the Inquisition, is decorated with paintings of Italian masters. St.

* Monsieur Dellon, a physician, was imprisoned in the dungeon of the Inquisition at Goa for two years, and witnessed an Auto da Fè, when some heretics were burned ; at which he walked barefoot. After his release he wrote the history of his confinement. His descriptions are in general very accurate.

Francis Xavier lies enshrined in a monument of exquisite art, and his coffin is enchased with silver and *precious stones.* The Cathedral of Goa is worthy of one of the principal cities of Europe! and the Church and Convent of the Augustinians (in which I now reside) is a noble pile of building, situated on an eminence, and has a magnificent appearance from afar.

But what a contrast to all this grandeur of the Churches is the worship offered within! I have been present at the service in one or other of the Chapels every day since I arrived; and I seldom see a single worshipper, but the ecclesiastics. Two rows of native Priests, kneeling in order before the altar, clothed in coarse black garments, of sickly appearance, and vacant countenance perform here, from day to day, their laborious masses, seemingly unconscious of any other duty or obligation of life.

The day was now far spent, and my companions were about to leave me. While I was considering whether I should return with them. Major Pereira said he would first introduce me to a Priest, high in office, and one of the most learned men in the place. We accordingly walked to the Convent of the Augustinians, where I was presented to Joseph a Doloribus, a man well advanced in life, of pale visage and penetrating eye, rather of a reverend appearance, and possessing great fluency of speech and urbanity of manners. At first sight he presented the aspect of one of those acute and prudent men of the world, the learned and respectable Italian Jesuits, some of whom are yet found, since the demolition of their order, reposing in tranquil obscurity, in different parts of the East. After half an hour's conversation in the Latin language, during which he adverted rapidly to a variety of subjects, and enquired concerning some learned men of his own Church, whom I had visited in my tour, he politely invited me to take up my residence with him, during my stay at old Goa. I was highly gratified by this unexpected invitation; but Lieutenant Kempthorne did not approve of leaving me in the hands of the *Inquisitor.* For judge of our surprize, when we discover that my learned host was one of the Inquisitors of the Holy Office, the second member of that august tribunal in rank, but the first and most active agent in the business of the department. Apartments were assigned to me in the College adjoining the Convent, next to the rooms of the Inquisitor himself; and here I have been now four days at the very fountain head of information, in regard to those subjects which I wished to investigate. I breakfast and dine with the Inquisitor almost every day, and he generally passes his evenings in my apartment. As he considers my enquiries to be chiefly of a literary nature, he is perfectly candid and communicative on all subjects.

Next day after my arrival, I was introduced by my learned conductor to the Archbishop of Goa. We found him reading the Latin letters of St. Francis Xavier. On my adverting to the long duration of the city of Goa, while other cities of Europeans in India had suffered from war or revolution, the Archbishop observed, that the preservation of Goa was owing to the prayers of St. Francis Xavier. The Inquisitor looked at me to see what I thought of this sentiment. I acknowledged that Xavier was considered by the learned among the English to have been a great man: what he wrote himself, bespeaks him a man of learning, of original genius, and great fortitude of mind; but what others have written for him, and of him, tarnished his fame, by making him the inventor of fables. The Archbishop signified his assent. He afterwards conducted me into his private Chapel, which is decorated with images of silver, and then into the Archiepiscopal Library, which possesses a valuable collection of books.—As I passed through our Convent, in returning from the Archbishop's, I observed among the paintings in the cloisters, a portrait of the famous Alexis de Menezes, Archbishop of Goa, who held the Synod of Diamper, near Cochin, in 1599, and burned the books of the Syrian Christians. From the inscription underneath I learned that he was the founder of the magnificent Church and Convent in which I am now residing.

On the same day I received an invitation to dine with the Chief Inquisitor, at his house in the country. The second Inquisitor accompanied me, and we found a respectable company of Priests, and a sumptuous entertainment. In the library of the chief Inquisitor I saw a register, containing the present establishment of the Inquisition at Goa, and the names of all the officers. On my asking the chief Inquisitor whether the establishment was extensive as formerly, he said it was nearly the same. I had hitherto said little to any person concerning the Inquisition, but I had indirectly gleaned much information concerning it, not only from the Inquisitors themselves, but from certain Priests, whom I visited at their respective convents ; particularly from a Father in the Franciscan Convent, who had himself repeatedly witnessed an Auto de Fé.

Goa : Augustinian Convent, **26th, Jan. 1808.**

On Sunday, after divine service, which I attended, we looked over together the prayers and portions of Scripture for the day. which led to a discussion concerning some of the doctrines of Christianity. We then read the third chapter of St. John's Gospel, in the Latin Vulgate. I asked the Inquisitor whether he believed in the influence in the spirit there spoken of. He distinctly admitted it; conjointly however he thought, in some obscure sense, with *water.* I observed that water was merely an emblem of the purifying effects of the Spirit, and could be *but* an emblem. We next adverted to the expression of St. John in his first Epistle : 'This is he that came by *water* and *blood* : even Jesus Christ ; not by water only, but by water and blood :...blood to atone for sin, and water to purify the heart ; justification and sanctification : both of which were expressed at the same moment on the Cross. The Inquisitor was pleased with the subject. By an easy transition we passed to the importance of the Bible itself, to illuminate the priests and people. I noticed to him that after looking through the colleges and schools, there appeared to me to be a *total eclipse* of Scriptural light. He acknowledged that religion and learning were truly in a degraded state....I had visited the theological schools, and at every place I expressed my surprize to the tutors, in presence of the pupils, at the absence of the Bible, and almost total want of reference to it. They pleaded the custom of the place, and the scarcity of copies of the book itself. Some of the younger Priests came to me afterwards, desiring to know by what means they might procure copies. This enquiry for Bibles was like a ray of hope beaming on the walls of the Inquisition.

I pass an hour sometimes in the spacious library of the Augustinian Convent, and think myself suddenly transported into one of the libraries of Cambridge. There are many rare volumes, but they are chiefly theological, and almost all of the sixteenth century. There are few classics; and I have not yet seen one copy of the original Scriptures in Hebrew or Greek.

Goa : Augustinian Convent, **27th Jan. 1808,**

On the second morning after my arrival, I was surprised by my host, the Inquisitor, coming into my apartment clothed in *black robes* from head to foot : for the usual dress of his order is white. He said he was going to sit on the Tribunal of the Holy Office. 'I presume, Father, your august Office does not occupy much of your time ?' 'Yes', answered he , 'much. I sit on the Tribunal three or four days every week.'

I had thought, for some days, of putting Dellon's book into the Inquisitor's hands ; for if I could get him to advert to the facts stated in that book, I should be able to learn, by comparison, the exact state of the Inquisition at the present time. In the evening he came in, as usual, to pass an hour in my apartment. After some conversation I took the pen in my hand to write a few notes in my Journal : and, as if to amuse him, while I was writing, I took up Dellon's book, which was lying with some others on the table, and handing it across to him, asked him whether he had ever seen it. It was in the French Language, which he understood well. 'Relation, de l'Inquisition de Goa,' pronounced he, with a slow articulate voice. He had never seen it before, and began to read with eagerness. He had not proceeded far, before he betrayed evident symptoms of uneasiness. He turned hastily to the middle of the book, and then to the end, and then ran over the table of contents at the beginning, as if to ascertain the full extent of the evil. He then composed himself to read, while I continued to write. He turned over the pages with rapidity, and when he came to a certain place, he exclaimed, in the broad Italian accent, 'Mendacium, Mendacium .' I requested he would mark those passages which were untrue, and we should discuss them afterwards, for that I had other books on the subject. 'Other books ,' said he, and he looked with an enquiring eye on those on the table. He continued reading till it was time to retire to rest and then begged to take the book with him.

It was on this night that a circumstance happened which caused my first alarm at Goa. My servants slept every night at my chamber door, in the long gallery which is common to all the apartments, and not far distant from the servants of the Convent. About midnight I was waked by loud shrieks and expressions of terror from some person in the gallery. In the first moment of surprise I concluded it must be the *Alguazils* of the Holy Office, seizing my servants to carry them to the Inquisition. But, on going out, I saw my own servants standing at the door, and the person who had caused the alarm (a boy of about fourteen) at a little distance, surrounded by some of the Priests, who had come out of their cells on hearing the noise. The boy said he had seen a *spectre*, and it was a considerable time before the agitations of his body and voice subsided.—Next morning at breakfast the Inquisitor apologised for the disturbance, and said the boy's alarm proceeded from a ' phantasma animi,' a phantasm of the imagination.

After breakfast we resumed the subject of the Inquisition. The Inquisitor admitted that Dellon's descriptions of the dungeons, of the torture, of the mode of trial, and of the Auto da Fé were, in general, just; but he said the writer judged untruly of the motives of the Inquisitors, and very uncharitably of the character of the Holy Church ; and I admitted that, under the pressure of his peculiar suffering, this might possibly be the case. The Inquisitor was now anxious to know to what extent Dellon's book had been circulated in Europe. I told him that Picart had published to the world extracts from it, in his celebrated work called ' Religious Ceremonies ' together with plates of the system of torture and burnings at the Auto da Fé. I added that it was now generally believed in Europe that these enormities no longer existed, and that the Inquisition itself has been totally suppressed ; but that I was concerned to find that this was not the case. He now began a grave narration to shew that the Inquisition had undergone a change in some respects, and that its terrors were mitigated.

I had already discovered, from written or printed documents, that the Inquisition of Goa, was suppressed by Royal Edict in the year 1775, and established again in 1779. The

Franciscan Father before mentioned, witnessed the annual Auto da Fé, from 1770 to 1775. "It was the humanity, and tender mercy of a good King," said the old Father, "which abolished the Inquisition." But immediately on his death, the power of the Priests acquired the ascendant, under the Queen Dowager, and the Tribunal was reestablished, after a bloodless interval of five years. It has continued in operation ever since. It was restored in 1779, subject to certain restrictions, the chief of which are the two following, 'That a greater number of witnesses should be required to convict a criminal than were before necessary;' and, 'that the Auto da Fé should not be held publicly as before; but that the sentences of the Tribunal should be executed privately, within the walls of the Inquisition.'

In this particular, the constitution of the new Inquisition is more reprehensible than that of the old one; for, as the old Father expressed it, 'Nunc sigillum non revelat Inquisitio.' —Formerly the friends of those unfortunate persons who were thrown into its prison, had the melancholy satisfaction of seeing them once a year walking in the procession of the Auto de Fé; or if they were condemned to die, they witnessed their death and mourned for the dead. But now they have no means of learning for years whether they be dead or alive. The policy of this new mode of concealment appears to be this, to preserve the power of the Inquisition, and at the same time to lesson the public odium of its proceedings, in the presence of British dominion and civilization. I asked the Father his opinion concerning the nature and frequency of the punishments within the walls. He said he possessed no certain means of giving a satisfactory answer; that every thing transacted there was declared to be 'sacrum et secretum'. But this he knew to be true, that there were constantly captives in the dungeons; that some of them are liberated after long confinement, but that they never speak afterwards of what passed within the place. He added that, of all the persons he had known, who had been liberated, he never knew one who did not carry about with him what might be called, 'the mark of the Inquisition;' that is to say, who did not shew in the solemnity of his countenance, or in his peculiar demeanor, or his terror of the Priests, that he had been in that dreadful place.

The chief argument of the Inquisitor to prove the melioration of the Inquisition was the superior *humanity* of the Inquisitors. I remarked that I did not doubt the humanity of the existing officers ; but what availed humanity in an Inquisitor ? he must pronounce sentence according to the Laws of the Tribunal, which are notorious enough ; and a *relapsed Heretic* must be burned in the flames, or confined for life in a dungeon, whether the Inquisitor be humane or not. ‘ But, if ’, said I, ‘ you would satisfy my mind completely on this subject, shew me the Inquisition ’. He said it was not permitted to any person to see the Inquisition. I observed that mine might be considered as a peculiar case ; that the character of the Inquisition, and the expediency of its longer continuance had been called in question; that I had myself written on the civilization of India, and might possibly publish something more upon that subject, and that it could not be expected that I should pass over the Inquisition without notice, knowing that I did of its proceedings ; at the same time I should not wish to state a single fact without his authority, or at least his admission of its truth. I added that he himself had been pleased to communicate with me very fully on the subject, and that in all our discussions we had both been actuated, I hoped, by a good purpose. The countenance of the Inquisitor evidently altered on receiving this intimation, nor did it ever after wholly regain its wonted frankness and placidity. After some hesitation, however, he said he would take me with him to the Inquisition the next day...I was a good deal surprized at this acquiescence of the Inquisitor, but I did not know what was in his mind.

Goa : Augustinian Convent, **28th January, 1808.**

When I left the Forts to come up to the Inquisition, Colonel Adams desired me to write to him ; and he added half-way between jest and earnest, “ If I do not hear from you in three days, I shall march down the 78th and storm the Inquisition.” This I promised to do. But, having been so well entertained by the Inquisitor, I forgot my promise. Accordingly, on the day before yesterday, I was surprised by a visit from Major Braamcamp, Aid-de-Camp to His Excellency the Vice-Roy, bearing a letter from Colonel

Adams, and a message from the Vice-Roy, proposing that I should return every evening and sleep at the Forts, on account of the *unhealthiness* of Goa.

This morning after breakfast my host went to dress for the Holy Office, and soon returned in his inquisitorial robes. He said he would go half an hour before the usual time for the purpose of shewing me the Inquisition. I thought that his countenance was more severe than usual; and that his attendants were not so civil as before. The truth was, the *midnight scene* was still on my mind. The Inquisition is about a quarter of a mile distant from the convent, and we proceeded thither in our *Manjeels*.* On our arrival at the place, the Inquisitor said to me, as we were ascending the steps of the outer stair, that he hoped I should be satisfied with a transient view of the Inquisition, and that I would retire whenever he should desire it. I took this as a good omen, and followed my conductor with tolerable confidence.

He led me first to the Great Hall of the Inquisition. We were met at the door by a number of well-dressed persons, who, I afterwards understood, were the familiars, and attendants of the Holy Office. They bowed very low to the Inquisitor, and looked with surprise at me. The Great Hall is the place in which the prisoners are marshalled for the procession of the Auto da Fé. At the procession described by Dellon, in which himself walked barefoot, clothed with the painted garment, there were upwards of one hundred and fifty prisoners. I traversed this hall for some time, with a slow step, reflecting on its former scenes, the Inquisitor walking by my side in silence. I thought of the fate of the multitude of my fellow-creatures who had passed through this place, condemned by a tribunal of their fellow-sinners, their bodies devoted to the flames, and their souls to perdition. And I could not help saying to him, 'Would not the Holy Church wish, in her mercy, to have those souls back again, that she might allow them a little further probation?' The Inquisitor answered

* The Manjeel is a kind of Palankeen common at Goa. It is merely a sea cot suspended from a bamboo, which is borne on the heads of four men. Sometimes a footman runs before, having a staff in his hand, to which are attached little bells or rings, which he jingles as he runs, keeping time with the motion of the bearers.

nothing, but beckoned me to go with him to a door at one end of the hall. By this door he conducted me to some small rooms, and thence, to the spacious apartments of the chief Inquisitor. Having surveyed these he brought me back again to the Great Hall; and I thought he seemed now desirous that I should depart. 'Now, Father,' said I, 'lead me to the dungeons below; I want to see the captives.'—'No' said he, 'that cannot be.' ...I now began to suspect that it had been in the mind of the Inquisitor, from the beginning, to shew me only a certain part of the Inquisition, in the hope of satisfying my Inquiries in a general way. I urged him with earnestness, but he steadily resisted, and seemed to be offended or rather agitated by my importunity. I intimed to him plainly, that the only way to do justice as to his own assertions and arguments, regarding the present state of the Inquisition, was to shew me the prisons and the captives. I should then describe only what I saw; but now the subjects was left in awful obscurity;...'Lead me down', said I, 'to the inner building and let me pass through the two hundred dungeons, ten feet square, described by your former captives. Let me count the number of your present captives, and converse with them. I want to see if there be any subjects of the British Government, to whom we owe protection. I want to ask how long they have been here, how long it is since they beheld the light of the sun, and whether they ever expect to see it again. Shew me the Chamber of Torture; and declare that modes of execution, or of punishment, are now practised within the walls of the Inquisition, in lieu of the public Auto da Fè. If, after all that has passed, Father, you resist this reasonable request, I shall be justified in believing, that you are afraid of exposing the real state of the Inquisition in India.' To these observations the Inquisitor made no reply; but seemed impatient that I should withdraw. 'My good Father,' said I, 'I am about to take my leave of you, and to thank you for your hospitable intentions, (it had been before understood that I should take my final leave at the door of the Inquisition, after having seen the interior), and I wish always to preserve on my mind a favourable sentiment of your kindness and candour. You cannot, you say, shew me the captives and the dungeons; be pleased then merely to answer this question; for I shall believe your word:...How many prisoners are there now below, in the cells of the Inquisition ?' The Inquisitor replied, 'That is a question which I cannot answer.' On his pronouncing these words, I retired hastily towards the door, and wished him farewell. We shook hands with as much cordiality as we could at the moment assume; and both of us, I believe, were sorry that our parting took place with a clouded countenance.

From the Inquisition I went to the place of burning in the *Campo Santo Lazaro*, on the river side, where the victims were brought to the stake at the Auto da Fé. It is close to the palace, that the Vice-Roy and his Court may witness the execution; for it has ever been the policy of the Inquisition to make these spiritual executions appear to be the executions of the State.

An old Priest accompanied me, who pointed out the place, and described the scene. As I passed over this melancholy plain, I thought on the difference between the pure and benign doctrine, which was first preached to India in the Apostolic age, and that bloody code, which, after a long night of darkness, was announced to it under the same name! And I pondered on the mysterious dispensation, which permitted the ministers of the Inquisition with their racks and flames, to visit these lands, before the heralds of the Gospel of Peace. But the most painful reflection was, that this tribunal should yet exist, unawed by the vicinity of British humanity and dominion. I was not satisfied with what I had seen or said at the Inquisition, and I determined to go back again. The Inquisitors were now sitting on the tribunal, and I had some excuse for returning; for I was to receive from the chief Inquisitor a letter, which he said he would give me before I left the place, for the British Resident in Travancore, being an answer to a letter from that officer.

When I arrived at the Inquisition, and had ascended the outer stairs, the doorkeepers surveyed me doubtingly, but suffered me to pass, supposing that I had returned by permission and appointment of the Inquisitor. I entered the Great Hall, and went up directly towards the tribunal of the Inquisition, described by Dellon, in which is the lofty Crucifix. I sat down on a form, and wrote some notes, and then desired one of the attendants to carry in my name to the Inquisitor. As I walked up the Hall, I saw a poor woman sitting by herself, on a bench by the wall, apparently in a disconsolate state of mind. She clasped her hands as I passed, and gave me a look expressive of her distress. This sight chilled my spirits. The familiars told me she was waiting there to be called up before the tribunal of the Inquisition. While I was asking question concerning her crime, the second Inquisitor came out in evident trepidation, and was about to complain of the intrusion; when I informed him I had come back for the letter from the Chief Inquisitor. He said it should be sent after me to Goa; and he conducted me with a quick step towards the door. As we passed the poor woman I pointed to her, and said to him with some emphasis, 'Behold, Father, another victim of the Holy Inquisition!' He answered nothing. When we arrived at the head of the great stair, he bowed, and I took my last leave of Josephus a Doloribus, without uttering a word.

It will be well understood for what purpose the foregoing particulars concerning the Inquisition at Goa, are rehearsed in the ears of the British nation. "The Romans," says Montesquieu, "deserve well of human nature, for making it an article in their treaty with the Carthaginians, that they should abstain from "SACRIFICING THEIR CHILDREN TO THEIR GODS." It has been observed by respectable writers, that the English nation ought to imitate this example, and endeavour to induce her allies "to abolish the human sacrifices of "the Inquisition;" and a censure has been passed on our Government for its indifference to this subject.* The difference to the Inquisition is attributable, we believe, to the same cause which has produced an indifference to the religious principles which first organized the Inquisition. The mighty despot, who suppressed the Inquisition in Spain, was not swayed probably by very powerful motives of humanity; but viewed with a jealousy a tribunal, which usurped an independent dominion; and he put it down, on the same principle that he put down the Popedom, that he might remain Pontiff and Grand Inquisitor himself. And so he will remain for a time, till the purposes of Providence shall have been accomplished by him.

* *Edin. Rev.* No. XXXII, p. 449.

But are we to look on in silence, and to expect that further meliorations in human society are to be affected by despotism, or by great revolutions? "If," say the same authors, "while the Inquisition is destroyed in Europe by the power of despotism, we could entertain the hope, and it is not too much to entertain such a hope, that the power of liberty is about to destroy it in America, we might, even amid the gloom that surrounds us, congratulate our fellow-creatures on one of the most remarkable periods in the history of the progress of human society, the FINAL ERASURE *of the Inquisition from the face of the earth.*" It will indeed be an important and happy day to the earth, when this final erasure shall take place ; but the period of such an event is nearer, we apprehend, in Europe and America, than it is in Asia ; and its termination in Asia depends as much on Great Britain as on Portugal. And shall not Great Britain do her part to hasten this desirable time ! Do we wait, as if to see whether the power of Infidelity will abolish the other Inquisitions of the earth ? Shall not we, in the meanwhile attempt to do something, on Christian principles, for the honour of God and of humanity ? Do we dread even to express a sentiment on the subject in our legislative Assemblies, or to notice it in our Treaties ? It is surely our duty to declare our wishes, at least, for the abolition of these inhuman tribunals, (since we take an active part in promoting the welfare of other nations,) and to deliver our testimony against them in the presence of Europe.

This case is not unlike that of the Immolation of Females in Bengal ; with this aggravation in regard to that atrocity, that the rite is perpetrated *in our own* territories. Our humanity in England revolts at the occasional description of the enormity ; but the matter comes not to our own business and bosoms, and we fail even to insinuate our disapprobation of the deed. It may be concluded, then, that while we remain silent and unmoved spectators of the flames of the Widow's Pile, there is no hope that we should be justly affected by the reported horrors of the Inquisition.

SELECT BIBLIOGRAPHY

Adler, Elkan Nathan: *Auto de Fé and Jews*, Oxford University Press, London 1908.

Albuquerque, Affonso: *Cartas de*, Tomo VI, (Academia de Sciencias de Lisboa), Lisboa 1915.

Albuquerque, Braz: *Commentaries of the Great Afonso Dalboquerque*, Vol. II, (Tr. by W. De G. Birch), London 1877.

Alorná, Marquez de: *Instrucção do Exmo Vice-Rei, ao seu successor o Exmo. Vice-Rei Marquez de Tavora* (Ed. by Felippe Nery Xavier), 3rd Ed., Nova Goa 1903.

Ayalla, Frederico Diniz de: *Goa: Antiga e Moderna*, Nova Goa 1927.

Baião, Antonio: *A Inquisição de Goa*, Vol. I, (Introdução a correspondencia dos Inquisidores da India 1569-1630), Lisboa 1949.

——*A Inquisição de Goa*, Vol. II, (Correspondencia dos Inquisidores da India 1569-1630), Coimbra 1930.

Barros, João de: *Da Asia*, Decada II, Lisboa 1777.

Bragança, Menezes and others: *A India Portuguesa*, Vol. II (Imprensa Nacional), Nova Goa 1923.

Bragança Pereira, A. B.: *Historia Religiosa de Goa*, Vol. I, Bastorá, (n.d.).

Brodrick, James: *Saint Francis Xavier*, London 1952.

Buchanan, Claudius: *Christian Researches in India*, (5th ed.) London 1812.

Carré, Abbé: *Travels of the, in India and the Near East*, (Tr. by Lady Fawcett and Ed. by Sir Charles Fawcett), 3 Vols., London 1947-48.

Castanheda, Fernão Lopes de: *Historia dos Descobrimentos e Conquista da India pelos Portugueses*, Livro III, (Ed. by Pedro de Azevedo), Coimbra 1928.

Castilo, D. Pedro de: *Regimento do Santo Officio da Inquisiçam dos Reynos de Portugal*, Lisboa 1640.

Correa, Gaspar: *Lendas da India*, 3 Vols, Lisboa 1858-64.

Cottinean de Kloguen, D. L.: *An Historical Sketch of Goa*, Bombay 1922.

Couto, Diogo: *Da Asia*, Decada VII, Lisboa 1782.

Cronin, Vincent: *A Pearl to India*, London 1959.

Cunha, J. Gerson da: " M. Dellon and the Inquisition of Goa," *J.B.Br. of the Royal Asiatic Society*, Vol. XVIII, pt. II (1887-1889), Bombay 1889.

Cunha Rivara, J. H.: *Archivo Portuguez Oriental*, Vols. IV-VI, Nova Goa 1862-75.

——*Ensaio Historico da Lingua Concani*, Goa 1958.

Dellon, C.: *Account of the Inquisition at Goa*, Hull 1812.

——*The History of the Inquisition as it is exercised at Goa*, London 1688.

——*Narração de Inquisição de Goa* (Tr. by Minguel Vincente D'Abreo), Nova Goa 1866.

——Relation de L' inquisition de Goa, Paris 1888.

——Voyages de, Avec Sa Relation de L'Inquisition de Goa, Tome Premier, A Cologne 1709.

——*Voyage to the East Indies*, Part II, London 1698.

Féréal, M. V. de: *Mystéres de l'Inquisition*, Paris 1845.

Fernandes, Braz A.: *Dellon and the Inquisition of Goa*, Bombay 1936.

Fonseca, J. N.: *An Historical and Archaeological Sketch of the City of Goa*, Bombay 1878.

Fryer, John: *A New Account of East-India and Persia*, London 1698.

Guimarães, Francisco Vaz de: *Declaração Novamente feita da muito Dolorosa Morte e Paixão do N.S. Jesus Christo*, Bombay 1845.

Heras, H.: *The Conversion Policy of the Jesuits in India*, Bombay 1933.

——" The Decay of the Portuguese Power in India," *Journal of the Bombay Historical Society*, Vol. I, Bombay 1928.

Herculano, Alexandre: *Historia da Origem e Estabelecimento da Inquisição em Portugal*, 9th Edition, Ed. by David Lopes, 3 Tomos, Lisboa (n.d.).

Lea, Henry Charles: *A History of the Inquisition of Spain*, 4 Vols., New York 1906-07.

Martins, J. P. Oliveira: *Historia de Portugal*, Tomo II, Lisboa 1886.

Miranda, J. C. Barreto : *Quadros Historicos de Goa*, 3 Cadernetas, Margão 1863.
Mocatta, F. D. : *The Jews of Spain and Portugal and the Inquisition*, London 1877.
Pais, Francisco : *Tombo da Ilha de Goa e das Terras de Salsete e Bardes*, (Ed. by P. S. S. Pissurlencar), Bastorá 1952.
Paranjpe, B. G. : *English Records on Shivaji* (1659-1682), Shiva Charitra Karyalaya, Poona 1931.
Penrose, Boies : *Sea Fights in the East Indies in the years* 1602-1639, Cambridge, Massachusetts 1931.
Picard, B. : *Exact description of Outward Rites, Ceremonies and Customs of all the Peoples of the World*, (Dutch), 6 Vols, Amsterdam 1727-38.
Pires, Tomé : *The Suma Oriental of*, (Tr. & Ed. by Armando Cortesão), London 1944.
Pissurlencar, P. : *Agentes de Diplomacia Portugueza na India*, Goa 1952.
——*Agentes Hindus da Diplomacia Portuguesa na India, I Cothari*, Nova Goa 1933.
——*Colaboradores Hindus de Afonso de Albuquerque*, Bastorá 1941.
——*Roteiro dos Archivos da India Portugueza*, Bastorá 1955.
Prescott, William H. : *History of the Reign of Ferdinand and Isabella, the Catholic of Spain*, Vol. I, London 1838.
Priolkar, A. K. : *The Printing Press in India*, Bombay 1958.
Pyrard, François : *The Voyage of, to the East Indies, the Maldives, the Molucas and Brazil*, (Tr. by Albert Gray), 3 Vols., London 1887-89.
Saldanha, M. J. Gabriel de : *Historia de Goa*, Vol. I, Bastorá 1925.
Silva Rego, Antonio de : *Documentação para a Historia das Missões do Padroado Portugues do Oriente*, 12 Vols, Lisboa 1947-1958.
Singer, Charles : *Studies in the History and Method of Science*, Oxford 1917.
Souza, Francisco de : *Oriente Conquistado a Jesus Christo*, 2 Parts, (2nd Edition), Bombay 1881.
Tavernier, J. B. : *Travels in India*, (Tr. by V. Ball), London 1925.
Valignano, Alessandro : *Historia del Principio y Progresso de la Compañia de Jesus en las Indias Orientales* (Ed. by J. Wicki), Rome 1944.
Wicki, Josephus : *Documenta Indica*, 6 Vols, Rome 1948-1960.

ANONYMOUS WORKS

Biographia Goana (The Anglo Lusitano Press), Bombay (unpublished).
A Inquisição (Enciclopedia pela Imagem), Porto (n.d.).

INDEX

ERRATA

Part I

P. 30,	l. 39,	*for*	C. B.	*read*	J. C.
P. 33,	l. 40,	,,	1945	,,	1949
P. 35,	l. 7,	,,	whic	,,	which
P. 48	l. 2,	,,	Ater	,,	After
P. 72,	l. 37,	,,	s	,,	is
P. 115,	l. 19,	,,	undersirable	,,	undesirable
P. 127,	l. 27,	,,	1546	,,	1646
P. 177,	l. 33,	,,	aiso	,,	also